Edited by
Björn Hettne and Bertil Odén

Global Governance in the 21st Century: Alternative Perspectives on World Order

Björn Hettne
Professor
Department of Peace and Development Research
Göteborg University
P.O. Box 700
SE-405 30 Gothenburg, Sweden
E-mail: b.hettne@padrigu.gu.se

Bertil Odén
Counsellor
Embassy of Sweden
P.O. Box 9274
Dar es Salaam, Tanzania
E-mail: bertil.oden@sida.se

Distributed by:
Almkvist & Wiksell International
P.O. Box 7634
SE-103 94 Stockholm, Sweden
Fax: +46 8 24 25 43
E-mail: order@city.akademibokhandeln.se

Edita Norstedts Tryckeri AB 2002

Table of Contents

List of Acronyms and Abbreviations

AIDS	acquired immune deficiency syndrome
APEC	Asia Pacific Economic Cooperation
ASEAN	Association of South East Asian Nations
CAP	Common Agriculture Policy (of the European Union)
CEO	Chief Executive Officer
CO_2	carbon dioxide
ECOSOC	Economic and Social Council (of the United Nations)
ECHO	European Commission Humanitarian Office
EP	European Parliament
EMU	European Monetary Union
EU	European Union
FDI	foreign direct investment
G7	Group of seven
G8	Group of eight
GATT	General Agreement on Tariffs and Trade
GDP	gross domestic product
GNP	gross national product
GPA	Global Peoples Assembly
HIPC	Heavily Indebted Poor Countries
HIV	human immunodeficiency virus
ICC	International Criminal Court
ICEM	International Federation of Chemical, Energy and Mine Workers' Union
IGOs	inter-governmental organisations
IFIs	international financial institutions
IMF	International Monetary Fund
IT	Information Technology
LDCs	least developed countries
MAI	Multilateral Agreement on Investment
MERCOSUR	Mercade Commún del Sur (Common Market of the South)
MDGs	Millenium Development Goals
MFN	most favoured nation
MNCs	multinational corporations
NAFTA	North American Free Trade Agreement
NICs	newly industrialised countries
NPV	net present value
NGO	non-governmental organisation
ODA	official development assistance
OECD	Organisation for Economic Co-operation and Development
PCM	Project Cycle Management
PPP	purchasing power parity

PRGF	Poverty Reduction and Growth Facility
PRSP	Poverty Reduction Strategy Paper
SFA	Strategic Framework for Afghanistan
SSA	Sub-Saharan Africa
TNC	transnational corporation
UN	United Nations
UNCTAD	United Nations Conference on Trade and Development
UNDP	United Nations Development Programme
UNHCR	United Nations High Commission for Refugees
UNICEF	United Nations Children's Fund
UNIDO	United Nations Industrial Development Organization
UNITA	National Union for the Total Independence of Angola
UNRISD	United Nations Research Institute for Social Development
WOMP	World Order Models Project
WTO	World Trade Organisation

Introduction

This is a small book about big issues. It addresses the question of possible frameworks for global governance with particular regard to development and security, which are two converging areas today. The book deals with alternative forms of global governance (or world orders). It discusses ideas ranging from optimistic globalist liberal visions to more pessimistic views to the effect that disorder has become a more or less permanent condition, at least in the so-called South.

Development assistance and conflict management are two international activities that necessarily take place within an international politico-juridical framework. Consequently, they are also largely shaped by this same framework. This is a neglected aspect in studies of these two activities. Furthermore this framework, often referred to as "the Westphalia order", is currently in process of transformation. We are not quite sure into what, and naturally this dilemma does not simplify the relationships involved. This increases the need for a study of the possible governance implications of emerging conflict patterns that are challenging the international system. Our aim is to contribute to the ongoing discussion regarding the interrelationship between conflict and development at global, regional, national and local levels. By systematising emerging tendencies and their interplay between various levels of the global political economy, taking the possible future roles of the nation-state as the point of departure, an inventory of various options or "world order scenarios" has been attempted

In the first chapter, by Björn Hettne, the future world order alternatives are spelt out in general terms with reference to earlier discourses on the fundamentals of international order and possible futures. We think it is meaningful to relate the art of political forecasting today to the methodology explored through earlier efforts in this difficult genre, and hope that this discussion will provide a relevant framework for the various contributions to this book.

The first strand identified is based on a strong belief in the virtues of globalism, where most decisions regarding resource allocation can be successfully left to the market and the role of the nation-state is consequently reduced. This vision is designated the *liberal globalist case*. The second strand focuses on the vicious side of the globalisation process, also with reduced influence for the nation-state. This scenario is called *durable disorder*. The third strand describes how the international community, based on existing nation-states or a reformed nation-states system, should meet the globalising factors. There are two possibilities: one is called *assertive multilateralism*, relating to a UN focused order: the other is *plurilateralism*, based on a great power concert, for instance G8 or NATO. The fourth and final strand is based on increased influence on international governance for civil society within a framework of a global "normative architecture". As part of this strand a move from national to regional governance can be envisaged. This scenario is called *global cosmopolitanism* combined with *new regionalism*.

In the next four chapters, which make up the bulk of the book, some of the trends identified are further explored by internationally well known authors, chosen for their expertise on the various dimensions of the alternative world orders discussed. They have not been asked to produce a rigid elaboration of exactly those forms of governance presented in chapter one, which would have been a rather artificial exercise, but rather to further pursue their own lines of reasoning from their previous work.

In chapter two, Indra de Soysa and Nils Petter Gleditsch, while not adhering to the hard globalist view that markets really can operate in a political vacuum, explore a link between globalisation and the growth of beneficent political institutions. Thus, they take their point of departure in the controversial phenomenon of globalisation that has such a surprising capacity for arousing diverging opinions. They stress the fact that the current debate is not very dissimilar to the old debate on modernisation vs. dependency, where the latter position blamed trade and foreign investment for making the poor countries poorer, whereas the former position considered underdevelopment was the result of bad governance and dirigiste practices. The authors build a case for the argument that increases in trade and investment will enhance the prospects for democracy and peace by strengthening interdependence among nations in a liberal world order.

In chapter three, Mark Duffield critically discusses the more pessimistic scenario, called "durable disorder" in chapter one, but does not define this as a permanent retrograde crisis. The new conflicts are seen less as temporary crises, more as distinct economic and political projects. To Duffield, the paradox of globalisation is that deregulation and liberalisation also create the conditions for autonomy and resistance in the "peripheries". The new wars are not forms of social regression but signs of actual development. In the emerging new political economy, the warring parties forge autonomous local-global networks as a means of marketing local resources and securing essential supplies. In the mainstream discourse, the new wars are interpreted as resulting from lack of development, which leads to a merger of development and security concerns for the purpose of conflict prevention, conflict resolution, and social reconstruction. The emerging forms of governance build on public-private networks of international assistance, convergence of development and security, and increasing coherence between various ministerial departments dealing with these issues. However, there are marked limits to international authority and governance in the "borderlands" in this new situation; hence the durability of disorder.

In chapter four, Raimo Väyrynen analyses opportunities to reform the international order either by means of assertive multilateralism or various plurilateral approaches, by which he means a multitude of actors other than states. The Asian financial crisis of 1997 was a wake-up call, underlining the need to strengthen global governance, if globalisation was to have a future. At present, a new consensus has emerged among governments, non-governmental organisations and international finance institutions, that the alleviation of poverty is a precondition for the creation of a more viable world order, globalisation with a human face. Even the transnational companies are in need of new ways to legitimise their behaviour. One lesson learnt from what happened to the Multilateral Agreement on Investment (MAI) as well as from subsequent anti-globalisation rallies may be that global rules for capitalism require that social, cultural and environmental standards are acceptable.

In chapter five, Falk gives his outline of what may be called a post-Westphalia model by looking at two trends: the normative trend toward *cosmopolitan democracy* and the economic and political trend toward *a new regionalism*, both representing a positive conception of a preferred future. Cosmopolitan democracy emphasises the importance of extending democratic notions of participation, accountability, transparency, rule of law, and social justice to all arenas of human interaction. The prospects for such "humane global governance" are crucially dependent on grassroots and transnational activism defining the reality of global civil society. It is the global civil society project. By contrast, regional initiatives reflect efforts by elites throughout the world to participate more effectively in the world economy. Such regionalism also expresses a sense of cultural, religious, and geographic affinity, representing erosion of allegiance to the sovereign state and a rise in regional civilisational identity. The stress on regional political community is also based on the assumption that the UN system, here designated assertive multilateralism, is not likely to be the core of a move toward humane global governance.

It should be noted that the authors include some of the existing economic and social trends when drawing their logical conclusion. This means that they deliberately argue in favour of a clear-cut version of each scenario, without elaborate discussion of the counter-arguments. The scenarios should thus not be mistaken as projections. The point is that by refining some trends, their possible effects become clearer. Applying this method, the study hopes to contribute to further discussion of the balance between various globalisation forces and their implications for international governance. It is clear that the policies and means by which global challenges in the areas of security and development will be handled, depend on how the global framework for governance develops in the next few years.

The great shock of September 11 happened as this book was being finalised, and it is legitimate to ask what impact it will have on the various forms of governance, or world orders, discussed in the book. The event and the counteractions that followed have been described as "the first war of the 21st century". They have also been referred to as a "war against terrorism", waged by an international coalition under the leadership of the USA. This can in fact be seen as an instance of global governance, but what kind of world order is it an expression of? Even if the concept of war can be questioned, it is relevant in the sense that a war normally concentrates decision-making powers, silences opposition, and focuses on one particular aim and one particular option; hence other options are excluded for the time being.

Furthermore, a war strengthens the state as well as its military arm and consequently weakens the subtler inter-state arrangements, not to mention more elaborate post-Westphalia forms of governance, such as a norms-based humane global governance. Thus, if a norms-based world order takes a long time to emerge, as Falk suggests, the current development is no improvement. Instead, the "unipolar movement" gains momentum.

Thus, in view of the state-strengthening influence of war, we should perhaps expect neo-Westphalia forms, such as assertive multilateralism, to crystallise. The question can be raised, as to whether the international coalition against terrorism can be transformed into a solid institutionalised regime based on generally accepted principles, or if this turns out to be unilateralism (or perhaps, in consideration of the Anglo-Saxon brotherhood, bilateralism) in disguise.

To the extent that the enemy can be dismissed as a sect with little popular support, the outcome of the first phase of the war may be seen as "the end of history" rather than "the clash of civilisations", thus showing the strength of the liberal, globalist case of beneficent globalisation. To the extent that future developments may be seen as a new and coercive phase in metropolitan rule over the margins, we should rather speak of a more serious and violent stage of "durable disorder". Thus, the events of September 11 will be interpreted differently within different paradigms, at least until the consequences are more evident than they are when this book goes to the printer.

In the final chapter, Bertil Odén discusses what common features can be traced in the four alternative forms of global governance, and what tentative conclusions may be drawn regarding the role of development cooperation within their framework. It is obvious that any conclusions, based on the type of tentative trends that form the content of the four chapters, are venturous. Yet, a few remarks may be made.

The authors agree that the state will not vanish or disintegrate. However, they also agree that the role of the state will change and the scope for governance at the nation-state level will change substantially. Whether the forces of change will be strong enough to transform the world order into something that could best be labelled *post-Westphalia* or whether *neo-Westphalia* is a more appropriate label is uncertain, particularly in the light of recent events.

It seems the authors in this volume also share the opinion that the impact of homogeneous and territorial authorities will be reduced, while the impact will increase of de-territorialised, heterogeneous collectivities, based on a multiplicity of rule systems in a world that in some areas becomes more multi-centric.

Alternative options can be offered concerning the implications for global governance and development cooperation. A highly simplified short version would be that the global liberalist case is closest to the prevailing pattern of development cooperation, which means that only marginal changes would be necessary in the present pattern. The multilateral and plurilateral routes would imply radical reforms of international institutions, particularly the UN system, and focus more on the provision of international public goods. It is also compatible with ongoing efforts to find new sources to finance such activities, including international tax bases.

"Durable disorder" implies that a political vision needs to replace the social claims of the development discourse. Instead of mainly providing an instrument for metropolitan monitoring and risk management in areas perceived as security threats, humanitarian and related development cooperation should solely focus on impartial humanitarian assistance. Finally, the role of development cooperation in order to facilitate "humane global governance" would largely be used for upgrading the rule of law, strengthening the impact of human rights and democratic governance at all levels, including at the global level, and improving the capacity of governments in poor countries and transnational civil society to participate in this process.

It remains to be seen whether in the next few years the balance changes between security policy strategic assessments, on the one hand, and factors such as human rights, democracy, good governance and prudent macro-economic policy, on the other, thereby moving closer to a Cold War pattern, but with a new definition of the enemy.

We would finally like to gratefully acknowledge valuable and constructive comments and suggestions on draft versions of the texts from members of the EGDI and from the participants in the RCA40/EGDI Workshop on New Regionalism and New/Old Security Issues in Göteborg 31 May–2 June 2001. In particular we want to thank the authors of the four world order perspectives, who participated in the workshop, commenting on each other's drafts.

Göteborg and Dar es Salaam in May 2002

Björn Hettne   *Bertil Odén*

1. In Search of World order

Björn Hettne

No political society, national or international, can exist unless people submit to certain rules of conduct. The problem why people should submit to such rules is the fundamental problem of political philosophy.
E. H. Carr, 1984 (1939, second ed. 1946), 41.

The true criticism of market society is not that it was based on economics – in a sense, every society must be based on it – but that its economy was based on self-interest
K. Polanyi, 1957 (1944), 249.

The guiding principle, that a policy of freedom for the individual is the only progressive policy, remains as true today as it was in the nineteenth century
F. A. Hayek, 1944, 246.

In this chapter, future world order alternatives are spelt out in general terms with respectful reference to well-known earlier discourses on the fundamentals of international order and possible futures by classic authors such as E.H. Carr, Fredric A. Hayek and Karl Polanyi, as well as Hedley Bull. The latter is one of the most frequently quoted authors as far as the concept of international order is concerned. It is meaningful in my view to relate the difficult art of political forecasting today to the methodology explored through earlier efforts in the hope that such a discussion will provide a relevant framework for the various contributions to this book. Furthermore, it is of interest to see to what extent there are persistent perspectives as far as possible world orders are concerned. Connected to this is the question as to whether a paradigmatic shift is needed in order to understand the current "globalised condition" as compared with the situation when the three classic thinkers preoccupied themselves with the emerging international order towards the end of the Second World War.

The contemporary point of departure, arguably making the current situation qualitatively new, is globalisation, which will therefore be dealt with in greater detail further on. In this context, globalisation is seen as a structural transformation of the international system away from traditional sovereignty, creating an urgent need for new forms of governance, because of a "governance gap" or a "governance dilemma". The greatest challenges to these new forms of governance are violent conflict and poverty, two negative phenomena which are related through complex and still little understood causational chains.

By global governance is meant authoritative, but not necessarily permanent or well-organised, decision-making and action by a number of actors in a globalised space, more or less beyond the full control of state governments. Thus, governance can be exercised by state or public sector actors, but also by non-state actors. Governance institutions may be of different types, *ad hoc* or created for specific purposes. Governance is not exclusive to any particular level of the world system but is a multi-level phenomenon. It can be seen as the content as well as the process of world order. Just as we may like or dislike a particular government, we may have different views on particular forms of global governance, although it is much more difficult to bring about changes at the global level.

New forms of governance represent the political content of the emerging transnational space created by globalisation, so far dominated by economic market forces. It is here assumed that any viable world order must rest upon an institutionalised balance between economic and political forces.

In the theory of economic history associated with Karl Polanyi, an expansion and deepening of the market is followed by political intervention. The expansion of market is the first movement and the societal response the second movement. Polanyi described this process as the Great Trans-formation, the title of his famous book. An institutionalised balance as a dialectic outcome of these two processes can be called a Great Compromise (Hettne, 2001). The Bretton Woods system that emerged after the Second World War was in fact such a compromise. Using a Polanyian term, John Ruggie (Ruggie, 1998: 62) labelled this system embedded liberalism, more precisely defined as transnational economic multilateralism combined with domestic interventionism (p. 73). If the last two decades have been characterised by the predominance of economics, the time seems to have come for a "return of the political" in order for another balance, or Great Compromise, to be established. The dysfunctions normally connected with the second movement, and particularly its various forms of regulation, lead to a renewed defence of market solutions. Thus Friedrich Hayek, disgusted with the ideological menu of the 1930s, warned against political intervention as "the road to serfdom", the title of his equally famous book, which was contemporary with Polanyi's.

Forecasting necessarily has to be a compromise between realism and utopianism. For the realist, the existing situation appears natural, and the problem of change plays a minor role, whereas the utopianist thinks of alternative futures, strongly contrasting with the present. E. H. Carr, the father of realist theory, created the conception of utopianism in international relations, whereas it is now usually referred to as idealism. Carr's realism was of the classical Machiavellian type, which could be used for both radical and conservative purposes, including what Robert Cox has called critical theory in contradistinction to problem-solving theory (Cox, 1995; 1996; 1997).

Carr also stated that any sound political thought must be based on elements of both utopia and reality.[1]

The Meaning of Order

First, however, a word on the concept of international order, or world order, is warranted. These terms can be seen as belonging to somewhat different historical contexts, *international order* normally referring to the relations among sovereign, territorial states in a Westphalia system. This concept refers to the territorial state, characterised by internal and external sovereignty that emerged after the Peace of Westphalia in 1648.[2] This international system is now in process of transformation due to changes in the basic constitutive principles on which it was based. The concept *world order* refers to a more complex post-Westphalia world – or a world beyond national sovereignty – where the familiar concept of government is being replaced by the more elusive concept of governance as defined above.

A useful point of departure for discussing how the meaning of order in the international system has been transformed, is the work of Hedley Bull. He not only explained the essence of international order, but also explored its limits, as well as the question of what, if anything, might emerge beyond classical sovereignty.[3] It is therefore not surprising that today's theorists, including some contributors to this book, are also engaging in Bull's path-breaking study on international order.[4]

Bull, who worked within the historically oriented group of scholars that

---

[1] In the preface to the 1946 edition (signed in November 1945) Carr made clear that he has chosen to retain the content of the 1939 edition with only minor changes. He also stated that the emphasis on power, which he deemed necessary in 1939, might be exaggerated in the perspective of the major war that followed. He also found the use of the concept of nation-state as the unit of international society superficial and instead felt that "the small independent nation-state is obsolete or obsolescent and that no workable international organisation can be built on a membership of a multiplicity of nation-states."

[2] See chapter five by Richard Falk for an elaborate discussion of the meaning of Westphalianism.

[3] To Hedley Bull (1977: 20) "world order" was for mankind. It was a more normative concept, whereas "international order" was simply order among states. The former thus had a moral priority, and the value of the latter was derived from its capability to promote the former.

[4] In this book, Mark Duffield takes Bull's work as a "benchmark for normalisation", showing the degree to which "intermediacy", or dangerous halfway movements towards post-sovereign structures, has now become part of the normal. Richard Falk, similarly but with different conclusions, makes the observation that Bull failed to see the power of global norms developing outside and beyond the Westphalia order (Falk, 1999: 35–36). The erosion of the state-centric paradigm has, however, not yet paved the way for a renewal of normative thinking. Falk, like Duffield, thus uses the realist backdrop, manifested in the English School, as the basis for commenting on globalisation and its implications for the future of the states system or international order. We certainly have moved some way towards a new international order, depending, of course, on how that is to be defined.

has become known as the English School in international relations, was rather sceptical about the possibility of any order beyond the "anarchical society". Somewhat reluctantly, however, he explored what he termed a new medievalism and also recognised situations of "intermediacy", in which aspects of sovereignty were transferred to institutions other than the state, thus modifying but not fundamentally changing the Westphalia logic. Bull saw a decline in international society but, in line with his theoretical analysis, he argued in favour of arresting this decline rather than hastening it, a process which in his view would have paved the way for something even worse than international anarchy. In his modest way, he also stated that such a conclusion stands in need of continual re-assessment (Bull, 1977: 319).

What then, did Bull mean by international order? He defined it as "a pattern of activity that sustains the elementary or primary goals of the society of states, or international society" (Bull, 1977: 8). It is important to note that Bull did not conceive of the international system as anarchy but as society, thus to a certain and varying extent bound by rules. He took his departure in the meaning of order in social life, security against violence, the honouring of agreement, and the stability of possession. The goals of the international system were – in addition to those associated with order in social life – the preservation of the states system, maintaining the external sovereignty of individual states, and peace, or rather, the absence of war.

The linkage between order in social life and international order underlines the fact that there are two dimensions to sovereignty, one external and one internal. External authority is emphasised in realist theory, but loss of internal sovereignty, i.e. the collapse of states, is an equally serious threat to international order. This new security situation is dramatically illustrated by recent national and ethnic conflicts. Depending on the level of interdependence between neighbouring national societies, these may lead to a more or less serious regional disorder or tensions, as has been demonstrated by Bosnia and Kosovo in Europe, Cambodia and Indonesia (East Timor, Kalimantan) in South-East Asia, Lebanon, Palestine/Israel in the Middle East, Liberia and Sierra Leone in West Africa, Somalia and Sudan in the Horn of Africa, Angola and Mozambique in Southern Africa, Burundi, Rwanda and Zaire in Central Africa, Nagorno-Karabakh and Tajikistan in the former Soviet Union, and some Indian states such as Assam, Kashmir, Punjab, as well as Sri Lanka, in South Asia.

Whether Bull, who in fact argued against the idea of a qualitative novelty of globalisation even before the concept was invented, would have seen these incidents as indications of a more fundamental erosion of sovereignty and signs of disorder is uncertain. To him, the number of political units was not a defining characteristic of international order. Of far greater importance was its structure. It is here assumed that an increase in the number of political units at some stage and above a certain threshold in fact indicates qualitative change.

Globalisation and World Disorder

Let us now turn to the question of what has undermined the once so well-established distinction between internal and external, and changed the historical preconditions for international order as it was once defined by Bull. In short, globalisation has taken place. As will be discussed in the concluding chapter, there are almost as many views on globalisation as there are authors. This should not come as a surprise, since globalisation is multidimensional, and it is perfectly legitimate to stress different dimensions for the purpose of analysis. Hence, no general definition of globalisation has been applied in this study. I will focus here on the more recent deepening and expansion of the market system in a transnational space, as well as the social and political implications of this process.

In many respects globalisation can undoubtedly be seen as a long-term historical process, but at the same time it is qualitatively new, in the sense that it is tooled by new information and communication technologies and a new organisational logic, that of networking (Holton, 1998; Castells, 1996).

In economic terms and in its current form, globalisation can be conceived of as a further deepening and expansion of the market system, a continuation of the great transformation, i.e. the 19th century market expansion that disrupted traditional society. Through the ensuing social disturbances, it provoked various kinds of political interventionism with very different ideological motivations, such as communism, fascism, social democracy, populism and social liberalism (or Keynesianism). As was noted earlier, Polanyi referred to this self-defence of society as the double movement of market expansion and political interventionism. This time the process of market expansion, including its social repercussions, is taking place on a truly global scale, which is likely to make the social and political counter-movements even more varying and hard to predict. This double movement can be seen as a "second great transformation" (Hettne, 2000).

It is important to identify the political actors behind this seemingly deterministic process. One may consider Polanyi's argument: "There was nothing natural about laissez-faire; free markets could never have come into being merely by allowing things to take their course" (1957: 139). This is also true today. States that are strong and competitive[5] can be deliberately instrumental through privatisation and liberalisation in order to promote certain interests in the globalised space. In many parts of the world, the Westphalia role was never even fulfilled, due to a lack of internal and external legitimacy as well as a lack of territorial control. By participating in globalisation on unequal terms, these poor states may gain external legitimacy and thereby access to credit. However, they lose in internal

---

[5] See also Cerny, 1990, on "competition states".

legitimacy and social cohesion as a consequence of fulfilling imposed conditionalities. This is obvious in the South, but can also be seen in the North. However, in the North the mechanisms of compensation are still fairly strong.

Globalism or, from the perspective of individual countries or national economies, global adjustment, is the current hegemonic development paradigm, with the growth of a free-functioning world market as its ideological core. Since this process is considered synonymous with increased economic efficiency and a higher world product, globalists consider "too much government" to be a systemic fault. Until recently, good governance was often equated to less government. Globalism as an ideology thus argued in favour of a particular form of globalisation, i.e. economic integration on a world scale. One should, however, not rule out other ideological forms of globalism, for instance Keynesian globalism. A revival of Keynesianism would probably be more rooted in the states system, but there have also been arguments, for instance in the Brandt Commission Report, for a "global Keynesianism". More recently the debate has focused on the Tobin tax and the need for global public goods.

What kind of political landscape is emerging from globalisation? Are more and more states becoming "pathological anarchies" (Falk, 1999: 74), or has the global village finally arrived? There is, as Bull also pointed out, a link between the stability of social and international order and the possibility of predictability in social science. To the extent there is less order, social scientists experience this by being overtaken by events as they occur. There is therefore little consensus as to the social consequences of globalisation but, undoubtedly, the process is putting a large number of nation-states under pressure, which they find increasingly hard to withstand (UNRISD, 1995; 2000). How should this pressure be understood?

In adapting to the market-led form of globalism, the state becomes the disciplining spokesman of external economic forces, rather than the protector of society against the disrupting consequences of these forces, which was one of the classical tasks of nation-building in Europe, and culminated in the modern welfare state. The retreat of the state from its historical functions also implies a changed relationship between the state and what is called civil society (Tester, 1992; Chandhoke, 1995), in particular a tendency for the state to become alienated from it. Inclusion as well as exclusion is inherent in the networking process implied in globalisation. The exclusionist implications may promote a politics of identity, as loyalties are in the process of being transferred from civil society to primary groups (here defined as the smallest "we-group" in a particular social context), competing for scarce natural resources, patronage, political influence, etc.

Political disintegration in a domestic context can be seen as part of the globalisation process, even if there are important domestic factors contributing to the process, as in Argentina. Particularly in the South, where

12

the redistributive (in terms of social justice) state never appeared in the first place, or was never firmly consolidated, there is an ongoing informalisation of the economy and fragmentation of society.

 Conventional view has it that such a disintegration of the state implies non-development. On the other hand, new fieldwork-oriented analyses of real substantive economies suggest a more complex picture of emerging local economies, de-linked from state control, run by a new type of entrepreneur, supported by private military protection, and drawing on international connections.[6] The poor who do not dominate the state, or the not so poor who face the end of state patronage, rely on collective identities, which enhance solidarity within the group but also can create hatred towards outsiders. Those who cannot control the state may turn to "war lord politics" (Reno, 1998).

There are also ordinary state actors involved, which may serve as an argument for those who say that the state is not in decline. Rival political projects are no longer necessarily competing nation-state projects, but rather economic competition by violent means, or the continuation of economics by other means. It is interesting to note that the new entrepreneurs sometimes rationalise their behaviour in accordance with the hegemonic liberal ideology. Hyperliberalism and warlordism have one thing in common – they both prefer the minimal state. They are both characteristic of the globalised condition.

Elsewhere one can, however, still discern a difference between the conventional nation-state strategy of maintaining sovereign rule over national territory and more parochial strategies of reserving local assets for local entrepreneurs, disregarding claims from the official, but no longer *de facto* existing nation-state. Thus the description of such situations as state disintegration, "black holes", and "failed states" is simplified. *It is not the state that disappears. It is everything else that changes.* The state remains an important actor in the new context, but in functional terms it is no longer the same kind of institution. Some of its traditional functions are debundled and transferred to new institutions on various societal levels. Security is one example.

Human Security as a Challenge to State Sovereignty

There is now a qualitatively new discourse on intervention called humanitarian intervention, which implies a coercive involvement by external powers in a domestic crisis for the purpose of preventing human rights abuses. The recent focus upon human security rather than state security is significant for understanding the change in the security and

[6] Cf. Duffield, 1998 and Chapter 3 in this book. See also Chabal and Daloz, 1999.

development discourse and the fundamental challenge to sovereignty. This security concept was launched in the 1994 Human Development Report from UNDP and consciously contrasted to state security:

> For too long, the concept of security has been shaped by the potential for conflict between states. For too long, security has been equated with threats to a country's borders. For too long, nations have sought arms to protect their security. For most people today, a feeling of insecurity arises more from worries about daily life than from the dread of a cataclysmic world event. Job security, income security, health security, environmental security, security from crime, these are the emerging concerns of human security all over the world (UNDP, 1994: 3).

Concepts such as human security, human development, human emergency, and humanitarian intervention, imply the idea of a transnational responsibility for human welfare. Protection of people and civil society by the state was implicit in the old Westphalia state-centric paradigm. Obviously, this is no longer taken for granted, and numerous examples show why it cannot be.

Until recently it has been taboo for states other than superpowers to intervene militarily in the affairs of another state. In international law there are only two *legal* types of intervention: (1) when a conflict constitutes a threat to international peace, and (2) when the behaviour of the parties to a conflict fundamentally violates human rights or humanitarian law. So far, the practice of external intervention in domestic affairs has been rather restricted. A counter-sovereignty operation is not compatible with what was originally stated in Article 2 of the UN charter, "Nothing in this charter shall authorise the United Nations to intervene in matters which are essentially within the domestic jurisdiction of any state". However, in the last decade the *legitimacy* factor with respect to intervention in "domestic affairs" has grown stronger relative to the *legality* factor and, consequently, the number of interventions in response to "complex humanitarian emergencies" has also increased.

Principles of legitimate humanitarian intervention should preferably be agreed upon beforehand. On an abstract and normative level this should not be so difficult, the problem is political will, consensus about identifying the individual cases and, of course, the practicalities of implementation. Dieter Senghaas has proposed a rather exhaustive, still relevant list of situations that call for such intervention: genocidal policies, policies displacing vast numbers of people, wars/civil wars and essential relief operations, internal persecution of people without external consequences, violation of minority rights, ecological warfare, attempts to acquire weapons for mass destruction and their proliferation (Senghaas, 1993; see also DUPI, 1999; Wheeler, 2000; Independent International Commission on Kosovo, 2000).

So far, external interventions have been *ad hoc* operations, and most of them controversial. We can distinguish between the interventions that took place during the Cold War which were almost universally criticised (East Pakistan 1971, Cambodia 1979, Uganda 1979) and the recent, more generally accepted, post-Cold War interventions, which took place in a radically new historical context and within a new security discourse.

The different cases of external intervention that we have seen so far have different degrees of legitimacy, not unrelated to the behaviour of the parties to the conflict. The more barbarian the behaviour, the more urgent and the more acceptable the external intervention will appear to public opinion.[7]

A New Medievalism?

Even if "new wars" or "new conflicts" are usually defined as internal, the new situation is actually characterised by an erosion of the external-internal distinction that was so central to the Westphalia model. As a state is dissolved, it can no longer be territorially defined. Occasionally various social forces in neighbouring states, or former states, are drawn into clashes. The phenomenon of state collapse may not only be a simple passing crisis for the state, but also in metaphorical terms "a new medievalism" (Cerny, 1998). The overall significance of this route is a downward movement of authority to subnational regions, localities, and social groups, while supranational forms of governance remain embryonic. Hedley Bull (1977: 254) was one of the first, if not the first, to make use of the medieval metaphor, describing it as "a system of overlapping authority and multiple loyalty". Thus a medieval order is not exclusively local:

> If modern states were to come to share their authority over their citizens, and their ability to command their loyalties, on the one hand with regional and world authorities, and on the other hand with sub-state or sub-national authorities, to such an extent that the concept of sovereignty ceased to be applicable, then a neo-medieval form of universal order might be said to have emerged (Bull, 1977: 254–55).

To Bull, the medieval metaphor was not normative but a structural description, emphasising multilevel governance and shifting authority structures, which can be referred to as universal medievalism (Gamble, 2001). For our purposes, however, the concept of *durable disorder* (or

---

[7] Of similar relevance in the new intervention discourse, reflecting the new political climate of global governance, are the recent attempts at creating international criminal courts and war crime tribunals (*The Economist*, June 16–22, 2001). See also the chapter by Richard Falk.

parochial medievalism), a more pessimistic interpretation of the same situation, is more appropriate. It implies a strong local focus, albeit not exclusively local. In security terms, the situation moves in a Hobbesian direction, and the mode of development in such a context may at best be some sort of primitive accumulation. In a more optimistic interpretation, which could be called stable chaos, some of the alternative development principles such as territorialism, sustainability and cultural pluralism (Hettne, 1995b), could take shape more easily.[8]

Obviously, standard definitions of development are hard to apply in the situation here described as durable disorder. In this context, development assistance has been reduced to a civil form of humanitarian intervention, and the major reason for intervention is violent conflict; to prevent it, to manage it, or to reconstruct societies in post-conflict situations. The record so far is not very impressive (Edwards, 1999). Development tends to be what development workers do and, more often than not, they do what they do in emergency situations. An additional relevant development dimension in a context of societal disintegration, is the role model for post-conflict reconstruction constituted by remaining "islands of civility" in a sea of civil war (Kaldor, 1999).

Development thinking forms part of the modern project. It believes in the rational human being, and remains stubbornly normative. Thus, the idea of purposeful change is not rejected. It shares that view with most theories of world order, although views on the room for manoeuvre differ. Again, it may be instructive to explore the classical discourse by authors like Hayek, Carr and Polanyi.[9]

Room for Manoeuvre in Retrospect

The search for world order is not new, neither is the frustration attending the pursuit of order at the international level (particularly a *just* order). Perhaps the most dramatic setback occurred during the so-called twenty years' crisis (1919–1939) "when the men of the 1930s returned shocked and bewildered to the world of nature" (Carr, 1984: 225). This Hobbesian image can be compared to the "new barbarism" of our present time, that followed the unfulfilled "new world order", the concept coined during the Gulf War 1991, reappearing with the recent war against terrorism. Order is not permanent, although it may be easy to believe so under periods of stability. It is therefore wise to look for emerging contradictions and structural openings in a particular order (Abrahamsson, 1997). They should first of all be looked for

[8] See also Hettne, 1995a.
[9] The discussion is for present purposes confined to certain key texts and not an assessment of the overall view of the respective authors

in structures, institutions and mechanisms that are constitutive for the existing political order.

If such constitutive principles change, we can assume that the whole system is in transformation. In the case of the Westphalia order *sovereignty*, *central authority*, based on various forms of legitimacy, and *territoriality*, are the most important constitutive principles. Since few would contest the argument that these principles are now under stress, we can conclude that some sort of structural change is in the making. As was noted above, the possibility of making prophetic statements melts down in such situations.

Changes in the structure of world order have often been connected to war situations, which tend to speed up the pace of change. The end of a major war is thus a situation in which a new international order is typically born. Let us therefore consider the situation when the Second World War was approaching its end, and it became relevant to debate the prospects of a post-war order. Interestingly, both Carr, in *The 20 Years' Crisis* (1939 with a second edition 1946) and Polanyi, in *The Great Transformation* (1944) speculated about future world orders, and they did so in their own characteristic ways. The liberal view was developed in a third classic work from this period of time, Friedrich Hayek's *The Road to Serfdom*, published in the same year as Polanyi's book. All three authors dealt with routes to the future in the last chapters, and all three said that they disliked utopias. However, they were referring to very different phenomena.

One important issue was that which more recently has been discussed as the hegemonic stability theory, asserting that an open world economy requires a dominant global power for its smooth functioning. Previously Great Britain fulfilled that task. Carr referred to the possible leadership of the USA as being a "young and untried nation" and quoted Woodrow Wilson: "Her flag is the flag not only of America, but of humanity" (Carr, 1984: 234).[10] He discussed, in classical realist terms, Pax Americana versus Pax Anglo-Saxonica, i.e. the partnership of English-speaking peoples or what we today refer to as the trans-Atlantic alliance. The winners of a war normally have the privilege to define the new order. Thus, power defines what is right and, according to Carr, those who do not understand that are utopians.

To Polanyi, taking a more normative position (however, compatible with his theory of structural change) on the future order, Pax Americana was precisely what should be avoided, since the market project associated with Pax Americana, like other universalisms which had been tried and had failed, constituted the great danger – a utopian project – to worry about. Instead, he hoped for a more planned, horizontal world order with "regional systems coexisting side by side" (Polanyi, 1945: 87). Thus, he retained his belief in

---

[10] This missionary attitude is lingering on, as in current statements from the White House that USA is fighting for the freedom of people everywhere.

some form of interventionism, but felt that something larger than the state was needed. These diverging perspectives can be seen as an early debate about what was later termed hegemonic stability.

To Hayek it was not the market but socialism, i.e. political interventionism in the economy that constituted the great utopia to be avoided, since this particular utopia according to him led to "serfdom" (Hayek, 1944). Hayek warned against planning, particularly at a transnational level, which would only create tensions and destroy the coming peace. In this context he made critical references to Carr. In Hayek's view there was certainly a need for an international authority with negative powers – to say no to all kinds of restrictions. Thus, the need was for a political order to maximise economic freedom. Hayek himself used the controversial *laissez-faire* concept. In spite of all his libertarianism, he was nevertheless prepared to accept milder forms of federalism. Just like the other authors discussed here, Hayek's ultimate concern in this book was peace, which is quite natural in view of the situation in which they all wrote.

These speculations about the emerging world order were made in a period of interregnum, which Antonio Gramsci once defined as a period in which "the old form of rule was dying, but a new one had not been born" (Hoare and Nowell Smith, 1971: 276). E. H. Carr (1969) also used this concept to describe a period of transition with an uneasy balance between contending forces. Today again, the first decade after the Cold War has been likened to such an interregnum.[11] Possibly, this interregnum has now ended with what has been called the first war of the 21st century, i.e. the war against terrorism showing a more assertive search for world order. Whether or not the concept of war is adequate, we have definitely entered a stage of increasing room for manoeuvre for a few important international actors. The actions they take will shape the new world order in the years to come.

What happens beyond this interregnum and in the wake of September 11 is the topic of this book. The new universalism, which Polanyi was so worried about, reappears in Fukuyama's triumphalist "end of history", in the form of market-led globalisation, or in the ideology of globalism, according to which capitalism and democracy are mutually supportive systems. I refer to this as ideology, since one might at least raise the concern that "globalising capitalism threatens the territorially based states in which liberal democratic values and practices are rooted" (Clark, 1997: 193). So far we have not seen a global democracy.

Returning to Bull, he also considered alternative systems in spite of his unwillingness to recognise any significant moves beyond the sovereign states-system, an unwillingness he shares with many contemporary observers who

---

[11] See the Special Issue (The Interregnum, Controversies in World Politics 1989–1999) of *Review of International Studies*, Vol. 25, December 1999.

keep repeating that the state is stronger than ever. The models he discussed are, of course, different from the scenarios we see today, but there are similarities as well. Bull's alternative models were (1) a Great Power Concert, which he called the Kissinger Model, (2) Global Centralism, or the Radical Salvationist Model, (3) Regionalism, considered to be a Third World Model, and finally (4) Revolution, the Marxist Model. We shall come back to three of these models while discussing the contemporary alternative world orders below. The fourth has lost relevance, at least for the time being.

Future World Orders

As stated above, in periods of interregnum, different models are still competing, but in a war situation – to which the current situation has been compared – the dominant actors will have more room for manoeuvre to choose and implement their preferred solution. To the extent that multilateralism rather than unilateralism prevails, the outcome will probably be a mixture of various models. For the present purpose, i.e. to provide a framework for the chapters to follow, we are more concerned with ideal models than hybrid forms.

The liberal view of globalisation, which still enjoys a hegemonic position, stresses the homogenising influence of market forces towards an open society. However, many liberal theorists agree that markets work through institutional frameworks that may be more or less beneficial and efficient. As we noted above, even Hayek could accept a milder form of federalist world order. Nevertheless, liberals normally take a minimalist view of political authority. The roots of this way of thinking are found in the doctrine of harmony of interests, expressed in its classical form by Adam Smith in *The Wealth of Nations*. It was again manifested in the theory of free trade, associated with David Ricardo.

The historical background to this argument was mercantilist regulation, but subsequently the negative other took the form of planning. The purpose of political order, according to liberal tradition, is to facilitate the free movement of economic factors. The breakdown of the socialist system seemed to confirm the liberal principle of evolution: the unnatural is sooner or later replaced by the natural. Any attempt to isolate oneself from market forces is thus a sentence to stagnation. The optimum size of an economy (and therefore its ultimate form) is the world market. All other arrangements, for instance regional trade arrangements, are only second best, but acceptable to the extent that they are stepping stones rather than stumbling blocks to the world market. This protectionist threat has been a predominant preoccupation of the international financial institutions (IFIs) in the last two decades.

To more interventionist thinkers, more concerned with the content of the second movement, i.e. to politicise the global, this is not realistic. They tend to see the unregulated market system as analogous to political anarchy. Many of the classical theorists, whether conservative or radical, held that the liberal ideology of ever expanding and deepening markets lacked ethical content. Similarly, the morality of the market system can, according to contemporary critics of what they call hyperglobalisation, only be safeguarded by some kind of organised purposeful will, manifested in a "return of the political", or reinvention of politics (Beck, 1997), for instance in the form of new social movements and a "new multilateralism" (Cox, 1997 and 1999; Gills, 2000).

The return of the political, or what Polanyi would have called the re-embedment of the market, may appear in various forms, strong or weak, good or bad. One possible form, assuming a continuous role for state authority, is a reformed neo-Westphalia order, governed either by a reconstituted UN system, which may be termed *assertive multilateralism,* or by a more loosely organised coalition of dominant powers, assuming the privilege of governance, including intervention, by reference to their shared system of values focused on order. This we can call *militant plurilateralism.*

The plurilateral model of political order (here defined in a rather state-centric way) has already been tested in the 19th century system of power balance called the European Concert. The concert arrangement was based on consultations among the great powers, who acknowledged their equal status and agreed to protect established members of the states-system and, consequently, prevent territorial change. The system was essentially conservative, and therefore in the long run bound to be undermined by the changing realities on the ground (Jervis, 1986; Elrod, 1976).

Polanyi referred to this historical period as "the hundred years' peace", the title of the famous first chapter of *The Great Transformation.* He emphasised that the balance-of-power system could not on its own ensure peace. This was actually achieved with the help of international finance, the very existence of which embodied the principle of the new dependence of trade upon peace (Polanyi, 1957:15). Financial interests could benefit from limited wars but were instrumental in preventing a general war. Similarly, today the global financial elites might share an interest in some kind of re-regulation in the interest of systemic stability (Helleiner, 2000).

Henry Kissinger (1992, 1996) again argued for a recreation of a power "concert" in the current situation. This is not surprising, since it is the most realistic model from a realist point of view. As noted above, more than two decades back Bull termed this model the Kissinger Mode. The concert will now be constituted by the USA, Europe (the EU), Russia, Japan, China and India. The 19th century Concert was a regional system, but this is no longer possible according to Kissinger: "Never before has a new world order had to be assembled from so many different perceptions, or on so global a scale" (Kissinger, 1996:180). Yet, many nations in the poorer areas are excluded, and as Bull has already stated with regard to this model, it is unlikely to be capable of achieving the kind of status that a sustainable world order will require.[12]

The multilateral model in a strengthened more assertive form has been suggested by the International Commission on Global Governance, headed by the former Swedish Prime Minister Ingvar Carlsson. This model is based on radical reform of the United Nations. For instance, the Security Council must be made more representative, and the General Assembly should have representatives also from civil society. A strengthened Economic and Social Council would take responsibility for global development (International Commission on Global Governance, 1995). The nation-states, at least the stronger among them, would remain in, or resume, control of their development, although they would have to operate "in a complex system of overlapping and often competing agencies of governance" (Hirst and Thompson, 1996: 183).

Both the neo-Westphalia models in fact imply a strong great power influence, in the case of *assertive multilateralism* not only Western powers but all regional great powers, in the case of *militant plurilateralism* most realistically the trans-Atlantic alliance. It is important to take note of the degree to which these two models really differ. How multi must multilateralism be?[13] Global alliance-building for a specific purpose, such as fighting terrorism, is not necessarily a solid base for multilateralism.

For there to be a significant difference between multilateralism and plurilateralism, the UN system has to undergo a major change, including a reasonable representation from various regions of the world; in fact a "multilateralisation". Both the League of Nations in its time and the United Nations today have been dominated by a number of great powers, i.e. plurilateralism, in spite of the principle of one nation, one vote.

---

[12] See the following quotation by Bull:
> The states system, as we have argued, can remain a viable means to world order only if it proves possible to preserve and extend the consensus within about common interest and values. No consensus is possible today that does not take account of the demands of Asian, African and Latin American countries and peoples for just change . . . (Bull, 1977: 300).

[13] The explicit distinction between multilateralism and plurilateralism, which has been made here, is not generally made in the literature. Raimo Väyrynen (inspired by Cerny, 1993) emphasises instead the multitude of actors in a process of structural differentiation towards a "complex structure", i.e. actors other than states, whereas the concept here is given a more state-centric orientation, since we are discussing neo-Westphalia models. Ruggie (1998: 102) defines multilateralism as based on a principle to which three or more parties adhere. It is inclusive. Plurilateralism can be defined as a shared interest among a limited number of countries, who do not form a regional group. Thus, a plurilateral grouping may be larger than a multilateral one, but the latter is always potentially larger, since it in principle is inclusive, provided the underlying principle is adhered to. To the degree that bilateral, plurilateral and regional organisations take on a more inclusive quality, they are "multilateralised", and such a non-multilateral organisation can in fact have "multilateralism (for instance free trade) as a long-term objective.

Assertive multilateralism still only exists on paper, since the various reform proposals dealing with the UN system have so far only been implemented to a marginal degree. The UN cannot but be an extension and function of the states system. It was never intended to be otherwise. Therefore it tends to decline as this system declines, and may therefore be unreformable. On the other hand in the last few years there has unquestionably been a new dynamics associated with the new leadership of Kofi Annan. Furthermore, the more realistic scenario of plurilateralism, particularly in its militant form demonstrated in Kosovo, is inconsistent with previously accepted principles of international law. It is true that the formation of international law is a process, and that the sovereignty argument is now contradicted by the human rights argument in favour of "humanitarian intervention". However, the question of who is the legal intervenor in domestic humanitarian emergencies remains. NATOs prominent role in this regard is due to its military strength and a high degree of institutionalisation, not its inherent legitimacy as a world police. Nor can an alliance of the type that was built after September 11 be maintained for long. Again, further multilateralisation seems to be the remedy. So far, the only legitimate humanitarian action that includes coercion comes from the UN. However, in a crisis situation unilateral or at best plurilateral solutions seem more likely.

Another possible form for the return of the political is a post-Westphalia order where the locus of power moves up to the transnational level. The state can be replaced or complemented by a regionalised order of political blocs, a New Regionalism (Hettne, *et al.*, 1999–2001) or by a strengthened global civil society with a new normative architecture of world order values. Richard Falk (1999) now prefers to call this model, to which he has contributed a lot over the years, *global democracy*. Elsewhere, (Kaldor, 1999; Held, 1995; Archibugi and Held, 1995) it is also referred to as *global cosmopolitanism* or *cosmopolitan governance*. It is a world order based on global values and norms, and the rule of law, monitored by a vigilant civil society, the result of which would be humane global governance.

Both these scenarios represent a firmer step towards supranational governance either on a regional or a global basis, possibly in combination, as in Falk's contribution to this book. Polanyi saw the post-World War II order as a horizontal world of regions. Bull later discussed regionalism as a purely utopian world order. Today it is much less utopian. There are some aspects derived from contrasting old and new regionalisms, which are theoretically significant. First, the focus on the multitude of actors which points beyond state-centric approaches. Second, the focus on the "real" region in the making, rather than the formal region defined by member states. Third, the focus on the global context – the process of globalisation – as an exogenous factor not really considered by old regionalism theory, concerned as it was with regional integration as a merger of national economies through co-operation between nation-states. Thus, with the concept of New

Regionalism the focus is on general characteristics and general conditions related to what is called globalisation.

Regionalisation as a new trend is worldwide albeit modest. In spite of that, it provokes nostalgic nationalism and may itself become introverted and fortress-like. For that reason it needs a strong civil society at the regional level. Regional multilateralism or multiregionalism rejects cultural hegemonism and accepts "the desirability of a world order reconstructed to accommodate inter-civilisational identities and aspirations" (Falk, 2000b, 157). In another context, Falk has stated that the normative possibilities for international society are now more compelling than ever, but the substantial displacement of a statist world makes it necessary to recast such aspirations, as well as rethink our conceptual tools for the framing of world order (Falk, 1999).

Global cosmopolitanism emphasises the role of community at the global level as well as the formation of global norms. However, it needs institutionalisation. Humanity does not constitute a political community, much less a political actor. Humanitarian intervention, as was discussed above, has been carried out in the name of humanity, by militarily co-operating states, sometimes in a formal UN context, sometimes in a plurilateral form, and sometimes complemented by various non-military forms through international non-governmental organisations, representing what is somewhat prematurely referred to as a global civil society.

References

Abrahamsson, H., 1997, *Seizing the Opportunity. Power and Powerlessness in a Changing World order: The Case of Mozambique*, Göteborg: Padrigu.

Archibugi, D. and D. Held (eds.), 1995, *Cosmopolitan Democracy. An Agenda for a New World order*, Cambridge: Polity Press.

Beck, U., 1997, *The Reinvention of Politics, Rethinking Modernity in the Global Social Order*, Cambridge: Polity Press.

Brandt Commission (Independent Commission on International Development Issues), 1980, *North – South. A Programme for Survival*, London: Pan Books.

Bramsted, E. and Melhuish, K. (eds.), 1978, *Western Liberalism. A History in Documents from Locke to Croce*, London: Longman.

Bull, H., 1977, *The Anarchical Society. A Study of Order in World Politics*, London: Macmillan.

Carr, E.H., 1969, *History of Soviet Russia: The Interregnum*, Harmondsworth: Penguin Books.

Carr, E.H., 1984 (1946), *The Twenty Years' Crisis 1919–1939*, London: Macmillan.

Castells, M., 1996, *The Rise of the Network Society* (The Information Age, Vol.1), Oxford: Blackwell.

Cerny, P., 1990, *The Changing Architecture of Politics, Structure, Agency, and the Future of the State*, London: Sage Publications.

Cerny, P., 1993, "Plurilateralism, Structural Differentiation and Functional Conflict in the Post-Cold War World Order", *Millennium*, vol. 22, no.1, pp. 27–51.

Cerny, P., 1998, "Neomediavalism, Civil War and the New Security Dilemma: Globalization as Durable Disorder", *Civil Wars*, vol. 1, no. 1, pp. 36–64.

Chabal, P. and Daloz, J-P., 1999, *Africa Works. Disorder as Political Instrument*, Oxford: James Currey.

Chandhoke, N., 1995, *State and Civil Society. Explorations in Political Theory*, New Delhi: Sage.

Clark, I., 1997, *Globalization and Fragmentation. International Relations in the Twentieth Century*, Oxford: Oxford University Press.

Cox, R., 1995, "Critical Political Economy", in Hettne, B. (ed.), *International Political Economy. Understanding Global Disorder*, London: Zed Books.

Cox, R. with T.J. Sinclair, 1996, *Approaches to World Order*, Cambridge: Cambridge University Press.

Cox, R. (ed.), 1997, *The New Realism. Perspectives on Multilateralism and World Order*, London: Macmillan, and Tokyo: United Nations University Press.

Cox, R., 1999, "Civil Society at the Turn of the Millennium: Prospects for an Alternative World Order", *Review of International Studies*, vol. 25, no. 1, pp. 3–28.

Duffield, M., 1998, "Post-modern Conflict, Warlords, Post-adjustment States and Private Protection", *Civil Wars*, vol. 1, no. 1, pp. 65–102.

DUPI, Copenhagen, 1999, *Humanitarian Intervention. Legal and Political Aspects.*

Edwards, M., 1999, *Future Positive. International Co-operation in the 21st Century*, Earthscan.

Elrod, R., 1976, "The Concert of Europe. A Fresh Look at an International System", *World Politics*, vol. 28, January, pp. 163–166.

Falk, R., 1999, *Predatory Globalism. A Critique*, Cambridge: Polity Press

Falk, R., 2000a, "Human Governance for the World, Reviving the Quest", in Nederveen Pieterse, J., *Global Futures. Shaping Globalization*, London: Zed Books.

Falk, R., 2000b, *Human Rights Horizons. The Pursuit of Justice in a Globalizing World*, New York and London: Routledge.

Gamble, A., 2001, "Regional Blocs, World Order and the New Mediaevalism", in Telo, M. (ed.), *European Union and the New Regionalism*, Alderhot: Ashgate.

Gill, S. and J. Mittelman (eds.), 1997, *Innovation and Transformation in International Studies*, Cambridge: Cambridge University Press.

Gills, B.K. (ed.), *Globalization and the Politics of Resistance*, London: Macmillan.

Hayek, F.A., 1944, *The Road to Serfdom*, London: Routledge.

Held, D., 1995, *Democracy and the Global Order. From the Modern State to Cosmopolitan Governance*, Cambridge: Polity Press.

Helleiner, E., 2000, *Globalization and Haute Finance – Deja vu?*, in McRobbie, K. and K. Polanyi Levitt (eds.), *Karl Polanyi in Vienna. The Contemporary Significance of The Great Transformation*, Montreal: Black Rose Books.

Hettne, B., 1995a, "Introduction: The International Political Economy of Transformation", in Hettne, B. (ed.), *International Political Economy. Understanding Global Disorder*, London: Zed Books.

Hettne, B., 1995b, *Development Theory and the Three Worlds*, London: Macmillan.

Hettne, B., 1997, "The Double Movement: Global Market versus Regionalism", in Cox, R.W., *The New Realism. Perspectives on Multilateralism and World Order*, Tokyo: United Nations University Press.

Hettne, B., 2000, "Rereading Polanyi. Towards a Second Great Transformation", in McRobbie, K. and K. Polanyi Levitt (eds.), *Karl Polanyi in Vienna. The Contemporary Significance of The Great Transformation*, Montreal: Black Rose Books.

Hettne, B., 2001, "Discourses on Peace and Development", *Progress in Development Studies*, vol. 1, no. 1, pp. 21–36.

Hettne, B., Inotai, A., and O. Sunkel (eds.), 1999/2001, *Studies in the New Regionalism. Volume I–V*, London: Macmillan Press.

Hoare, Q. and G. Nowell Smith (eds.), 1971, *Selections From The Prison Notebooks of Antonio Gramsci*, London: Lawrence and Wishart.

Hobsbawn, E., 1994, *The Age of Extremes. The Short Twentieth Century 1914–1991*, London: Abacus.

Hirst, P. and G. Thompson, 1996, *Globalization in Question, the International Economy and the Possibilities of Governance*, Cambridge: Polity Press.

Holton, R. J., 1998, *Globalization and the Nation State*, London: Macmillan.

Huntington, S.P., 1993, "The Clash of Civilizations", *Foreign Affairs*, vol. 72, no. 3, pp. 22–42.

Independent International Commission on Kosovo, 2000, *The Kosovo Report*, Oxford University Press.

International Commission on Global Governance, 1995, *Our Global Neighbourhood*, Oxford University Press.

Jervis, R., 1986, "From Balance to Concert. A Study of Security Cooperation", in Oye, K. (ed.), *Cooperation Under Anarchy*, Princeton: Princeton University Press.

Kaldor, M., 1999, *New & Old Wars. Organized Violence in a Global Era*, Cambridge: Polity Press.

Kaplan, R., 1994, "The Coming Anarchy", *Atlantic Monthly*, February, pp. 44–76.

Kissinger, H., 1966, *A World Restored, Metternich, Castlereagh and the Problems of Peace 1812–22*, Boston: Houghton Mifflen.

Kissinger, H., 1992, "Balance of Power Sustained", in Allison, G. and G. Treverton (eds.), 1992, *Rethinking America's Security. Beyond Cold War to New World Order*, New York: W.W. Norton.

Kissinger, H., 1996, "The New World Order", in Crocker, C.A. and Hampson, F.O. with P. Aall (eds.), *Managing Global Chaos. Sources of and Responses to International Conflict*, Washington: United States Institute of Peace Press.

Nederveen Pieterse, J., 2000, *Global Futures. Shaping Globalization*, London: Zed Books.

Paul, T.V. and Hall, J. (eds.), 1999, *International Order and the Future of World Politics*, Cambridge: Cambridge University Press.

Polanyi, K., 1945, "Universal Capitalism or Regional Planning", *London Quarterly of World Affairs*, January 1945, pp. 86–91.

Reno, W., 1995, *Corruption and State Politics in Sierra Leone*, Cambridge: Cambridge University Press.

Reno, W., 1998, *Warlord Politics and African States*, London: Lynne Rienner.

Rist, G., 1997, *The History of Development*, London: Zed Books.

Ruggie, J., 1998, *Constructing the World Polity. Essays on International Institutionalization*, London and New York: Routledge.

Sadowski, Y., 1998, *The Myth of Global Chaos*, Washington: Brookings Institution Press.

Tester, K., 1992, *Civil Society*, London and New York: Routledge.

UNDP, 1994, *Human Development Report 1994*, New York and Oxford: Oxford University Press.

UNRISD, 1995, *States of Disarray, The Social Effects of Globalization*, Geneva.

UNRISD, 2000, *Visible Hands. Taking Responsibility for Social Development*, Geneva.

2. The Liberal Globalist Case

Indra de Soysa and Nils Petter Gleditsch

The Globalisation Debate

Globalisation is currently *the* catchphrase for the perils and promises facing humanity in the 21st century.[1] Globalisation is generally understood as economic, political, and social integration of states and societies, both horizontally and vertically in tighter webs of interdependence. Globalisation is a *process* and not a qualitatively different end-state where politics has receded and the market has taken over. Integration of national states in the global economy is currently taking place via at least two major visible and measurable processes – the rapid spread of foreign capital and trade and the spread of the ideas of political democracy and market economy to an extent never before witnessed in modern history. The debate on the desirability of globalisation takes place between those who see this trend as mutually beneficial and those who see it as the intensification of exploitation, at least where the so called international capitalist forces are concerned.

Most governments in the developed and developing worlds, and many international organisations such as the International Monetary Fund (IMF), the World Bank and United Nations Conference on Trade and Development (UNCTAD), are generally favourable to the idea of international integration.[2] In the public debate, however, globalisation is often portrayed as exploitation by the strong (multinational corporations and industrialised states) of the weak (the developing states), which will ultimately lead to social disarray and conflict.[3] Today, most developing countries welcome foreign capital and wish to open up to the international trading system. This is in clear contrast to the 1960s and 1970s, when many practised import substitution and formed what seemed to be a solid bloc around the group of 77, which called for a New International Economic Order to replace a biased system that was ostensibly exploitative (Bhagwati, 1999; Birdsall and Lawrence, 1999).

The debate on globalisation has moved beyond the academic arena. As

---

[1] For overviews of the debate, see Burtless, Lawrence, Litan and Shapiro, 1998; Dunning and Hamdani, 1997; Giddens, 1999; Gilpin, 2000; Held and McGrew, 2000; Nye and Donahue, 2000; Sakamoto, 1994.

[2] See, for instance, UNCTAD, 1998; UNDP, 1999; World Bank, annual.

[3] The best-known attack on globalisation is Martin and Schumann, 1997. Other critical accounts of globalisation are Mittelman, 1997; Gray, 1999; Rodrik, 1997.

shown by the violent demonstrations in Seattle, Prague, Gothenburg and elsewhere, anti-globalisation forces have been galvanised into action on the streets. Movements such as Attac, that are devoted to challenging the liberalisation of the global economy, are spreading. Coalitions against globalisation are formed by some unlikely partners. They include supporters of such populist American politicians as Patrick Buchanan and Ross Perot, who want to see an end to US involvement in multilateral treaties and an end to the United Nations system, the World Bank and the IMF, organised labour interested in protecting domestic markets and jobs, supporters of the Third World devoted to opposing what they see as imperialistic processes, anarchists and environmentalists (Micklethwait and Wooldridge, 2000). Even the European Commission has been known to lay blame on globalisation for unemployment in Europe (Krugman and Venables, 1995).

It may well be true that these disparate protesters are beginning to influence a political discourse that has started to question whether the process of globalisation lacks a human face and that proposes to make globalisation work for the poor. We argue that the weight of the evidence suggests that globalisation already benefits the poor. As Jagdish Bhagwati and others have suggested, Seattle and the noisy protests since have led to the privatisation of policymaking, rather than to promoting the liberalisation of markets and encouraging free trade (Bhagwati, 1999).

There is a mountain of books on the subject. Most of the literature is journalistic and anecdotal. The confusion and contentiousness of the issues are captured in popular epithets, which are slung back and forth, such as global-babble, globaloney and globaldegook. There is much confusion surrounding definitions and terms, making it difficult to evaluate findings, and as a result, to formulate optimal policies. A few scholars have tried to synthesise the debate more systematically, but their voices can barely be heard above the transnational clamour.[4] Given the collapse of the bipolar configuration that dominated the post-war years, the future of global prosperity and peace depends in large measure on the sound and timely management of these processes.[5]

The developing world is faced with an array of options for development and political change. Improving the prospects of the 20 percent of the world's population who live in the developing world on little less than $1 per day (estimated at 1.3 billion people) has replaced the nuclear arms race as the world's most problematic issue (Boutros-Ghali, 1995). Some formerly third-world states are doing remarkably well in terms of raising incomes, instituting good governance and creating social peace, while others have imploded

---

[4] For balanced overviews of the main issues see, for instance, Held and McGrew, 2000; Nye and Donahue, 2000; Väyrynen, 1999; Østerud, 1999.

[5] See for instance Gilpin, 2000; Heilbroner, 1995; Nye and Donahue, 2000; von Laue, 1987.

in violence and disarray, largely due to a lack of good governance and failure to improve people's living conditions. While the term globalisation is relatively new, the issue of whether or not global structures and agents benefit poor countries, or indeed exploit them, has been at the core of social research on the problems of development for decades. Issues of development and underdevelopment were discussed within the framework of modernisation theory and dependency theory, discussions mirrored in the current debate.

While neoliberal, modernisation theorists view closer international economic contact as a strong factor in the modernisation of poorer countries, structuralists (or world-system theorists) view such contact as the continuation of neo-colonial processes. They appeal to structural theories of imperialism and theories of unequal exchange to argue that international contact between strong and weak states results in adverse socio-economic outcomes for the poor.[6] They argue, in particular, that foreign direct investment (FDI) and trade are forms of international capitalist exploitation of developing societies, and that greater contact perpetuates poverty and leads to societal disarray and conflict within the developing world.[7]

In contrast, neoliberal models blame internal processes of bad government and dirigiste policies, and do not see international processes as the cause of underdevelopment. They argue that the subversion of domestic and international markets, not their fair functioning, is to blame for underdevelopment. These theories suggest that globalisation can prevent narrow interests from dominating the market. The narrowing of ideological schisms and the spread of democracy will improve social welfare, since the created wealth can be redistributed in an accountable, if not consensual, manner.

We have been commissioned to produce a scenario for the liberal globalist case based on the idea that most decisions regarding resource allocation can be left to the market, and that political intervention in general is less efficient and in the long run suboptimal for all. In line with this mandate, we focus mainly on literature and statistical evidence that illuminate the liberal globalist case. We cannot engage in all lines of argument of those who challenge the forces of globalisation, but we show that the fears of those who see market forces as being disruptive of progress, thought of in terms of prosperity and peace, are misplaced. As the mandate suggests, we agree that most decisions about resource allocation are best left up to the market.

However, well-functioning markets also require good governance. States which have tried to do too much have failed, but government is needed for the proper regulation of markets, in order to correct market failure. Well-

---

[6] See Hoogvelt, 2001, for a synthesis.
[7] Neomarxist dependency arguments continue to be expounded by some scholars, such as Amin, 1990 and Mittelmann, 1997. See also Hettne, 1995, and Hoogvelt, 2001.

functioning markets serve to strengthen government in an organic relation-ship between state and society (Hall and Ikenberry, 1989; Lal, 2000). Mar-kets and states are not mutually exclusive.[8]

Few liberal globalists will argue that the World Trade Organisation (WTO), that governs the global free trade regime, is unimportant for stability and the institutionalisation of rules. Neither would it be prudent to dissolve the IMF and the World Bank as lenders of last resort. We argue that globalisation is, in the long run, likely to strengthen rather than weaken states and demo-cratic forces, because open markets require institutional development and afford governments larger budgets to do what is necessary for generating greater growth and socio-economic development. Open markets create pros-perity, strengthen institutions and indirectly create the conditions that pro-mote democracy. Social peace also follows under these conditions as an intended and unintended consequence.[9]

While we draw on some theory and evidence that demonstrates the ben-efits of greater integration for peace and prosperity globally, we particularly focus on the effects of globalisation on developing countries. We do not want to discount the active debate on globalisation's effects on workers in rich countries, a topic that is widely discussed in the literature (Rodrik, 1997; Burtless, et al., 1998; Williamson, 1997). However, our primary concern is the enormous problem of poverty, inequality, crises of governance, and con-flict in the developing world, problems that are increasingly becoming sa-lient to us all, regardless of where we live. Violent conflict, disease, state collapse, environmental degradation or uncontrolled human migration – all of these phenomena carry spillovers to everyday life in the farthest corners of the globe. As we show, these problems are not located among the states, largely located in East and South East Asia, that practise open economics, show high trade to gross domestic product (GDP) ratios and attract much of the world's FDI, but among those states that have largely been bypassed by the forces of globalisation. Many of these states have been hostile to liberal economic principles of free markets, and are plagued by political and social conditions that perpetuate their marginalisation.

---

[8] See Tanzi, 2000, for an enumeration of arguments and for an excellent historical sketch of the growth of government, its failure and success.

[9] In his treatise, The Wealth of Nations, Adam Smith argued against the mercantilistic practices of the day, which he saw as the creation of wealth for national glory that benefited only the politically powerful. Contrarily, he gave birth to classical liberal economic principles that view the importance of each individual's desires to maximise his/her wealth as contributing more effectively towards increasing national wealth and well-being. For Smith, as for other liberals, self-interested pursuit in economic life was more harmonious than conflictual, but harmony and productivity were to be guaranteed by the sovereign or commonwealth with the creation of institutions that safeguarded property rights, law and order, and provided public goods. For Smith, the state has a role in promoting economic development, albeit a limited one. Many developing countries do indeed have big govern-ments, but not ones that devote their time effectively to the tasks Adam Smith prescribes.

In the following section we define the main dimensions of globalisation and attempt to assess its emergence and growth. Subsequently we enumerate what we see as the most important yardsticks for human progress – democracy, development, environment and peace – and perform a brief audit on the state of the world. Next, we assess the influence of globalisation on human progress before summing up our arguments in the last section. Given the enormity of the literature and the scope of the debate, combined with the limited resources, we have had to cut many corners. However, we hope that our basic message comes across: although globalisation presents many challenges, it also represents an opportunity for building a more humane world, for strengthening the socio-economic position of the largest segment of humanity and for protecting social peace.

The most immediate challenge for governments and peoples around the globe will be to distinguish clearly the promises and perils of globalisation and formulate the necessary policies that will yield the optimum outcomes. This task will become increasingly difficult given the incoherence of noisy protests, but it is more surmountable today than decades ago when ideology played such a divisive role. Twentieth century history has been one of unprecedented progress and of massive disruption, but the relatively peaceful end of a decades-long arms race and tense rivalry between the two superpowers suggests the importance of human agency and humanity's capacity for acting constructively in this new century.

The Advance of Globalisation

What is globalisation and how do we assess its consequences? These are contested issues. As Robert Keohane and Joseph Nye argue, the importance of faraway places in the history of peoples has ebbed and flowed to varying degrees, during various forms of globally consequential phenomena and in various arenas from politics to microbes (Keohane and Nye, 2000). The current period of economic liberalisation is such a flow-phase. We concur with their view that the best way to understand waves of globalisation is by assessing their "thickness". Europe and China were once connected by the silk route, plied mainly by bands of traders who transferred such culturally pervasive goods as noodles and gunpowder from China to Europe.

The present wave of globalisation, however, is thicker, in that a variety of issues become salient across the globe almost instantaneously, through television images and instant communication. At the same time, relatively short periods of time are required for the consequences of human migration, financial crises, war, human rights and environmental issues to be manifested transnationally. The current wave of globalisation is clearly being driven by highly visible and measurable economic processes, such as the growth of trade and rapid spread of foreign capital (Bordo, *et al.*,1999; Milner and Keohane, 1996). This is also evident in the spread of democratic institutions and an unprecedented adherence to the ideology of the market economy. A newer element of globalisation that is still difficult to assess in a balanced way is the emergence of virtual communities through electronic communications.

Massive declines in transportation costs and the development of electronic means of communication have shrunk the globe. There is a vast difference between what is possible in the market today (even if it is not fully realised) as opposed to when goods were transferred along the silk route or when the age of empire globalised economic activity in the 19th century. Today we live in a truly global age. This section begins with a discussion on the expansion of economic integration, followed by a brief examination of the revolution in electronic communications. The spread of democracy is discussed in the next section.

When did the present wave of globalisation begin? In the political arena, the start of the liberalising trend has been dated to the mid-1970s (Huntington, 1991). If we look to economic liberalisation as a key, we might place the turning-point in the late 1970s, when far-reaching deregulation began in the USA under Jimmy Carter and was later reinforced under Ronald Reagan (Henderson, 2000). The United Kingdom embraced liberal economic policies after the Thatcher victory in 1979, and extensive liberalisation was subsequently introduced in France (from 1982), Australia (from 1983), Canada and New Zealand (both from 1984). More surprisingly, China started a "rush to capitalism" in 1978, followed by a number of smaller third-world countries and, more significantly, by India from 1991. For Eastern Europe and the Soviet Union, the fall of the Berlin Wall in 1989 marked a turning-point.

But changes in world politics had been brewing before that, in what has been referred to as a "quiet cataclysm" (Mueller, 1995). Some even heralded the changes as the "end of history" (Fukuyama, 1991). Others have viewed the primary driver of globalisation as the "death of distance" (Cairncross, 2001) brought on by the revolution in information and communications technology, also in the late 1970s. Some others interpret what happened during this period as a culture shift that recognised the failure of a modernist project which sought to force-march and force-feed society. Development had to be kinder and more gentle to be legitimate, or in fact to be considered as development at all (Sen, 1999). Initially, countries liberalised their internal economies, but in turn this also had consequences for the international economies. Significant steps in this regard were the decision in 1986 to establish a Single Market in the European Union, the expansion of ASEAN (originally formed in 1967), the growth of regional groupings such as NAFTA, Mercosur, APEC and others, and the re-emergence of GATT and the WTO as international instruments for governing the free-trade regime. The economic interchange has not simply consisted in the movement of goods and money, but has also been increasingly accompanied by a movement of labour.

Trade

Integration in the form of trade is not, of course, a new phenomenon. By the end of the 19th century, trade exceeded thirty percent of GDP in several European countries. Alberto Alesina and his associates show that for nine European countries with long data series, the average trade/GDP ratio was roughly stable until about 1930, when it dropped and stayed down during the depression and war years. After World War II, it rose rapidly to the pre-1930 level where it stayed until it started rising again in the early 1970s (Alesina, *et al.*, 2000: Figure 1). In Figure 1 we reproduce a time-series for a larger sample of sixty-one countries from 1950, which shows that trade open-ness has picked up remarkably during the period we have identified as the globalisation years.[10] Of course, during that same period GDP has increased immensely, and the absolute value of trade even more so.

Figure 1. Trade as Share of GDP, 1950–95 (%)

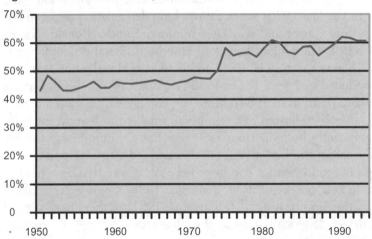

Source: Alesina, *et al.* (2000: 1277). We are grateful to the authors for providing a copy of their dataset. The original data sources are from Summers and Heston (1991) and later updates of the Penn World Tables, as well as World Bank data.

Trade in manufactures and intermediate goods appears to have increased considerably more than trade in general (Bordo, *et al.*, 1999). There are also significantly different policymaking environments between the two waves

[10] Other sources, such as Russett and Oneal (2001: 178, Figure 5.1) report a steady long-term decline after 1885, and with little or no evidence of globalisation. Their aggregate figures are, however, based on whatever trade data are available for any given year and are probably also heavily influenced by the emergence of new states. Russett and Oneal themselves point out that information on trade (outside of the major powers) was under-reported before the foundation of the IMF and OECD. Cf. Maddison, 1989 and 2001.

(Baldwin and Martin, 1999). The 19th century's wave of globalisation came with imperial, political control of much of the world, so that international trade often meant trade among the powerful states, a handful of actors. At least since the end of World War II, the number of actors in the global trading system has exploded and the political environment of independent, sovereign, national states makes a qualitative difference when trying to assess outcomes of globalisation. Moreover, to obtain a correct picture of the extent of globalisation one should perhaps compare the current situation with a situation of perfect integration, rather than with the 19th century (See Frankel, 2000). The movement of goods and capital is still subject to overt and covert barriers, and the free movement of labour is highly restricted.

National borders still matter in other ways too. Some studies of the USA and Canada, two countries with a long history of free trade, show that despite physical proximity, Americans and Canadians are far more likely to trade within their own borders than across them. Moreover, our own computation of regional averages from 1960–98 shows great gaps in the share of trade to GDP. Figure 2 shows that all regions have increased their share of trade to GDP, but East and South East Asia outpace other regions, particularly the low income countries as a group and Sub-Saharan Africa, to a considerable degree.[11]

Figure 2. Trade to GDP by Region 1960–98 (%)

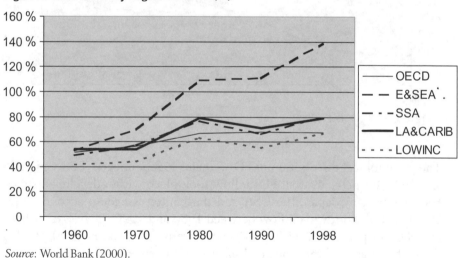

Source: World Bank (2000).

---

[11] Low income countries and the OECD countries have the same average trade-to-GDP ratio. This of course does not mean that international trade cannot be important for well-being. This result simply means that rich countries contain larger domestic markets that drive demand.

Foreign direct investment

While trade has been important for a long time, the extent of economic globalisation is far wider and deeper today than in the previous wave of globalisation in the 19th century. Foreign direct investment now accounts for one-third of global output, three-quarters of commercial technological capacity, and about three-quarters of all world trade (Dunning, 1992: 12). Between 1980 and 1990, FDI quadrupled, increasing at an annual average of 15 percent.[12] Between 1983 and 1990, FDI grew at an unprecedented 27 percent per annum, three times faster than the growth of exports and four times that of world output. Indeed, the 1980s have seen what UNCTAD (1994 and 1995) calls a bulge in the trend in FDI flows, but the 1980s have been outpaced by the 1990s. In 1990, the stock of FDI globally had reached approximately 2,000 billion dollars from a figure a bit under half that. By 1999, a period of just nine years, the stock of FDI more than doubled to reach approximately 4,400 billion dollars (Figure 3).

Figure 3. Global Stock of FDI, 1980–99 (billions 1996 USD)

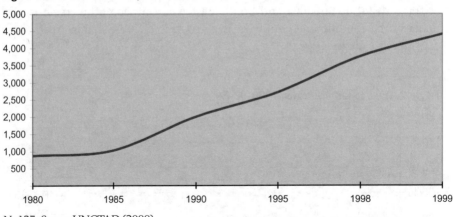

N=127. *Source*: UNCTAD (2000).

The geographical distribution of FDI remains highly uneven. Between 1985 and 1990, 83 percent of all FDI inflow took place within developed states. France, Germany, Japan, the USA and the United Kingdom accounted for 56 percent of worldwide inflow between 1980 and 1990 (UNCTAD, 1994). In 1960, 48 percent of all FDI originated from the USA. In 1990, the US share of FDI around the globe had shrunk to 26 percent, with Japan becom-

---

[12] Except where other sources are cited, the figures in this subsection are based on UNCTAD, 2000; World Bank, 2000, and our own calculations from these sources.

ing a major capital exporter. In 1990, approximately 79 percent of the total inward FDI stock globally could be found in twenty developed states. By 1999, this figure had fallen to 69 percent, with China alone accounting for almost 7 percent of global stock. All of Africa, with its abundant natural resources accounts for a mere 2 percent of global stock. With regard to FDI, globalisation still has a long way to go, and there is even some evidence that certain areas are becoming less globalised in terms of trade and investment ratios to GDP.[13] For many developing countries, the problem is how to attract FDI, not how to repel it.

Recent trends show, however, that more investment is now flowing to poorer countries. Between 1980 and 1990, the mean annual rate of investment for least developed countries (LDCs) was 9 percent, which increased to 13.4 percent between 1990 and 1997. Moreover, the FDI stock to GDP ratio (a standard measure of the internationalisation of the economy) increased from 8 percent in 1980 to 14 percent by 1990 and 27 percent in 1998. The correlation between the level of trade to GDP and the FDI stock to GDP ratio increased from 0.47 for 1980 to 0.58 for 1990 and 0.62 for 1997. Higher levels of international capital seem to be tied to increasing levels of international trade within economies. Some studies suggest that FDI is responsible for driving greater levels of trade but that initially more open economies also seemed to have attracted greater amounts of FDI (De Melo, 1999).

For a sample of twenty rich countries (the main capital exporters), the average stock of FDI to GDP ratio was 7 percent in 1980, 13 percent in 1990, and 23 percent in 1998 respectively. Clearly, both poorer countries and the richest ones are becoming internationalised at a rather rapid rate according to the FDI stock to GDP ratio. The level of internationalisation is now almost equal in rich and poor countries (Figure 4). FDI in the rich countries is clearly driven by technological and market factors. For the poor countries, much of this is owed to drastic changes in the attitude of governments towards FDI, a major impediment in the past.

---

[13] See Hoogvelt, 2001, for similar statistics and conclusions.

Figure 4. FDI stock to GDP ratio (MNC penetration) 1980–98

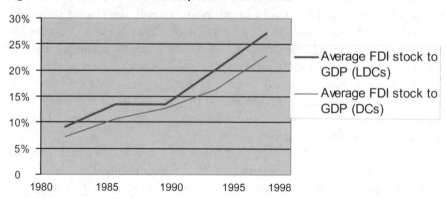

Sources: FDI stock data are from UNCTAD (2000) and GDP from *World Bank* (2000).

Electronic communications

International interaction, positive as well as negative, has traditionally been constrained by distance. Goods to be traded, immigrants, tourists, troops – all are subject to the time and costs involved in transactions between distant points. Until recently, even telephone calls and cables were subject to pricing roughly proportional to the distance travelled by the message, making long-distance very expensive and often cumbersome

Modern electronic communications, such as e-mail and the Internet, counteract the "tyranny of distance". Figure 5 gives an indication of how these forms of communication have exploded in the era of globalisation. While the use of these means of communication is still subject to a 'digital divide' within and between nations, this is no different than the pattern found for any new technology.[14] The decreasing user costs of the electronic forms of communication promise that they will continue to grow very rapidly.

Supporters and critics of globalisation agree that the rapidly expanding integration – economic and virtual – cannot fail to have a lasting impact on human affairs in a number of ways. Before we examine their dissenting claims, we ask what standards they should be evaluated against.

---

[14] For data on the digital divide in the US, see Hanson, 1999. For data by nation, see Juliussen and Petska-Juliussen, 1998: 315. For Danish data on the spread of consumer goods over time, see Lomborg, 1998: 72.

Figure 5. Economic and Virtual Globalization, 1981–98

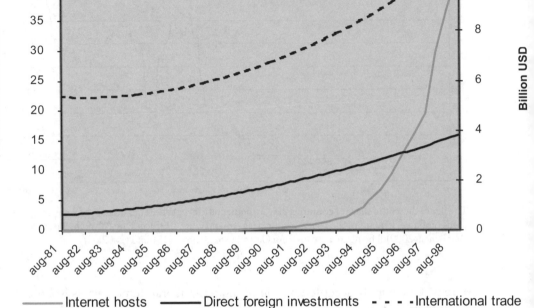

——— Internet hosts   ——— Direct foreign investments   - - - -International trade

The growth of the Internet is measured by the number of registered addresses in the world, as recorded by Network Wizards at http://www.nw.com/zone/host-count-history. The figures for world trade are taken from the UN *Statistical Yearbook* (annual) and the data for FDI from *World Investment Report*, UNCTAD (several years). The two economic indicators are measured in 10^9 1992 US$, corrected for inflation by figures from US Department of Commerce, Bureau of Economic Analysis at http://www.stls.frb.org/ fred/data/gdp/gdpdef. The trade data have been smoothed. The level of virtual integration cannot be compared with the level of economic integration. The point of the graph is to compare the growth of the three indicators of globalisation over time.

Measuring Human Progress

As already noted, globalisation is frequently portrayed as a source of most of the world's perils – and promises. We need some measuring-rods in order to assess the accuracy of these portrayals. We have chosen to concentrate on four relatively consensual values: democracy, development, environment, and peace

Democracy

By democracy we broadly mean governance by the people. There are numerous suggestions as to how to define it more precisely, and how to mea-

Figure 6. The Growth of Democracy 1800–1998

Percentage of democratic countries, 1800-1998

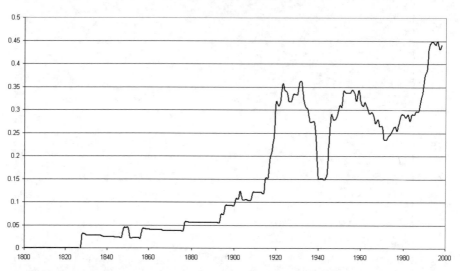

The figure shows the share of countries that are democratic over time. The measure of democracy used combines elements of the Polity measure (Jaggers and Gurr, 1995) and the Polyarchy measure (Vanhanen, 2000). The figure is taken from Gates, Hegre, Jones and Strand (2002: 1).

sure it. One widely accepted notion of modern, liberal democracy is Robert Dahl's concept of polyarchy (Dahl, 1971). Polyarchy is the combination of *political competition* and *political participation*. This is closely in line with a measure of democracy developed by Tatu Vanhanen (2000). Polity, another frequently-cited measure, conceptualises democracy largely in institutional terms, with particular emphasis on *restraints on executive power* (Jaggers and Gurr, 1995). A third approach starts from *civil and political rights*, incorporating factors relating to human rights (Freedom House, annual).

Democratic government has spread over time, but not in a linear fashion. Samuel Huntington (1991) identifies three broad waves of democratisation, which have been verified in quantitative studies. The first wave peaked after World War I and was followed by a period when the two totalitarian movements that arose in Europe reversed democracy in their home countries as well as in many of their neighbouring countries. After the fall of Fascism in 1945 followed soon by decolonisation, democracy was once again on a rising trend, as illustrated in Figure 6. The second wave of democratisation was soon reversed, however, with the continued growth of Communism and the failure of many post-colonial democracies to take hold.

Not until the mid-1970s did the third wave begin, initially with the decline of military rule in Southern Europe, and then after the fall of Communism in 1989, when it was powerfully reinforced. The third wave is still continuing, and has brought the world to a point where more countries and a higher proportion of its peoples live under democratic rule than ever before. Although there have been reversals in some countries, and pessimistic voices about the end of the third wave have made themselves heard from time to time, the trend continues to point upwards.

The third wave of democratisation, then, largely coincides in time with the period that we have identified as the boom-period of globalisation. Only a little over a decade ago, many prognosticated the limits of democratisation because of what they saw to be the growth of "bureaucratic authoritarianism", with the advance of modernisation in the developing world (O'Donnell, 1973). Dependency theorists, in particular, would not have been able to predict such a transformation under liberal economic conditions of increased trade and investment. We may not have reached the "end of history", because movement in reverse has been the historical pattern, but the transformation is remarkable. What about the other indicators of human progress?

Development

One standard measure of the rate of development is the rate of increase of the level of per capita income. Standard neo-classical theory predicts that poorer countries grow faster on average than richer countries because of diminishing returns on capital, usually called the Solow model after the Nobel prize-winning economist. Poor countries were expected to converge with the rich over time because of their higher capacity for absorbing capital. Convergence, however, failed by and large to occur. As Figure 7 shows, the pattern of income growth between rich and poor states overall is roughly equivalent over the period 1950–95, yet this results in divergence, or an increasing gap in the standard of living.

New growth theories have discarded the notion of diminishing returns on capital, showing instead increasing returns on human capital (technology and ideas), which explains why the rich do not always slow down and why some poor countries have failed to grow at all. Poorer countries with higher initial endowments of human capital grew faster than the rich countries in the post-war years (Barro, 1991; Temple, 1999). East and South East Asia's spectacular growth performance is explained partly as a result of having had higher levels of human capital initially. In Africa, on the other hand, the recent growth record is dismal, with a few striking exceptions (Botswana, Mauritius).

There are many objections to GDP per capita as a measure of welfare: wealth can be unevenly distributed (even to the point where a growing average is accompanied by increasing impoverishment), it can be created at the cost of pollution, hazardous work, etc. The United Nations provides several alternative indices of welfare, such as the Human Development Index (a composite measure of life expectancy, education and material stan-

Figure 7. GDP per capita at Purchasing Power Parity (PPP), 1950–95

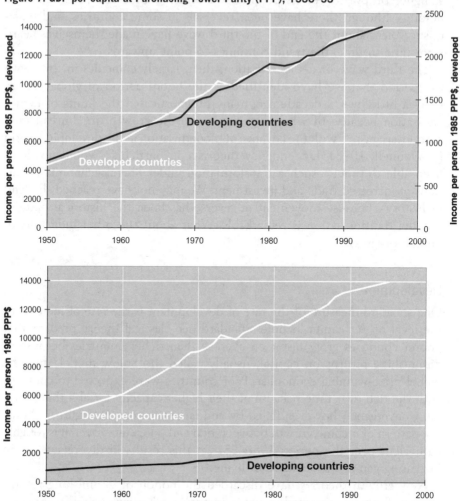

Gross domestic product per capita at 1985 purchasing power parity $. The lower curve shows that the gap is widening. In the upper curve the scales have been adjusted to coincide at 1995, showing that the growth rates are roughly equal. Source: see Lomborg (1998: 67) and Lomborg (2001a), on the basis of Summers and Heston (1991) and World Bank (1996).

dard of living) and the Rate of Progress, which measures the rate of reduction of under-five mortality. While it has often been argued that economic growth and human welfare do not work in tandem, the weight of the evidence suggests that they most certainly do (Chen and Ravaillon, 1998; Dollar and Kraay, 2000; Lal and Mynt, 1996). Using data for 1990–99 (UNICEF, 2000), we find that growth and level of income account for 35 percent of the variance in the rate of reduction of under-five mortality.

Of course, growth is not enough, but increasing income and taxable wealth allow governments to implement the right policies for achieving other objectives. Clearly, some countries fail to ensure progress on indicators such as health and education and policy has a big role to play, but even well-meaning policymakers must create the conditions that allow them the financial means for achieving ends. A plethora of recent studies find that economic growth is strongly related to human welfare, defined in terms of socio-environmental dimensions, such as longevity and education, access to basic needs and the reduction of income inequality (Deininger and Squire, 1997; Lal and Mynt, 1996; Chen and Ravillon, 1998; Dollar and Kraay, 2000). One study concludes that:

> the developing countries suffering from low growth . . . are generally worse off with respect to macro-economic stability and redistributive justice as compared to those enjoying medium growth to high growth (Naqvi, 1996: 977).

In Figure 8 we examine the life expectancy for the world as a whole and separately for industrialised and developing countries. Life expectancy is a welfare measure that is not inflated by extremely high inequalities, within or across nations. All three curves show progress. There are some countries both in the developed part of the world (notably Russia) and among the LDCs where the trends are not as positive, but it is encouraging that progress is being made for the LDCs as a whole.

Figure 8. Life Expectancy, 1950–2050

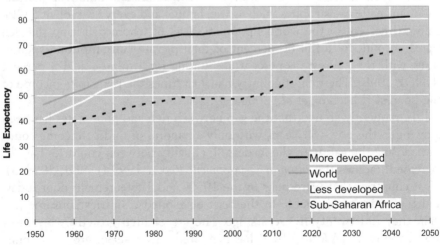

Source: Lomborg (1998: 409; see also 2001a), based on data from Keyfitz and Flieger (1990). The projections are from 1990.

Human welfare can also be measured in terms of consumption of goods weighed against the time spent on acquiring them. Interesting data on this score are provided by Bradford DeLong (2000). The material standard of living and human productive capability have exploded in the 20th century. For example, what took a worker in 1890 an hour's worth of labour to produce on average can be done in seven minutes today. DeLong looks at the prices of various commodities in a Montgomery Ward Catalogue and compares them with hourly wages, so that the relative time spent acquiring a product can be compared over time. A bicycle would have cost 260 hours of work in 1895 for an average working person compared to 7.2 hours in 2000 – 1/36th as much in labour time. A six-volume set of books by Horatio Alger costs 1/34th the labour time, a hundred-piece dinner set costs 1/12th the labour time etc.

Only silverware costs more today, but given the availability of stainless steel, this is hardly a necessary commodity – a teaspoon made of stainless steel would be 1/50th the cost in labour time. Much of DeLong's analysis is only valid for the United States and some rich countries, but the analysis surely holds for many developing countries that have been part of 'the world that trade has created' since at least the 1400s (Pomeranz and Topik, 1998).

Inequality

In the case against globalisation, inequality – alleged to be rising – plays a central role. And, indeed, the gap in income and other forms of welfare between rich and poor citizens of the world is enormous. This is true whether one thinks in terms of disparities in consumption, human development in-dicators such as literacy and health, or of risks to life and limb from natural and man-made catastrophes, such as war, famine and everyday violence. Glo-bally, 20 percent of the world's population, all of whom hail from the rich states, account for a full 86 percent of total private consumption expendi-tures, with the poorest 20 percent accounting for a minuscule 1.3 percent (UNDP, 1998). The richest country had 115 times the per capita income of the poorest (Melchior, et al., 2000a: 9).

It is frequently argued that the gap between rich and poor states has been growing in the post-war years, with only a handful of middle-income coun-tries closing the gap with the leaders. "Inequality between countries has . . . increased", argues the *Human Development Report 1999* (UNDP, 1999: 3). Most countries that were poor in the 1950s and 1960s remain poor today, and the majority of people in the least developed countries consume less than they did twenty-five years ago. The era of high growth, which fol-lowed the end of World War II has benefited only a select group of coun-tries (Gilpin, 1987; Maddison, 1989; Olson, 1996; Spero, 1990). Growth is going to be the major source of poverty alleviation, given that foreign aid budgets are now at the lowest levels in recent history. The end of the Cold War has certainly facilitated the reduction in foreign aid budgets, now a mere 0.25 percent of the GNP on average of the donor countries, and the decline will most likely continue (UNDP, 1998).

The view that inequality has been increasing during the period of globalisation is contested. Comparisons on the basis of income measures adjusted for purchasing power indicate that inequality seems to have decreased over the period 1965–97, when using a measure that takes account of the entire range of income distribution (the Gini index) (Melchior, et al., 2000: 14). Studies using income data that are not adjusted for price differences generally report rising income inequality. For studies using more limited parts of the income distribution, the results depend on what comparisons are made: comparing the richest and poorest 20 percent, Arne Melchior et al. (2000: 15–16) found lower inequality. Reports of higher inequality are usually based either on figures not adjusted for price differences or on more limited parts of the income distribution (highest/lowest 10 percent or even highest/lowest country).

Prior to 1960, world income inequality seems to have increased. The more recent decline is consistent with the inverted U-curve posited by Simon Kuznets (1956). Given that so many developing countries are struggling to come out of stagnation and poverty, we should expect many of them to be on the upturn of the Kuznets curve, but this will not go on forever. Robert Barro (2000) confirms the Kuznets curve on recent data and O'Rourke (2001) argues that the growth of inequality in the past two hundred years may be attributed to between-country inequality, but that the recent trend is one of convergence.

While there is compelling evidence to show that between–country inequality in particular has been rising in the post war years, particularly between 1980 and 1999, much of the increase in the Gini index may be attributed to the growth failures of Africa and Latin America and the collapse of the middle classes in the former Soviet bloc (Milanovic, 2001). If, however, the sample is weighted by population, there is a net decline of inequality, largely driven by the rapid growth of Chinese income, which has quadrupled in comparison with mean world income. Moreover, urban China's rapid growth relative to rural China and India and the steady growth-rate of the industrialised countries in Western Europe and North America accounts for much of the inequality in global terms. The findings of this in-depth study, which uses household surveys and purchasing power parity-based GDPs to measure world income, underline the importance of generating growth where it has failed. As we outline below, trade and investment will be instrumental in generating some of this badly needed growth, and good macro-policies will also contribute towards achieving social peace, which is threatened by absolute poverty.

Eliminating poverty – now a key element of the policy of the World Bank and other international agencies – might well be given priority over the reduction of inequality per se.

Environment

Is our physical environment improving or deteriorating? Are conditions for human survival better or worse? This is a long-standing controversy. Thomas Malthus (1798) predicted extensive famine on the basis of the reasoning that population growth would exceed the growth of food production. He was wrong at the time, but today many neomalthusian thinkers argue that the carrying capacity of the earth is being eroded, and that population pressure, excessive resource consumption (particularly in rich countries) and environmental destruction will combine to produce a major resource crisis that could lead to declining standards of living, impaired governance and armed conflict.[16] Taking the opposite view, cornucopian thinkers argue that population pressures are abating, that the higher value placed on the environment in rich countries bodes well for our environmental future, and that traditional environmental indicators are improving.[17]

The cornucopians point out that many traditional indicators of pollution, such as air pollution in cities and industrial areas (SO_2, soot), human intake of toxic metals like lead, etc., show improvements in the highly developed countries, where environmental improvement is given priority (Lomborg, 1998; 2001a). Likewise, concerns about impending global scarcities in oil, food or minerals have also repeatedly been shown to be exaggerated. Prices of such products have generally fallen, rather than risen, as shown in Figure 9 for food.

The oil crisis of 1974 was a political boycott instigated by the Arab countries in response to the Yom Kippur War, rather than a production crisis. Since then, the main concern of the same countries has been to avoid producing so much that prices would tumble. Water scarcity, often posited as a potential cause of war, is largely a function of wasteful use and lack of sensible pricing. Although sharing a river may increase the probability of conflict between water-constrained countries, such conflict usually leads to co-operative solutions to handle the scarcity rather than to war (Antweiler, *et al*, 1998; Grossman and Krueger, 1993; 1995).

If environmental degradation had been increasing generally, we would expect consequences for human health, such as a declining life expectancy.

---

[16] Prominent spokespeople for the group we label as neomalthusians are Ehrlich and Ehrlich, 1968 and 1996; the World Watch Foundation, annual; Homer-Dixon, 1999.
[17] Broad cornucopian positions are argued in Lomborg, 1998 and 2001a; Simon, 1996. A balanced assessment can be found in Neumayer, 2000.

Figure 9. World Bank Price Index for Foodstuffs, 1957–2000

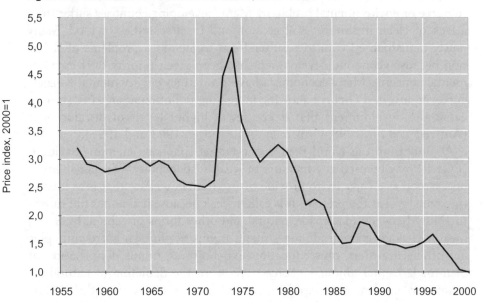

If the neomalthusian prediction of an impending crisis in the production of food were to become true, we should at some point see a sharp increase in food prices. While short-term rises have been observed on a number of occasions, the long-term development of food prices is downward, as illustrated in the World Bank index for foodstuffs. The sharp rise of food prices around 1975 is due to the higher price of energy (and fears of energy shortages) following the Arab oil embargo of 1974. *Source*: Lomborg (2001a; see also 2001b: 130), on the basis of the *International Statistical Yearbook* of the International Monetary Fund.

Such consequences have been observed in the parts of the former Soviet Union which were subject to the worst environmental excesses (Feshbach and Albert, 1992).[18] However, we observe no such decline for the world as a whole, or for most countries caught up in the process of globalisation. This includes poor countries. Indeed, one of the most drastic recent cases of famine in the world is in one of the least globalised countries – North Korea. While environmental degradation and the mismanagement of resources must be safeguarded against, Malthusian crises seem more likely to be corrected than promoted by a policy that encourages trade and exchange on liberal principles.

The fact that the threat of global scarcity in traditional resources so far has

[18] The deterioration of life expectancy in the former Soviet Union is, of course also related to other factors, such as the breakdown of health care, increases in violent crime, drunkenness and deterioration of the social services.

proven to be a red herring does not mean, of course, that there are no resource or environmental problems. Many developing countries suffer from a lack of clean freshwater, soil erosion and local scarcities of food. Many newly-industrialised countries suffer from tremendous problems of pollution because economic development has been given priority over environmental concerns. Many economists have posited an environmental Kuznets curve, an inverted U-curve showing increasing pollution at an early stage of economic development that decreases at higher levels of development (Antweiler, *et al.*, 1998; Grossman and Krueger, 1993 and 1995).

A study from the World Bank suggests that Extended Genuine Saving II (EGS II) may be used as a measure of weak sustainability.[19] Sustainability is understood as a capacity to provide future human welfare that is at least at the same level as the present. It is called weak because it assumes full substitutability between man-made, natural and other forms of capital. EGS II is measured as gross domestic investment, minus net foreign borrowing, plus net official transfers, plus education expenditures, minus depreciation of man-made capital, minus resource rents from the depletion of natural resources, minus damage caused by CO_2 emissions as a proxy for other pollutants. The World Bank finds that the world as a whole, as well as the high-income countries, are safely weak sustainable, while many countries in Sub-Saharan Africa (SSA), North Africa and the Middle East are not. The World Bank data, nevertheless, show that weak sustainability for the lower-income groups has increased in the twenty-year period that we particularly focus on here, as well as for North Africa and the Middle East. Here, as elsewhere, SSA remains the most worrisome region.

Global warming perhaps poses one of the biggest challenges for policy, in terms of ensuring increases in economic activity and safeguarding the global commons. While there is no consensus on the issue, the bulk of the evidence appears to be leaning increasingly towards the position that observed long-term increases in temperature have a man-made component. The consequences of this for human welfare are still very difficult to predict. Some areas of the world will no doubt gain from global warming, while others will lose. Siberia may bloom, while the Maldives and part of Bangladesh may go under water. The Kyoto Protocol aiming at reducing CO_2 emissions remains a concern due to the United States' withdrawal from the process. On the other hand, new technology may provide opportunities for storage of large quantities of CO_2 or reduced emissions, with little change to present production patterns or lifestyles. International agreements to alleviate the effects of global warming may be easier to achieve than agreements to reduce greenhouse gases.

We conclude that there is no evidence for an overall decline in environ-

---

[19] In our summary of World Bank, 1997, we draw heavily on Neumayer, 2000.

mental quality to date. On the contrary, at least in richer countries, environmental quality is improving. The uncertainty lies in the possibility that processes such as global warming might create problems for all inhabitants on this planet in the future.

Below, we will discuss how trade and the transfer of technology from rich to poor may in fact be a way for poor countries to avoid polluting while increasing their standards of living and sustaining social peace.

Peace

At the end of the Cold War, there were two sharply contrasting predictions for the future of human conflict. Realists feared that the collapse of the Soviet empire would unsettle the balance of power and eliminate the nuclear deterrence that had allegedly provided stability after World War II. John Mearsheimer (1990) likened the ending of the Cold War to taking the lid off a pressure cooker at full power; the contents of the pot would quickly scatter all over. Old conflicts that had been held in check by nuclear deterrence would re-emerge and take Europe back to its conflict-ridden past. Mearsheimer even argued that Germany and Ukraine needed nuclear forces to balance their nuclear neighbours, France and Russia respectively (Mearsheimer, 1990; 1993).

In a somewhat different, but also highly pessimistic scenario, Samuel Huntington (1996) argued that conflict in the post-Cold War world would follow age-old faultlines of civilisations, with the Muslim world vs. the West as a particularly unhealthy combination. Radical, structuralist interpretations of world politics in the post-Cold War world have also tended towards the pessimistic. These views focus on the ills that befall the world in the absence of a counterweight to Western economic and military power. Exploitation of the Third World will be exacerbated, because third-world countries can no longer play the Soviet card to obtain concessions from the West. Development assistance will decline, capitalism will run rampant, inequality will increase along with environmental quality – and the net result will be increased turmoil and armed conflict.

The liberal perspective on the post-Cold War world is much more optimistic. It views the passing of the Cold War as an opportunity for ending ideological rivalry, settling military conflict, building peace on a firm basis of democracy and prosperity, strengthening the role of the United Nations in the world order and reducing military expenditure.[20]

Statistics on armed conflict in the post-Cold War world yield a measure of support for the realist pessimism in the former Yugoslavia and in the

---

[20] See, for instance, Gleditsch, *et al.*, 1996 on the peace dividend. On the future of conflict, see Gleditsch, *et al.*, 1998; Mueller, 1995 and 2001; Russett and Oneal, 2001.

Caucasus. In both these areas, the removal of a repressive overlay resulted in violence. However, these conflicts have to be attributed more to the break-down of two authoritarian states, the Soviet Union and Yugoslavia, than to the decline of nuclear deterrence. And despite this, the dissolution of the Soviet empire proceeded in a remarkably peaceful fashion compared, for instance, to the end of the Tsarist, Habsburg or Nazi empires.

Figure 10 shows the development of armed conflict (down to a thresh-old of 25 battle-deaths) after World War II. The figure includes interstate as well as internal conflicts. The data show clearly that the number of ongoing conflicts increased during most of the Cold War. In the aftermath of the great changes in 1989, the number of conflicts increased briefly, mainly due to the new conflicts in the former Yugoslavia and the Soviet Union. Soon, however, that development was reversed, thanks to the new potential for settling conflicts that had been fuelled by the Cold War, particularly in Central America and in some parts of Africa. Moreover, the

Figure 10. Armed Conflicts 1946–2000

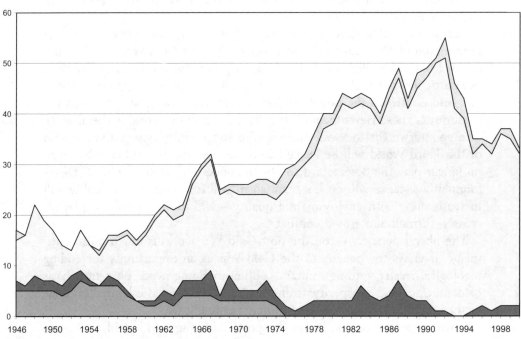

Source: Gleditsch, *et al.*, 2001. Following the guidelines of the Uppsala University Conflict Data project, a conflict is an incompatibility between two actors, where at least one is the government of a country, which leads to at least 25 battle-deaths in a given year. For a more detailed definition, see Wallensteen and Sollenberg, 2001. The lowest area represents extra-systemic conflict (mostly colonial conflict), the next interstate conflict, then internal conflict, and finally internationalised internal conflict.

rising trend during the entire post-war period reflects the increase in the number of states from just under 60 states in 1950s to over 200 today. Much of the state-making and state-breaking process has been disorderly and violent.

Most conflicts in the post-Cold war world, as in the bulk of the Cold War years, have been internal conflicts. There have always been very few inter-state armed conflicts, and in the last few years there have been almost none. Many of the conflicts classified as interstate in recent years (Yugoslavia, Eritrea-Ethiopia and others) have been borderline cases where the warring parties have recently been part of the same national state. An encouraging trend is that there has not been a single interstate war in the post-Cold War era claiming more than 100,000 lives, whereas such wars occurred in every earlier decade in the twentieth century. Most recently, the Iran-Iraq War (1980–88) claimed more than one million lives.

There have been some large wars in terms of the number of countries involved, the amount of military materiel and the number of combat troops (notably the Gulf War of 1991 and the Kosovo war of 1999) but neither war claimed human life anywhere near this scale. The large wars that oc-curred during the Cold War, after all, may also be traced to the ways in which the superpowers played each other off by picking their preferred side and aiding the war with the supply of finance and materiel, as was the case in the war between Iraq and Iran.

The large number of internal conflicts is closely linked to the state-formation process in the decolonisation period, with shifting governance structures and power coalitions, and with numerous unsettled claims for secession. During the Cold War, any such local conflict could become a globally significant issue if the superpowers allied themselves with the war-ring parties, as they did in Afghanistan, Angola, Nicaragua, Vietnam, the Middle East and elsewhere.[21] In the post-Cold War world, the major powers have, to an unprecedented extent, worked together to contain the conflicts rather than exploit them in wars by proxy. The swift and relatively one-sided war to evict Iraq from Kuwait would most certainly have played out differently had US-Soviet rivalry been a major factor.

Many of the dire predictions for the post-Cold War world have been based on a projected increase in ethnic conflict. Indeed, many of the new states have been ethnically divided and the state-formation conflicts have frequently been fought along ethnic lines. However, most countries are eth-nically divided without suffering from state collapse or armed struggle. Re-cent data indicate that ethnic conflict is now on the wane, along with other forms of armed conflict (Sadowski, 1998; Gurr, 2000; Mueller, 2000).

---

[21] In fact, in two Middle East crises, the United States nuclear forces prepared to launch nuclear attacks against the Soviets.

Figure 11. Internal Armed Conflict and Poverty, 1989–2000

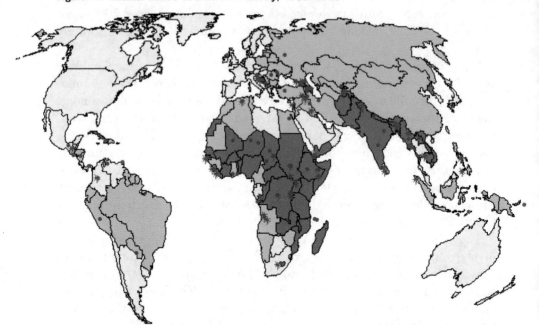

The conflict data were taken from the same source as Figure 10. Dots represent small armed conflicts (more than 25 battle-deaths in at least one of these years), stars are large conflicts (more than 1,000 battle-deaths in a year). The symbol for conflict is placed in the geographical center of the conflict. For internal conflicts that affect the whole country, the symbol is placed in the geographical center of the country. The countries are divided into three groups of equal size according to GDP per capita around 1995; darker shading indicates greater poverty.

The geographical distribution of conflict, shown in Figure 11, shows clearly that most internal conflicts take place in poor countries. The figure also shows that in the post-Cold War world there have been three broad areas of conflict. One is a long, but fairly narrow band of conflict running from the Balkans through the Middle East and the Caucasus to India. Many of these conflicts have an ethnic (or perhaps "civilisational" basis) that may be hard to erode. But armed conflict in the former Yugoslavia appears to be declining, and even in the Middle East there has not been a major war pitting Israel against an Arab country since 1982, even though in the previous decades such wars occurred about every 6–9 years. The second is a shorter band of conflict from Central America into South America. Most of the Central American conflicts have now been settled, or are in the process of being settled, and the conflict in Peru is at a lower level than during the active days of the Shining Path. The one remaining serious armed conflict in South America is in Colombia, where it is too early to tell if the peace negotiations will be successful in the short run. The third area of turmoil is Africa, where armed conflicts are going on in several countries.

The number of armed conflicts continued to rise in the 1980s, in the early part of the period that we have identified as the heyday of globalisation. But after the end of the Cold War it has declined to a lower level than before globalisation started to make its mark. The one region where conflict is endemic is Africa, which of course is also the region that has benefited the least from the advantages of the recent globalisation. Later, we discuss the evidence for the benefits of growth and trade on civil peace. Earlier work in the structuralist tradition maintained that global capitalist forces were responsible for internal conflict within the developing world by arguing that the structure of the world system drove income inequality, leading to relative deprivation and conflict (Boswell and Dixon, 1990). New evidence suggests strongly that structural change brought on by economic growth is not a driving force of conflict, but rather that it is economic stagnation that drives conflict (Collier and Hoeffler, 2000; Hegre, et al., 2001; Henderson and Singer, 2000).

Summary

Increasing globalisation has gone hand in hand with greater democracy, improvements in development and increasing peace. In the environmental area, prospects look reasonably good too, with a big question mark for global warming. We believe that this is not a historical accident, and that these trends are interrelated. We will now examine the specific links between globalisation and measures of human progress. To underpin the argument we have made in the preceding section about how globalisation has been accompanied by progress, we now present the theoretical foundations and empirical evidence in support of the connection between globalisation and each of the indicators of progress.

Globalisation and Human Progress

In this section we discuss the four measures of human progress and their links to globalisation in the same order as in the previous section.

Globalisation and democracy

Development does not just happen, it has to be organised. Social activity aimed at achieving peace and prosperity must be directed by a competent, neutral state. Contemporary scholars have found that governance matters for bringing about good developmental outcomes, beyond arranging a sound macro-environment and getting prices right (Kaufmann, et al., 1999; Government of Britain, 2000; Collier, 2000). The capacity of government is crucial for determining whether or not and to what extent society benefits from development. Good governance can insure quality institutions that provide a stable environment for economic growth, supply public services such as health and education, and serve to moderate forces that may be detrimental to peace and social well-being (Olson, 2000; Bates, 2001).

Most have moved away from the simplicity of pitting states against markets with the insight that the state is crucial for the efficient functioning of markets since it is vested with the power to protect property, supply public goods, and is, at least in theory, the social entity entrusted with an encompassing interest in society. Properly functioning democratic states will be more encompassing, even if authoritarian regimes are successful in organising some aspects of development.

We have already noted that the growth of democracy in this era of globalisation is not just intrinsically valuable, but also brings about a qualitatively different form of development (Sen, 1999). Gradually, globalisation will increase wealth by promoting growth and democracy, which lead to peace in a virtuous circle. Democracy and development are intimately related to the question of how state capacity and social capacity are organically related in mutually reinforcing ways. However, it is good institutions that make a state and determine the quality of its policy and polity, especially in the short-run.

Good institutions obtain socially efficient outcomes and provide the right incentives for the production of wealth. Alternatively, bad institutions result in socially wasteful behaviour (even if individually rational) and create perverse incentives that stifle broad-based productive activity, sending what productive activity there is underground. Such environments are unable to create the interconnectedness of state, society and economy in webs of interdependence, which are important for both social harmony and the attainment of good institutions (De Soto, 2000; Varshney, 1997). The "grabbing hand" of the state (which has the longest reach and heaviest hold because of its monopoly on the use of force) is dodged, causing much economic activity to go underground, denying the state revenue and leading to economic inefficiencies.

Conditions that prevent the growth of trade and development ultimately result in socially corrosive outcomes, which in turn result in violence and conflict – both organised and disorganised. Such environments do not allow the growth of specialisation from trade to growth of technology, human capital, or efficient institutions, or what some refer to as social technologies of peace and prosperity (Nelson and Sampat, 2000). Such states drive productive economic activity underground. Shadow economies are pervasive around the world, especially where governments have been and are traditionally hostile to liberal trade and investment policies, and do not contain the institutional environments conducive to encouraging contracting, protection of property rights, the diversification of the economy out of extractive activity, and provision of other infrastructures for maximising productive enterprise (De Soto, 2000).[22] The estimates of shadow economies for places such as the former Soviet states and India are as high as 60–70 percent of GDP, economic activity that is in effect lost in terms of taxes.

Somewhat ironically, we draw on arguments that caution against globalisation to make the case that state strength and social peace stem from the very processes that supposedly lead to welfare losses and social disarray in industrialised countries. The critique by Dani Rodrik of the optimistic arguments for globalisation emphasises the impact of free trade on unskilled workers (Rodrik, 1996; 1997). He bases some assumptions on political science literature that finds a relationship between the growth of government and increasing openness of the economy as measured by trade-to-GDP ratios.

This literature, beginning with David Cameron (1978) asserts that the increasing importance of trade in small open economies within the OECD countries led to the development of strong labour movements and left-oriented political parties, which have resulted in the expansion of the public economy. Rodrik argues that the expansion of the public economy was coterminous with the risks that an open economy faces, given the loss of economic autonomy from interdependence. The rationale for the expansion of government, thereby, was for compensation against shocks. Moreover, Rodrik argues that openness increases the elasticity of unskilled labour within the rich countries, thereby lowering the bargaining power of this group, and in turn resulting in depressed wages.[23]

According to Rodrik, the problem with growing openness is that governments will find it increasingly difficult to extract the necessary revenue through taxes, since capital has become highly mobile. He finds evidence suggesting that increased openness lowers government consumption as a percentage of GDP. He concludes that increasing risk and decreasing state capacity for compensating the losers will result in social disarray and threaten globalisation in the long run. Mixed in with such scenarios is the so-called race to the bottom, where governments will relax taxation to attract continued inflows of capital.[24] There has been little evidence to support this view. In fact, evidence from World Bank surveys of companies around the

[22] Schneider and Enste, 2000, shows the pervasiveness in many developing countries of state involvement in business life and the perverse ways in which such activity hinders people from translating their talents and wealth into productive uses.

[23] For critiques of Rodrik, see Panagariya, 2000; Bhagwati, 1999.

[24] Rogowski, 1998, demonstrates convincingly that there is no evidence from trade and taxation theory, nor is there any empirical evidence to expect policy convergence. As he shows, within federal states such as Australia, Germany, Switzerland, and the US, free movement of labour, goods, and capital has led to diverging policies, with governments at the sub-national level setting tax policies according to diverse agendas. There is no evidence that globalisation emasculates policy choice, or hampers the growth of government.

world as well as from statistical analyses suggests that businesses do not mind paying higher official taxes, although they shy away from corruption, which often ends up being more burdensome (see Friedman, *et al.*, 2000).

If globalisation – as even some of the critics find – does not constrain the growth of government and policy choice, how can we find support for arguments that it will ultimately create social polarity and disarray? The evidence that income disparity will lead to serious social instability is very thin. Recent research on civil conflict finds no evidence to suggest that income inequality has led to serious conflict. On the contrary, the evidence suggests that stagnant economies and very poor ones experience serious conflict, and that the size of income differentials among individuals and groups does not matter (Collier, 2000). A host of earlier studies on relative deprivation as a cause of conflict have also come to similar conclusions (Weede, 1998).

The crux of the matter is that trade and investment that promote growth will also allow governments the badly-needed revenue with which to make social and institutional changes, and prevent the type of societal and governmental disarray that continues to ravage many parts of the developing world. The evidence from the industrialised countries is quite clear; trade has led to the growth of government and to greater compensation to people who seem to lose relatively, even while gaining in absolute terms. Of course, job security and related issues in the North are trivial compared with the problems faced by the masses of poor in the developing world, as we have tried to outline above.

We focus below on recent theoretical and empirical evidence on the incidence of state corruption, institutional underdevelopment, and violent conflict that continues to marginalise large portions of the population in the developing world. We believe that investment, trade and growth are instrumental to understanding the new forms of social disarray in the post-Cold War world.

Keeping the economy open to trade, diversifying exports, and making a solid tax base out of society have enormous economic and social payoffs. If state capacity increases through diverse sources of revenue, society also becomes more interdependent across groups and regions, since diversified trade requires a variety of inputs based on specialisation. External trade and investment will also spill over into domestic economic activity, creating various forms of specialisation that necessarily create interdependencies. Since trade and production require stability, state and society – on the whole – will have a large interest in solving collective-action problems for peace.

Ashutosh Varshney (1997) has shown quite convincingly in the case of Indian cities how civic exchange between the Hindu and Muslim communities that are interwoven in webs of interdependence create islands of peace, as a result of which people from across communities come together to prevent conflict from starting and spreading. On the other hand, cities without such ties often break down in complete violence. The islands of peace are achieved despite the provocations of state actors and institutions. In other words, social capital causes peace because it develops autonomously as a result of the pursuit of self-interested, mutually beneficial objectives among groups within society.[25]

At the same time, states that depend on society will build the institutions through which communities and individuals can find redress for grievance and prevent socially wasteful behaviour. Strong institutions form the infrastructure that allows state penetration of society. This, in turn, provides for the stable environment required for peace – or for the development of what some call the organic state (Hall and Ikenberry, 1989).[26] As in the case of international hegemony, a state's power is strongest when it is recognised as legitimate, a recognition that comes with the way in which a state uses its power in ensuring the common good.

Trade also influences the type of economy, which has a bearing on the development of the polity. Openness of the economy is strongly correlated with less corruption (Ades and Di Tella, 1999; Gatti, 1999; Wei, 2000). The links from openness to trade and good governance work in two ways. Open trade creates high levels of competition that lower the payoffs associated with offering bribes and corrupting officials. Moreover, less state involvement in the economy will reduce opportunities for corruption. Second, high levels of government regulation and involvement in the economy afford opportunities for state officials to set up trade barriers for rent extraction, which drives down openness and is a reverse link. In weak states, trade barriers drive economic activity into the shadows, where huge profits can be realised from smuggling.

These activities may resemble crime, but the existence of these groups solves the problem of organising violence whenever state capacity is weakened for whatever reason (democratisation, economic shocks, growth collapses, death of a despot, etc). The kinds of groups that have ducked in and out of the shadows in the Balkans and were some of the most active participants in the so called ethnic conflicts illustrate the point well (Kaldor, 1999; Mueller, 2001). Organising in the shadows generally happens around kin (family, ethnic group, territorial group) as this minimises transaction costs, and trust takes on new virtue. Such set-ups have an organisational advantage, based on the underground economy.

In such situations, kin-based groups are bound to have antagonistic relations with officialdom and coexist in a vicious circle of corruption and violence around the yields from smuggling and other illegal activity, with the discourse of grievance around identity and territory-based issues serving as a

---

[25] Recently, there has been much anecdotal evidence from the Palestinian-Israeli violence to suggest that business leaders with trade- and production-related ties highly desire peace, and that those who prefer to see an embargo on Palestinian labour and goods do not stand to lose much.
[26] Models of predatory states in the field of political science are based on similar arguments, Levi, 1998.

convenient cover.[27] Conflict and bad governance are tied together in a vicious circle in what some term "the black hole of graft" (Marcouiller and Young, 1995).

The State Failure Project reports trade to GDP ratio as one of the most robust correlates of political stability, from among 600 variables that were analysed (Esty, *et al.*, 1995, 1998, 1999).[28] Using large sets of quantitative data spanning the entire post-war years, the project sought to find the correlates of state failure, defined as civil conflict at various levels, revolutionary wars, ethnic wars, genocides and politicides, as well as serious government crises and regime changes. The project conducted logistic regression analyses and neural network analyses and narrowed down a single-best model relying on three variables, which were trade to GDP (imports + exports/GDP), level of democracy and the infant mortality rate. All these factors were related to stability independent of each other, so that the effects of trade on stability were not dependent on democracy and vice versa. In the global model and a Sub-Saharan subset, countries that were above the median in trade openness were only half as likely to experience a major instability.

Given the scope and magnitude of the study and all relevant social, economic and political variables that were identified, we feel that the finding on trade is significant, even if under-theorised. We believe that trade influences civil order and peace because it aids the development of social capital, increases state capacity, and lowers corruption and shadow activity, while raising the standard of living for all. This is not to say that liberal trade policies alone will deliver all the goods, but that they allow good politicians to pursue good policies, build institutions, and accede to society's wishes about creating climates conducive to increasing mutually productive activity.

Our discussion of civil violence below will illustrate how the lack of good institutions and an organic state may, in fact, be driven by the availability of lootable income tied to resource wealth rather than to liberal economic forces of free trade and foreign capital investment. We will examine the evidence for this proposition and show how trade and FDI may aid countries to grow out of dependence on extractive industry, which corrupts politics and provides the incentive for organising violence.

---

[27] In many such situations it is very difficult to separate the good guys from the bad. State officials and private actors overlap. Bad governance, corruption, and weak state capacity are mixed in with 'robinhoodism', grievance and greed. The language of identity often becomes a convenient vehicle for claims and counterclaims. Recent events in Macedonia illustrate this point quite well.

[28] The State Failure Task Force was commissioned by the Vice President Al Gore to find the causes of state failure. The task force comprised a host of eminent independent scholars and published two phases of their findings. The information and data are available at http://www.bsos.umd.edu/cidcm/stfail/index.htm (as of 18 March 2001).

Globalisation and development

Classical economists recognised the benefits of mutual gain from trade and exchange. John Stuart Mill observed that "the opening of foreign trade . . . sometimes works a sort of industrial revolution in a country whose resources were previously underdeveloped" (quoted in Todaro, 1977: 331). With the flow of goods, capital and technology, LDCs are expected to gain through an open market. The example of enormous gains made by the miracle economies of East and South-East Asia that practised export-led growth strategies is often contrasted with the failure of the import-substitution strategies that were followed by many other states, notably those in Latin America, Africa and South Asia (Gilpin, 1987). As one scholar has put it, "trade, trade, and more trade was what propelled the pacific-rim states out of agrarian destitution or post-World War II destruction and decline into world economic prominence" (Aikman, 1986: 10). Foreign capital and trade played a crucial role in developing the technological capabilities in some of the East Asian NICs, such as Taiwan (Amsden, 1988).

New evidence challenges the view held by structural theorists that foreign capital and trade worked against the poor countries. Theoretically, neoliberals have long argued that there are substantial benefits from foreign capital for creating economic development. According to standard neoclassical theories, economic growth is based on the utilisation of land, labour and capital in the productive process. Since developing nations in general have under-utilised land and labour and exhibit low savings rates, the marginal productivity of capital is likely to be greater in these areas.

Thus, neoliberal theories of development assume that interdependence between the developed and the developing countries can serve to benefit the latter because capital will flow from rich to poor areas where the returns on capital investments will be highest, helping to bring about a transformation of "backward" societies. Therefore, capital-poor developing states should benefit from the expected infusion of capital from the capital-rich, industrialised states. Moreover, neoliberals place particular emphasis on FDI to act as an engine of growth through the transfer of technology.

Indeed, Simon Kuznets linked the productivity of the industrialised, Western states to the extended application of science and technology to the problems of production. According to Kuznets (1966), the basis of modern society is inextricably linked to the application of advanced technologies, and the economic prospects of developing states depend mostly on the transfer of transnational knowledge and technology from rich to poor states.

In this sense, investments by multinational corporations (MNCs) from the richer states are a basic mechanism for the transfer of technology from those who have it to those who do not. Poor states are not merely capital depositories, they also benefit from the technologies embodied in the capital invested from abroad, especially in the case of foreign direct investment as opposed to other forms of capital transfers from rich to poor states. Since developing countries lack the managerial and technical skills required for fuelling development, FDI in particular has been seen as a key element in North-South interaction that has aided the process of economic growth and the convergence of incomes between rich and poor. Through this process of diffusion of capital and technology, developing countries were expected to take off into self-sustaining growth, achieving higher stages of development and catching up with the rich (Rostow, 1960).

At the same time as FDI brings technology, the MNC also transfers a package of institutional attributes of the modern corporation that helps to transform tradition-bound, particularistic societies in developing regions. Indeed, some recent studies conclude that FDI has been one of the most effective means for the transfer of technology and knowledge (Dunning and Hamdani, 1997). These studies have concluded that multinational capital is crucial for improving productivity and standards of living in developing areas.

Neoliberals also argue the importance of open markets for economic development. They maintain that LDCs benefit from such an arrangement because states with small markets, as is the case with most LDCs, gain access to the much larger markets of the industrialised areas. This process allows small states to exploit economies of scale. Moreover, trade is expected to diffuse knowledge because it encourages learning by doing. The growth of the productive capacity of an economy is best realised through continued specialisation and exposure to the global marketplace.[29]

The recent evidence on openness and rapid economic growth is less ambiguous than the findings on FDI. According to one widely cited study that estimates the robustness of a multitude of variables thought to influence growth, trade to GDP (openness) was one of two variables exhibiting a robust relationship with growth, working through investment (Levine and Renelt, 1992). Recent findings are even less ambiguous about the effects of trade on income (Baldwin and Seghezza, 1996) and on the growth of the income of the poor (Dollar and Kray, 2001). Below, we focus particularly on FDI, which is the more contentious issue.

The opponents of neoliberal policies and globalisation have focused on the exploitative nature of MNCs. These arguments formed the basis of a theory that came to reflect the views of LDC governments on foreign direct investments. By the 1960s and 1970s, the dependency perspective challenged the neoliberal, modernist bias, especially its emphasis on blaming LDC failures

[29] Not all neoliberal economists agree with every facet of the argument presented here. However, there is very wide agreement that market forces and free-trade – and the efficiency they promote – benefit LDCs.

on internal factors.[30] These theorists, hailing largely from within the LDCs, questioned the Western bias and ethnocentrism of neoliberal theories on economic development, blaming instead external factors for development failure. Taking their cue from theories of imperialism, dependency theorists blamed the unequal exchange taking place between the North and South as a result of the structural power of Western capital (Arghiri, 1972). According to this view, unequal exchange was predicated on the basis of the dominant position enjoyed by the advanced industrial countries and the resultant dependency of the poor countries on the rich. This perspective was so far-reaching that, by the mid-1970s, it had galvanised the LDCs as a powerful bloc against global liberalism, and they seemed to be united in their call for a New International Economic Order (Krasner, 1985: 68).

The arguments about dependency and underdevelopment were supported by empirical studies in sociology and political science, and the debate continues to this day. Volker Bornschier and Christopher Chase-Dunn spearheaded more than a decade of so-called PEN research named after the crucial variable measuring penetration of LDCs (Bornschier, 1980; Bornschier and Chase-Dunn, 1985). They argued that FDI flows should have short-term beneficial effects but that the long-term effects of the accumulation of FDI stock as a percentage of GDP was negative on growth over time. They concluded that the larger the proportion of the economy of an LDC in the hands of MNCs, the greater the negative externalities.

Subsequently, a host of studies, using the PEN data on MNC stocks reported a host of ills on LDCs emanating from the penetration of MNC capital of host economies. These ills ranged from the effects of policy emasculation of national governments for providing basic human needs, mortality and nutrition to income inequality and conflict (Boswell and Dixon, 1990; London and Williams, 1990; Wimberley, 1990; Wimberley and Belo, 1992). Such evidence was seen as definitive proof of the various transgressions of powerful MNCs in the developing world.

This was generally the case until Glenn Firebaugh (1992) demonstrated that the findings of PEN researchers were based on a misinterpretation. He showed that the negative sign on FDI stock/GDP holding flows constant was due to a denominator effect of flows over stock. The larger the stock,

[30] The early dependency theorists came primarily from the Latin American region, aiming their critiques at US imperialism. There is clearly no one unified body of dependency theory, nor a clearly articulated position that is accepted by all, but André Gunder Frank, Samir Amin, and Immanuel Wallerstein are probably the most influential and theoretically most closely allied. Their views are clearly opposed to the modernisation and Marxist (diffusionist) paradigms. They may loosely be termed 'structuralists' because of the theory's emphasis on the capitalist world system's structural barriers against development in LDCs, see Browett, 1985.

the smaller the investment rate, and vice versa. These studies find that flows are positive and stock negative because smaller investment rates are related to lower economic growth – exactly as orthodox theories would predict. Firebaugh found foreign investment rates as well as domestic investment rates to be positively and significantly related to growth, but foreign investment had a smaller impact. He concluded that domestic investment was more effective than FDI.

While disagreeing with Firebaugh on several points, William Dixon and Terry Boswell (1996) agreed that the less-good foreign capital is likely to displace the better domestic capital over time and thereby contribute towards lower economic growth in the long-run. Indra de Soysa and John Oneal (1999), using newer data, found that foreign and domestic investment rates both show positive effects on growth. They also demonstrated that previous studies had been mistaken in concluding that foreign capital was less good than domestic capital based on the absolute size of the coefficients, because a percentage increase in foreign capital was not of the same magnitude in terms of dollar value compared with a percentage increase in domestic capital.

Since domestic stock on average was 13 times larger than foreign, a one percent increase in foreign investment was only 1/13 the size of a similar increase in domestic investment. They estimated that foreign capital is at least three times as productive as domestic investment dollar for dollar. Using Granger causality tests they also found that foreign capital is more likely to attract domestic capital than to displace it. Others have complemented these findings with different data and alternative specifications to provide the rather unambiguous finding that FDI benefits rather than hurts poor countries (Borenzstein, et al., 1998; de Melo, 1999).

The problem is that not all poor countries will be able to attract FDI in sufficient quantities because of factors wholly internal, largely hinging on state capacity and societal conditions currently prevalent in much of the developing world. The accumulated results on growth also call into question the earlier studies on the negative externalities of FDI in poor countries. At least one recent study finds FDI to be significantly negatively related to human rights violations in developing states (Richards, et al., 2001).

Globalisation and Inequality

The relationship between globalisation and inequality has been the subject of much argument, but little analysis. A study conducted by economists at the Norwegian Institute for International Affairs for the Norwegian Ministry of Foreign Affairs finds that there is insufficient evidence for concluding one way or the other (Melchior, et al., 2000: 32–37). However, in view of the lack of evidence of increasing global inequalities, the question of the role of globalisation is less pressing. It is indeed possible – contrary to the common assumption in the international debate – that globalisation may have contributed to the recent decrease in inequality, but to make such a conclusion would be premature. Where there has been an increase in inequality, it has been driven by labour-saving technology and not by free trade. Moreover inequality is not a key problem if welfare is generally increasing. States can compensate globalisation's losers with policy, but such compensations can only be made by being open to trade and building institutions that ensure social cohesion.

Globalisation and the environment

Trade can effect the environment in three important ways (Grossman and Kreuger, 1993). First, increases in levels of trade increase the scale effect of economic activity, which in turn can have an impact on the environment. Increases in the sheer volume of activity can rapidly lead to the degradation of air, water and soil quality and the depletion of non-renewable resources. This is true if production practices remain the same.

Second, there can be a composition effect where the product being traded in will be composed of an abundant factor. Liberalisation, therefore, will drive countries to shift their production where they have a competitive advantage. If the advantage comes from a sector where regulation is low because of abundance, each country will over-exploit causing a rapid depletion of resources. Third, the environment can be affected by the technique effect, whereby liberalisation encourages foreign capital, which brings cleaner production technologies, decreasing levels of pollution in poor countries. Moreover, liberalisation will gradually increase wealth and raise the population's awareness of environmental concerns, which will promote a demand effect for a cleaner environment. This effect essentially explains the environmental Kuznets curve.

The evidence from hard data is limited despite heated debate. Gene Grossman and Alan Krueger find evidence for the Kuznets curve effect from the maquiladores in Mexico, and no evidence for the pollution-haven hypothesis that views liberalisation as a convenient vehicle for rich countries to dump their waste on poor countries. Recent evidence from hard data on sulphur-dioxide emissions from the Global Environmental Monitoring data for a large number of countries demonstrates similar findings (Antweiler, *et al.*, 1998). This study found that freer trade does not increase the intensity of pollution. Combining their findings on dimensions relating to scale and technique effects, they actually find that if trade increases GDP per capita by one percent, it will reduce sulphur-dioxide emissions by an equal amount. They conclude that free trade might in fact be good for the environment.

Globalisation and peace

Towards the end of the Cold War and particularly afterwards, there has been a resurgence of interest in how liberal factors might promote peace. Prominent among these is the view that trade promotes internal and external peace. There are three main reasons why this is the case. First, trade promotes development, and rich countries rarely fight interstate wars against each other. Rich countries also rarely experience civil war or serious internal violence. Secondly, development promotes democracy, as argued in a classic article by Seymor Martin Lipset and supported in a great deal of later empirical work (Lipset, 1959; Burkhart and Lewis-Beck, 1994). Thirdly, trade creates ties of dependence that states will be anxious to maintain.

Bruce Russett and John Oneal (2001) see trade as one of the three foundations of a liberal (or "Kantian") interstate peace – the others are shared democracy and shared memberships in international organisations. In a series of articles, they have responded to numerous substantive objections and methodological challenges to the liberal peace.

Liberals also see trade as a factor reducing internal conflict. Again, the links via wealth and democracy are decisive (Gissinger and Gleditsch, 1999; Hegre and Gleditsch, 2001). While trade can also create inequality, which in turn may stimulate lower-level conflict, the net effect seems to be greater internal peace.

In recent years, research on conflict has found that greed-driven factors are more powerful than grievance-driven factors in explanations of civil conflict. Several key findings in this literature point to state and social capacity as crucial for preventing greed-driven forces from causing conflict. The main assertions of this literature are based on the key finding that extractable wealth in terms of large natural resources provide the incentive for organising large-scale violence, often driven by loot-seeking behaviour. As Paul Collier (2000) argues, conflict is not universally harmful, but a few "do well out of war". Since the provision of justice is a public good, altruistic individuals rarely spring up to serve justice by bearing all the costs. Groups organise for violence because of private gain. Likewise, peace is a public good, which often prevents the majority from organising for peace (larger groups are harder to organise according to the theory of collective action).

However, given the destruction caused by conflict, people who are productive in society have the necessary incentive to organise for peace. The more society stands to lose, the easier will be the organisation for solving collective-action problems – this is the main message in the plethora of literature on social capital (Putnam, 1993).

We argue that the evidence in recent empirical work on civil conflict, which demonstrates that natural resources and weak institutions are intimately related to the ways in which social technologies of peace erode, supports the argument that globalisation should work towards supporting civil peace. In this sense, trade and investment and continued globalisation will allow state (institutional) and social capacities (informal institutions) to develop, creating the webs of interdependence required for stable peace. We view this both as supply driven through state institutions and demand driven through the organisational abilities of social forces from below.

The finding that resource wealth is related to greed-driven conflict is a key result. Resource wealth does not only provide lootable income to private actors; it also leads to semi-private states, or what some call shadow states (Reno, 1995). Shadow states, are states that are captured by a few private interests. Moreover, the nature of the economic payoff, or viability of the state, provides the rationale for institutional development and strength. A convenient resource stream, such as extractable mineral wealth, leads to the withering of institutions around the collection of taxes, thereby weakening the social contract necessary for building a tax base from society. Moreover, a convenient resource stream renders social bases of taxation superfluous, which leads to semi-privatised states that will be disinterested in providing the optimal level of public goods, ultimately eroding social and human capital (Aury, 2000).

Resource wealth also allows states to close their economies and practice industrial substitution policies, which some have referred to as precocious keynesianism for state building along nationalist lines (Waldner, 1999). This, according to others, is the paradox of plenty and the natural resource curse that seems to be at the heart of some of the social ills facing many poor countries (Karl, 1997; Ross, 1999). Moreover, all these pernicious effects form a powerful cocktail that often leads to state and social disarray, violent civil wars and continued marginalisation. There is, however, nothing automatic about resource wealth that leads to disarray – as Botswana, Norway or Canada might attest to. The problems can often be corrected by policy (Auty, 2000).

To sum up, the major sources of social instability and violence in poor countries do not stem from global processes but from processes internal to states that trap them in a vicious circle which ensures their continued marginalisation.

The Promise of Globalisation

Globalisation has come to mean many things to many people. We have addressed the issue in terms of the growth of the global economy which creates interdependence between states through trade and investment. Without discounting the fears within the developed world that increased globalisation runs the risk of marginalising the unskilled workers there, we have focused on the effects of globalisation on the developing states, many of whom face serious problems that threaten to spill over across the globe.

These problems are largely due to poverty and misgovernment, both causes and symptoms of the political, economic and social disarray that currently afflict many poor nations. We have argued that the process of global integration holds promise, not peril for poor states and that greater integration should be seen as a global public good (Birdsall and Lawrence, 1999). However, as is the case with all public goods, it has to be provided and managed, and it remains to be seen whether the current global institutions will be successful at this task.

Globalisation, defined as the increasing integration of states and societies in tighter webs of interdependence, holds promises on many fronts. At the same time, the end of the Cold War signals new possibilities for channelling policy energies that in the past were largely spent on maintaining global peace and a balance of power between the rival superpower blocs rather than on redressing great economic and social disparities between peoples. The unleashing of market forces, given the failure of state-led promises of socialism, is already beginning to be felt in positive terms in many parts of the globe.

Political democracy has taken root around the world to a remarkable extent. Not only are civil societies springing up within previously repressed areas, there is also a culture of global civil society with an explosion in the number and forms of activities of non-governmental organisations (NGOs) and other bodies devoted to such problems as human rights and good governance. Such a turn of events could only have been seen as idealistic, romantic dreams a few decades ago. Deep integration through trade leads to cooperation between states on many fronts (Birdsall and Lawrence, 1999). We have chosen to focus on the economic agents of globalisation and to hold them up against a set of outcomes associated with prosperity and peace.

While much of the debate on globalisation centres on its effects on unskilled labour in the rich countries, we believe that the globally consequential problems stem from the problems of want, which face the mass of humanity in poor societies. These wants do not just concern commodities, but also institutions, policies and good governance in general – factors that simultaneously keep many of these areas from becoming globalised. To find the right policies that can break the vicious circles is the main policy challenge facing global and local policymakers.

The differences of opinion on whether or not globalisation supports or hinders the development prospects of states have been based on the theoretical frameworks offered by liberal (modernisation) theories and neo-marxist (world-systems) theories. We believe that the weight of the evidence, as we have tried to present above, supports the view that trade and foreign investment are likelier than not to benefit poor societies.

While the process of development never comes easy, economic growth does not necessarily have to be accompanied by great woe, as even some modernisation theorists believed during the disruptive days of the Cold War (Huntington, 1968). Many countries have made the transition from poor to middle income, or from poor to rich without too much disruption.

The problem areas in terms of poverty and peace seem to be areas that have by and large been bypassed by global economic forces.

We have tried to incorporate new insights into the causes of civil conflict to demonstrate that conflict and bad governance, which seem to be closely allied, are not related to global processes but to conditions that favour predation over production within poor states. These conditions, however, are not produced because of market forces but because of the capture of states and state-instituted macro policies that provide the wrong incentives, discourage contracting, and destroy social and institutional capital. We believe that it is a mistake to talk in terms of states versus markets, the question is sooner one of the degree to which the state is involved in governing the economic life of citizens, as Adam Smith highlighted in 1776, giving birth to classical liberal principles.

It is private enterprise that will respond most effectively to global conditions and opportunities, and smart states that will try to capture the gains from it. Unfortunately, many parts of the world, that are being marginalised, such as much of Sub-Saharan Africa, do not exhibit the conditions that favour such a turn (Collier and Gunning, 1999; Freeman and Lindauer, 1999).

The crux of the matter for many developing states is how to build up a base for meaningful trade with neighbouring countries and attract FDI to help in this process. In most cases, the factors that attract FDI are the same factors that strengthen development – peace, good governance, and social and physical infrastructure. These factors can indeed be affected by appropriate policy, given the commitment of political leaders. As Paul Romer has written,

> One of the legacies of colonialism is an aversion in some developing countries to any contact or exchange with firms from industrial economies. Interaction with multinational firms is sometimes permitted, but only on terms that are so restrictive and unattractive that few foreign firms decide to participate (Romer, 1993: 547).

Democracy and imperialism have been the most salient political terms of the 20th century. With imperialism having lost much of its currency at the beginning of the 21st century, we are now in an era of post-imperialism (Becker and Sklar, 1999). It is heartening that with more and more states and political leaders recognising the promises of globalisation, the right policy environments will be instituted to capture the benefits for ordinary people around the world. This factor is, after all, what eroded the post-war structure of bipolarity with all its attendant costs and has offered the world an array of options. The world is not yet united in one borderless marketplace, but it is an option available to most societies that wish to join. We believe that the current trends point in the right direction.

References

Ades, A. and R. Di Tella, 1999, "Rents, Competition, and Corruption", *American Economic Review*, vol. 89, no. 4, pp. 982–993.

Aikman, D., 1986, *Pacific Rim: Area of Change, Area of Opportunity*, Boston, MA: Little, Brown.

Alesina, A., Spolaore, E. and R. Wacizarg, 2000, "Economic Integration and Political Disintegration", *American Economic Review*, vol. 90, no. 5, pp. 1276–1296.

Amin, S., 1990, *Maldevelopment: Anatomy of a Global Failure*, Tokyo and London: United Nations University Press and Zed.

Amsden, A.H., 1988, "Taiwan's Economic History: A Case of Etatisme and a Challenge of Dependency Theory", in Bates, R.H. (ed.), *Toward a Political Economy of Development: A Rational Choice Perspective*, Berkeley, CA: University of California Press.

Antweiler, W., Copeland, B.R. and M. Scott Taylor, 1998, "Is Free Trade Good for the Environment?", *Working paper*, 6707, Cambridge, MA: National Bureau of Economic Research.

Arghiri, E., 1972, *Unequal Exchange: A Study of the Imperialism of Trade*, with additional comments by C. Bettelheim, New York: Monthly Review Press. [Originally published in French as *Échange inégal.*]

Auty, R.M., 2000, "How Natural Resources Affect Economic Development", *Development Policy Review*, vol. 18, no. 4, pp. 347–364.

Baldwin, R.E. and P. Martin, 1999, "Two Waves of Globalisation: Superficial Similarities, Fundamental Differences", in Siebert, H. (ed.), *Globalisation and Labour*, Tübingen: Mohr Siebeck.

Baldwin, R.E. and E. Seghezza, 1996, "Trade-Induced Investment-led Growth", *NBER Working Paper*, 5582, Cambridge, MA: National Bureau of Economic Research.

Barro, R.J., 1991, "Economic Growth in a Cross Section of Countries", *Quarterly Journal of Economics*, vol. 106, no. 2, pp. 407–443.

Barro, R. J., 2000, "Inequality and Growth in a Panel of Countries", *Journal of Economic Growth*, vol. 5, no. 1, pp. 5–32.

Bates, R. H., 2001, *Prosperity and Violence: The Political Economy of Development*, New York: Norton.

Becker, D.G. and R.L. Sklar (eds.), 1999, *Postimperialism and World Politics*, Westport, CT: Praeger.

Berdal, M. and D.M. Malone (eds.), 2000, *Greed and Grievance: Economic Agendas in Civil Wars*, Boulder, CO: Lynne Rienner.

Bhagwati, J., 1999, "Globalisation: Who Gains, Who Loses?", in Siebert H. (ed.), *Globalisation and Labour*, Tübingen: Mohr Siebeck.

Birdsall, N. and R.Z. Lawrence, 1999, "Deep Integration and Trade Agreements: Good For Developing Countries?", in Kaul, I., Grunberg, I. and M. Stern, (eds.), *Global Public Goods: International Cooperation in the 21st Century*, Oxford: Oxford University Press.

Bordo, M.D., Eichengreen, B. and D.A. Irwin, 1999, "Is Globalisation Today Really Different Than Globalisation A Hundred Years Ago?", *NBER Working Paper*, 7195, Cambridge, MA: National Bureau of Economic Research.

Borenzstein, E., de Gregorio, J. and J-W. Lee, 1998, "How Does Foreign Investment Effect Economic Growth?", *Journal of International Economics*, vol. 45, no. 1, pp. 115–135.

Bornschier, V., 1980, "Multinational Corporations and Economic Growth: A Cross-National Test of the Decapitalisation Thesis", *Journal of Development Economics*, vol. 7, pp. 191–210.

Bornschier, V. and C. Chase-Dunn, 1985, *Transnational Corporations and Underdevelopment*, New York: Praeger.

Boswell, T. and W. Dixon, 1990, "Dependency and Rebellion: A Cross-National Analysis", *American Sociological Review*, vol. 55, no. 4, pp. 540–559.

Boutros-Ghali, B., 1995, *An Agenda for Development, 1995: with related UN documents*, New York: Department of Public Information, United Nations.

Browett, J., 1985, "The Newly Industrializing Countries and the Radical Theories of Development", *World Development*, vol. 13, no.7, pp. 789–309.

Brown, L. *et al.*, annual, *State of the World. A World Watch Institute Report on Progress Toward a Sustainable Society*, New York and London: Norton.

Burkhart, R.E. and M.S. Lewis-Beck, 1994, "Comparative Democracy: The Economic Development Thesis", *American Political Science Review*, vol. 88, no. 4, pp. 903-910.

Burtless, G., Lawrence, R.Z., Litan, R. and R. Shapiro, 1998, *Globaphobia: Confronting Fears About Open Trade*, Washington, DC and New York: Brookings, Progressive Policy Institute and Twentieth Century Fund.

Cairncross, F., 2001, *The Death of Distance: How the Communications Revolution is Changing Our Lives*, Cambridge, MA: Harvard Business School Press.

Cameron, D.R., 1978, "The Expansion of the Public Economy", *American Political Science Review*, vol. 72, no. 4, pp. 1243–1261.

Chen, S. and M. Ravallion, 1998, "How Did the World's Poorest Fare in the 1990s?", *Working Paper*, 2409, Washington, DC: World Bank.

Collier, P., 2000, "Doing Well Out of War: An Economic Perspective", in Berdal, M. and D.M. Malone (eds.), *Greed and Grievance: Economic Agendas in Civil Wars*, Boulder, CO: Lynne Rienner.

Collier, P. and J. W. Gunning, 1999, "Explaining African Economic Performance", *Journal of Economic Literature*, vol. 37, no.1, pp. 64–111.

Collier, P. and A. Hoeffler, 2000, "Greed and Grievance in Civil War", *Policy Research Working Paper*, 2355, Washington DC: Development Research Group, World Bank.

Dahl, R.A., 1971, *Polyarchy: Participation and Opposition*, New Haven, CT: Yale University Press.

De Melo Jr, L.R., 1999, "Foreign Direct Investment-Led Growth: Evidence From Time Series and Panel Data", *Oxford Economic Papers*, vol. 51, no. 1, pp. 133–151.

de Soto, H., 2000, *The Mystery of Capital: Why Capitalism Triumphs in the West and Fails Everywhere Else*, New York: Basic Books.

de Soysa, I., 2000, "The Resource Curse: Are Civil Wars Driven by Rapacity or Paucity?", in Berdal, M. and D. Malone (eds.), *Greed and Grievance: Economic Agendas in Civil War*, Boulder, CO: Lynne Rienner.

de Soysa, I. and J. Oneal, 1999, "Boon or Bane? Reassessing the Effects of Foreign and Domestic Capital on Economic Growth", *American Sociological Review*, vol. 64, no. 5, pp. 766–782.

Deininger, K. and L. Squire, 1997, "A New Data Set Measuring Income Inequality", *World Bank Economic Review*, vol. 10, no. 3, pp. 565–591.

DeLong, B. J., 2000, *The Economic History of the Twentieth Century: Slouching Towards Utopia?*, Berkeley, CA: Department of Economics, University of California, Berkeley. [Electronic manuscript available on http://econ161.berkeley.edu.]

Dixon, W.J. and T. Boswell, 1996, "Dependency, Disarticulation, and Denominator Effects: Another Look at Foreign Capital Penetration", *American Journal of Sociology*, vol. 102, no. 2, pp. 543-562.

Dollar, D. and A. Kraay, 2000, "Growth *is* Good for the Poor", *Working Paper*, forthcoming. Washington, DC: Development Economics Group, World Bank, http://www.worldbank.org/research/growth/.

Dunning, J.H., 1992, "Governments, Markets, and Multinational Enterprises: Some Emerging Issues", *International Trade Journal*, vol. 7, no. 1, pp. 111–129.

Dunning, J.H. and K.A. Hamdani, 1997, *The New Globalism and Developing Countries*, Tokyo and New York: United Nations University Press.

Ehrlich, P.R., 1968, *The Population Bomb*, New York: Ballantine.

Ehrlich, P.R. and A.H. Ehrlich, 1996, *Betrayal of Science and Reason: How Anti-Environmental Rhetoric Threatens Our Future*, Washington, DC and Covelo, CA: Island Press.

Esty, D.C., Goldstone, J.A., Gurr, T.R., Surko, P.T. and A.N. Unger, 1995, *Working Papers State Failure Task Force Report*, McLean, VA: State Failure Project.

Esty, D.C. *et al.*, 1998, "State Failure Task Force Report: Phase II Findings", McLean, VA: Science Applications International Corporation.

Esty, D. *et al.*, 1999, "Environmental Task Force Report: Phase II Findings", *Environmental Change and Security Project Report*, Summer, vol. 5, pp. 49–79.

Feshbach, M. and F. Albert, 1992, *Ecocide in the USSR: Health and Nature under Siege*, New York: Basic Books.

Firebaugh, G., 1992, "Growth Effects of Foreign and Domestic Investment", *American Journal of Sociology*, vol. 98, no.1, pp. 105–130.

Frankel, J.A., 2000, "Globalisation of the Economy", in Nye, J.S. and J.D. Donahue (eds.), *Governance in a Globalizing World*, Cambridge, MA and Washington, DC: Visions of Governance for the 21st Century and Brookings.

Freedom House, annual, *Freedom in the World: The Annual Survey of Political Rights and Civil Liberties*, New York: Freedom House.

Freeman, R.B. and Lindauer, D.L., 1999, "Why Not Africa?", *NBER Working paper*, 6942, Cambridge, MA: National Bureau of Economic Research.

Friedman, E., Johnson, S., Kaufmann, D. and P. Zoido-Lobaton, 2000, "Dodging the Grabbing Hand: The Determinants of Unofficial Activity in 69 Countries", *Journal of Public Economics*, vol. 76, pp. 459–493.

Fukuyama, F., 1991, *The End of History and the Last Man*, Oxford: Oxford University Press. [Also 1992, New York and Toronto: Free Press and Macmillan.]

Gates, S., Hegre, J., Jones, M.P. and H. Strand, 2002, *Democratic Waves? War, New States, and Global Patterns of Democratization, 1800-1998*, Paper presented at the 43rd Annual Convention of the International Studies Association, New Orleans, LA, 24-27 March.

Gatti, R., 1999, "Explaining Corruption: Are Open Countries Less Corrupt?" Working Paper, Washington, DC: World Bank.

Giddens, A., 1999, *Runaway World: How Globalisation is Reshaping Our Lives*, London: Profile. [Also in 2000, New York: Routledge.]

Gilpin, R. with the assistance of J.M. Gilpin, 1987, *The Political Economy of International Relations*, Princeton, NJ: Princeton University Press.

Gilpin, R. with the assistance of J.M. Gilpin, 2000, *The Challenge of Global Capitalism: The World Economy in the 21st Century*, Princeton, NJ: Princeton University Press.

Gissinger, R. and N.P. Gleditsch, 1999, "Globalisation and Conflict: Welfare, Distribution, and Political Unrest", *Journal of World-Systems Research*, no. 2, pp. 327–365. [www.sv.ntnu.no/iss/ranveig.gissinger/data/global.html]

Gleditsch, N.P., *et al.*, 1998, *Det nye sikkerhetsbildet: Mot en demokratisk og fredelig verden?* [The New Security Picture: Towards a Democratic and Peaceful World?] Trondheim: Tapir.

Gleditsch, N.P., Bjerkholt, O., Cappelen, Å., Smith, R.P. and J.P. Dunne (eds.), 1996, *The Peace Dividend*, Amsterdam: North-Holland.

Gleditsch, N.P., Strand, H., Wallensteen, P. and M. Sollenberg, 2001, *Armed Conflict 1945–99: A New Dataset*, Paper presented at the conference on Identifying Wars: Systematic Conflict Research and Its Utility in Conflict Resolution and Prevention. Uppsala University, 8–9 June

Government of Britain, 2000, "Eliminating World Poverty: Making Globalisation Work for the Poor", *White Paper on International Development*, London: Department for International Development.

Gray, J., 1999, *False Dawn: The Delusion of Global Capitalism*, London: Granta.

Grossman, G.M. and A.B. Krueger, 1993, "Environmental Impacts of a North American Free Trade Agreement", in Garber, P. (ed.), *The Mexico–US Free Trade Agreement*. Cambridge, MA: MIT Press.

Grossman, G.M. and A.B. Krueger, 1995, "Economic Growth and the Environment", *Quarterly Journal of Economics*, vol. 110, no. 2, pp. 353–377.

Gurr, T.R., 2000, "Ethnic Warfare on the Wane", *Foreign Affairs*, vol. 79, no. 3, pp. 52–64.

Hall, J.A. and J.G. Ikenberry, 1989, *The State*, Minneapolis, MN: University of Minnesota Press.

Hanson, E.C., 1999, *The Diffusion and Distributional Effects of the Internet*, Paper presented at the 40th Annual Convention of the International Studies Association. Washington, DC, 16–20 February.

Hegre, H., Ellingsen, T., Gates S. and N.P. Gleditsch, 2001, "Toward a Democratic Civil Peace? Democracy, Political Change, and Civil War, 1816-1992", *American Political Science Review*, vol. 95, no.1, pp. 33-48.

Hegre, H. and N.P. Gleditsch, 2001, *Political Institutions, Globalisation, and Conflict*, Paper presented at the World Bank Conference on The Economics and Politics of Civil War: Launching the Case-Study Project. Soria Moria Conference Center, Oslo, 11–12 June. [Also available at Http:// www.prio.no/CWP/conference/0601/]

Heilbroner, R., 1995, *Visions of the Future: The Distant Past, Yesterday, Today, and Tomorrow*, New York: Oxford University Press.

Held, D. and A.G. McGrew (eds.), 2000, *The Global Transformations Reader: An Introduction to the Globalisation Debate*, Cambridge: Polity.

Henderson, D., 2000, "Anti-Liberalism 2000", *Wincott Lecture*, 28 September, London: Institute of Economic Affairs, http://www.iea.org.uk.

Henderson, E. A. and D. J. Singer, 2000, "Civil War in the Post-Colonial World, 1946–92", *Journal of Peace Research*, vol. 37, no.3, pp. 275–299.

Herbst, J., 2000a, *States and Power in Africa: Comparative Lessons in Authority and Control*, Princeton, NJ: Princeton University Press.

Herbst, J., 2000b., "Economic Incentives, Natural Resources and Conflict in Africa", *Journal of African Economies*, vol. 9, no. 3, pp. 270–294.

Hettne, B. (ed.), 1995, *International Political Economy: Understanding Global Disorder*, Halifax, NS, Cape Town, Dhaka, London and Atlantic Highlands, NJ: Fernwood, SAPES SA, University Press and Zed.

Homer-Dixon, T.F., 1999, *Environment, Scarcity and Violence*, Princeton, NJ: Princeton University Press.

Hoogvelt, A., 2001, *Globalisation and the Postcolonial World: The New Political Economy of Development*, 2nd. ed., Houndmills: Palgrave. [First edition published in 1997. Reprinted in 1998, 1999, and 2000.]

Huntington, S.P., 1968, *Political Order in Changing Societies*, New Haven, CT: Yale University Press.

Huntington, S.P., 1991, *The Third Wave: Democratisation in the Late Twentieth Century*, Norman, OK and London: University of Oklahoma Press.

Huntington, S.P., 1996, *The Clash of Civilisations and the Remaking of World Order*, New York: Simon and Schuster.

Jaggers, K. and T.R. Gurr, 1995, "Tracking Democracy's Third Wave with the Polity III Data", *Journal of Peace Research*, vol. 32, no. 4, pp. 469-482.

Juliussen, E. and K. Peteska-Juliussen, 1998, *Internet Industry Almanac*, San Jose, CA: Peer-to-Peer Communications (61–70), http://www.c-i-a.com/www.peer-to-peer.com.

Kaldor, M., 1999, *New and Old Wars: Organized Violence in a Global Era*, London: Blackwell.

Karl, T.L., 1997, *The Paradox of Plenty: Oil Booms and Petro-States*, Berkeley, CA: University of California Press.

Kaufmann, D., Kraay, A. and P. Zoido-Lobaton, 1999, "Governance Matters", *Working Paper*, 2196, Washington, DC: World Bank.

Keohane, R.O. and J.S. Nye, 2000, "Introduction", in Nye, J.S. and J.D. Donahue (eds.), *Governance in a Globalizing World*, Cambridge, MA and Washington, DC: Visions of Governance for the 21st Century and Brookings.

Keyfitz, N. and W. Flieger, 1990, *World Population Growth and Aging*, Chicago, IL: University of Chicago Press.

Krasner, S.D., 1985, *Structural Conflict: The Third World Against Global Liberalism*, Berkeley, CA: University of California Press.

Krugman, P. and A.J. Venables, 1995, "Globalisation and the Inequality of Nations", *Quarterly Journal of Economics*, vol. 110, no. 4, pp. 857–880.

Kuznets, S., 1956. "Economic Growth and Income Inequality", *American Economic Review*, vol. 45, no. 1, pp. 1–28.

Kuznets, S., 1966, *Modern Economic Growth: Rate, Structure, and Spread*, New Haven, CT: Yale University Press.

Lal, D., 2000, *The Poverty of Development Economics*, Expanded US 2nd ed., Cambridge, MA: MIT Press.

Lal, D. and H. Mynt, 1996, *The Political Economy of Poverty, Equity, and Growth*, Oxford: Clarendon.

Levi, M., 1988, *Of Rule and Revenue*, London: University of California Press.

Levine, R. and D. Renelt, 1992, "A Sensitivity Analysis of Cross-Country Growth Regressions", *American Economic Review*, vol. 82, no. 4, pp. 942–963.

Lipset, S.M., 1959, "Some Social Requisites of Democracy: Economic Development and Political Legitimacy", *American Political Science Review*, vol. 53, pp. 69–105.

Lomborg, B., 1998, *Verdens sande tilstand*, Viby: Centrum. [The True State of the World]. [English edition: Cambridge, MA: Cambridge University Press, 2001.]

Lomborg, B., 2001a, "Resource Constraints or Abundance?", in Diehl, P.F. and N.P. Gleditsch (eds.), *Environmental Conflict*, Boulder, CO: Westview.

Lomborg, B., 2001b, *The Skeptical Environmentalist*, Cambridge: Cambridge University Press.

London, B. and B.A. Williams, 1990, "National Politics, International Dependency, and Basic Needs Provision – A Cross-National Analysis", *Social Forces*, vol. 69, no. 2, pp. 565–584.

Maddison, A., 1989, *The World Economy in the 20th Century*, Washington, DC: OECD.

Malthus, T., 1798, *An Essay on the Principle of Population*. Oxford: Oxford University Press. [Reprinted 1993.]

Marcouiller, D. and L. Young, 1995, "The Black Hole of Graft: The Predatory State and the Informal Economy", *American Economic Review*, vol. 85, no. 3, pp. 630–646.

Martin, H-P and H. Schumann, 1997, *The Global Trap: Globalisation and the Assault on Democracy and Prosperity*, London and New York: Zed and St. Martin's. [Originally published in 1996 as *Die Globalisierungsfalle. der Angriff auf Demokratie und Wohlstand*, Reinbek bei Haimburg: Rowohlt.]

Mearsheimer, J.J., 1990, "Back to the Future: Instability in Europe After the Cold War", *International Security*, vol. 15, no.1, pp. 5–56.

Mearsheimer, J.J., 1993, "The Case for a Ukrainian Nuclear Deterrent", *Foreign Affairs*, vol. 72, no. 3, pp. 50–66.

Melchior, A., Telle, K. and H. Wiig, 2000, "Globalisering og ulikhet – verdens inntektsfordeling og levestandard 1960–88", *Aktuelle utenrikspolitiske spørsmål*, 6a, Oslo: Royal Ministry of Foreign Affairs. Available online at http:// odin.dep.no/ud/norsk/publi/rapporter. Shorter

English version 2000b, "Globalisation and Inequality. World Income Distribution and living Standards, 1960–88", *Studies on Foreign Policy Issues*, 6b, available online at http://odin.dep.no/archive/ udvedlegg/01/01/rev__016.pdf. [Summary as 2000c, "Globalisation and Inequality: A Norwegian Report", *Population and Development Review*, vol. 26, no. 4, pp. 843–848.]

Micklethwait, J. and A. Wooldridge, 2000, *A Future Perfect: The Challenge and Hidden Promise of Globalisation*, New York: Crown.

Milanovic, B., 2001, "World Income Inequality in the Second Half of the 20th Century" Development Research Group, Washington, DC: World Bank.

Milner, H. and R.O. Keohane, 1996, "Internationalisation and Domestic Politics: An Introduction", in Milner, H. and R.O. Keohane (eds.), *Internationalisation and Domestic Politics*. Cambridge, MA: Cambridge University Press.

Mittelman, J.H. (ed.), 1997, *Globalisation: Critical Reflections*. Boulder, CO: Lynne Rienner.

Mueller, J., 1995, *The Quiet Cataclysm: Reflections on the Recent Transformation of World Politics*, New York: Harper Collins.

Mueller, J., 2000, "The Banality of 'Ethnic War'", *International Security*, vol. 25, no.1, pp. 42–70.

Mueller, J., 2001, *The Remnants of War: Thugs as Residual Combatants*, Paper presented at the conference on Identifying Wars: Systematic Conflict Research and Its Utility in Conflict Resolution and Prevention. Uppsala University, 8–9 June.

Naqvi, S.N.H., 1996, "The Significance of Development Economics", *World Development*, vol. 24, no.6, pp. 975–987.

Narula, R. and J.H. Dunning, 1999, "Developing Countries versus Multinational Enterprises in a Globalising World: The Dangers of Falling Behind", *Forum for Development Studies*, vol. 2, no. 2, pp. 261–287.

Nelson, R.R. and B.N. Sampat, 2000, "Making Sense of Institutions as a Factor Shaping Economic Performance", *Journal of Economic Behavior and Organisation*, vol. 44, no.1, pp. 31–54.

Neumayer, E., 2000, "Resource Accounting in Measures of Unsustainability: Challenging the World Bank's Conclusions", *Environmental and Resource Economics*, vol. 15, no.3, pp. 257–278.

Nye Jr., J.S. and J. D. Donahue (eds.), 2000, *Governance in a Globalizing World*, Washington, DC: Visions of Governance for the 21st Century and Brookings.

O'Donnell, G., 1973, *Modernisation and Bureaucratic Authoritarianism: Studies in Latin American Politics*. Berkeley, CA: University of California Press.

Olson, M., 1996, "Big Bills Left on the Side Walk: Why Some Nations are Rich, and Others Poor", *Journal of Economic Perspectives*, vol. 10, no. 2, pp. 3–24.

Olson, M., 2000, *Power and Prosperity: Outgrowing Communist and Capitalist Dictatorships*, New York: Basic Books.

O'Rourke, K.H., 2001, *Globalisation and Inequality: Historical Trends*, Paper presented at the World Bank, Annual Bank Conference on Development Economics. Washington, DC.

Panagariya, A., 2000, *Trade Openness: Consequences for Poverty and Income Distribution*, Paper presented at the Third Anniversary Symposium of the Asian Development Bank Institute, Tokyo, 3 December.

Pomeranz, K. and S. Topik, 1998, *The World That Trade Created: Society, Culture, and the World Economy, 1400–The Present*, New York: Sharp.

Putnam, R., 1993, *Making Democracy Work: Civic Traditions in Modern Italy*, Princeton, NJ: Princeton University Press.

Reno, W., 1995, *Corruption and State Politics in Sierra Leone*, New York: Cambridge University Press.

Richards, D.L., Gelleny, R.D. and D.H. Sacko, 2001, "Money With a Mean Streak? Foreign

Economic Penetration and Government Respect for Human Rights in Developing Countries", *International Studies Quarterly*, vol. 45, no. 2, pp. 219–239.

Rodrik, D., 1996, "Why Do More Open Countries Have Bigger Governments", *NBER Working Paper*, 5537, Cambridge, MA: National Bureau of Economic Research.

Rodrik, D., 1997, *Has Globalisation Gone Too Far?*, Washington, DC: Institute for International Economics.

Rogowski, R., 1998, *Globalisation and Convergence: Getting the Theory and the Evidence Right*, Manuscript, Los Angeles, CA: University of California Los Angeles.

Romer, P.M., 1993. "Idea Gaps and Object Gaps in Economic Development", *Journal of Monetary Economics*, vol. 32, no. 3, pp. 543–573.

Ross, M., 1999, "The Political Economy of the Resource Curse", Book review of *Natural Abundance and Economic Growth* by Sachs, J.D. and A. Warner', *World Politics*, vol. 51, no. 2, pp. 297–322.

Rostow, W.W., 1960, *Stages of Economic Growth*, New York: Cambridge University Press.

Russett, B. and J. Oneal, 2001, *Triangulating Peace. Democracy, Interdependence, and International Organisations*, New York and London: Norton.

Sadowski, Y., 1998, *The Myth of Global Chaos*, Washington, DC: Brookings.

Sakamoto, Y. (ed.), 1994, *Global Transformation: Challenges to the State System*, New York: United Nations University Press.

Schneider, F. and D.H. Enste, 2000, "Shadow Economies: Size, Causes, and Consequences", *Journal of Economic Literature*, vol. 38, no. 1, pp. 77–114.

Sen, A., 1999, *Development as Freedom*, New York: Knopf.

Simon, J.L., 1996, *The Ultimate Resource 2*, Princeton, NJ: Princeton University Press.

Spero, J.E., 1990, *The Politics of International Economic Relations*, New York: St. Martin's.

Summers, R. and A. Heston, 1991, "The Penn World Table (Mark 5): An Expanded Set of International Comparisons, 1950-1988", *Quarterly Journal of Economics*, vol. 106, no. 2, pp. 327–368. [Version 5.6 of the data, released January 1995, available at http://datacentre.chass.utoronto.ca/pwt/]

Tanzi, V., 2000, *Policies, Institutions, and the Dark Side of Economics*, Cheltenham: Elgar.

Temple, J., 1999, "A Positive Effect of Human Capital on Growth", *Economic Letters*, no. 65, pp. 131–134.

Todaro, M.P., 1977, *Economic Development in the Third World: An Introduction to Problems and Policies in a Global Perspective*, New York: Longman.

Toset, H., Wollebæk, P., Gleditsch, N.P. and H. Hegre, 2000, "Shared Rivers and Interstate Conflict", *Political Geography*, vol. 19, no. 8, pp. 971–996.

UN, annual. *Statistical Yearbook*, New York: United Nations.

UNCTAD, 1994, *Foreign Investment Directory: The Developed Countries*, New York: United Nations.

UNCTAD, 1995, *World Investment Report: Transnational Corporations and Competitiveness*, New York: United Nations.

UNCTAD, 1998, *Trade and Development Report*, New York: United Nations.

UNCTAD, 2000, *World Investment Report: Cross-border Mergers and Acquisitions and Development*, New York: United Nations.

UNDP, 1998, *Human Development Report*, New York: Oxford University Press.

UNDP, 1999, *Human Development Report: Globalisation with a Human Face*, New York: Oxford University Press.

UNICEF, 2000, *The State of the World's Children*, Geneva: United Nations Children's Fund.

Vanhanen, T., 2000, "A New Dataset for Measuring Democracy, 1810–1998", *Journal of Peace Research*, vol. 37, no. 2, pp. 251–265. [Data available at http://www.prio.no/jpr/datasets.asp]

Varshney, A., 1997, "Postmodernism, Civic Engagement, and Ethnic Conflict: A Passage to India", *Comparative Politics*, vol. 30, no.1, pp. 1–20.

von Laue, T., 1987, *The World Revolution of Westernisation: The Twentieth Century in Global Perspective*, New York: Oxford University Press.

Väyrynen, R. (ed.), 1999, *Globalisation and Global Governance*, Lanham, MD: Rowman and Littlefield.

Waldner, D., 1999, *State Building and Late Development*, Ithaca, NY: Cornell University Press.

Wallensteen, P. and M. Sollenberg, 2001, "Armed Conflict, 1989-2000", *Journal of Peace Research*, vol. 38, no. 5, pp. 635–650.

Weede, E., 1998, "Are Rebellion and Transfer of Power Determined by Relative Deprivation or by Rational Choice", *Guru Nanak Journal of Sociology*, vol. 19, no. 2, pp. 1–33.

Wei, S-J., 2000, "Natural Openness and Good Government", *Working Paper*, 7765, Cambridge, MA: National Bureau of Economic Research.

Williamson, J.G., 1997, "Globalisation and Inequality Past and Present", *World Bank Research Observer*, vol. 12, no. 2, pp. 117–135.

Wimberley, D.W., 1990, "Investment Dependence and Alternative Explanations of 3rd World Mortality: A Cross-National Study", *American Sociological Review*, vol. 55, no. 1, pp. 75–91.

Wimberley, D.W. and W. Belo, 1992, "Effects of Foreign Investment, Exports and Economic Growth on Third World Food Consumption", *Social Forces*, vol. 70, no. 4, pp. 895–921.

Wolf, A.T., 1999, '"Water Wars" and Water Reality: Conflict and Cooperation Along International Waterways', in Lonergan, S.C. (ed.), *Environmental Change, Adaptation, and Human Security*, Dordrecht: Kluwer.

World Bank, 1996, *World Development Report: From Plan to Market*, New York: Oxford University Press.

World Bank, 1997, *Expanding the Measure of Wealth: Indicators of Environmentally Sustainable Development*, Washington, DC: World Bank.

World Bank, 2000, "World Development Indicators CD-Rom", Washington, DC: World Bank.

World Bank, annual, *The World Development Report*, New York: Oxford University Press.

Østerud, Ø., 1999, *Globaliseringen og nasjonalstaten*, [Globalisation and the Nation-State] Oslo: Ad Notam Gyldendal.

3. Reprising Durable Disorder: Network War and the Securitisation of Aid

Mark Duffield

The Changing Perception of Private Intermediacy
From new medievalism to network society

During the 1970s, it was becoming increasingly noticeable to commentators and analysts that associations other than sovereign states were growing in social, economic and political importance. Multinational companies, regional organisations, trade cartels, multilateral financial bodies, international terrorist groups, and so on, were making themselves felt in new and insistent ways. A widespread concern was established among political classes that state sovereignty and the long-standing system of international security that it had shaped was now being questioned (Derlugian, 1996).

From the perspective of international relations, Hedley Bull was prompted to question whether the inroads of such associations on the authority of states was likely to "to deprive the concept of sovereignty of its utility and viability" (Bull, 1977: 264). Such a possibility was expressed in the metaphor of a new medievalism. That is, without the cohesion provided by independent states now under threat, the world may be witnessing a secular reincarnation of a system of segmented, overlapping and competing authorities and jurisdictions that characterised medieval Christendom. Bull's approach to the worrying prospect of a new medievalism was one of caution. Providing such trends did not develop much further, the state-based system of international security existing at the time was sufficiently resilient to avoid this fate.

In examining the continuing influence of Bull's analysis, a key aspect of his work involves the concept of *intermediacy* in relation to the opposing tendencies of state integration and disintegration. A contemporary and contiguous example of these tendencies would be deepening of the European Union (EU) while, on its borders, Yugoslavia was wrenched into a number of successor states during the early 1990s (Kaldor, 1999). In relation to both tendencies, the issue for Bull was not these processes *per se*. If carried to their logical conclusions they would, respectively, lead to either fewer or greater numbers of sovereign entities. They do not necessarily challenge the principle of sovereignty itself. The main concern was the possibility that processes of integration or disintegration might fall short of their logical conclusions, leading to conditions of intermediacy in which private, that is, non-state associations hold sway. It was this middle condition, in which states are neither completely integrated nor totally disintegrated, that provided the real threat to sovereignty (Bull, 1977: 267). Under such ambiguous intermediate conditions, grey zones of overlapping and competing private associations come to predominate and define political space; states become one among the many organisations claiming legitimacy. For Bull, to the extent that the metaphor of a secular medievalism is given substance, the principle of sovereignty is undermined and hollowed-out.

Over the past quarter-century, not only have there been new departures within the trends highlighted by Bull, all of them have continued to augment and deepen. In some cases this has been significant. Multinational companies, regional associations, multilateral bodies, religious movements, trade organisations, criminal networks, non-governmental organisations (NGOs), and so on, have greatly extended their scope and continued to develop new roles that radically impacted upon the sovereignty of states. Indeed, the augmentation of such trends shapes the debate on what we now call *globalisation* (Held, *et al.*, 1999: 1–29; Hirst and Thompson, 1996: 1–17; Waters, 1995). In relation to Bull's work, what is interesting about the globalisation debate – or at least the official aspects of it – is that the concern over a new medievalism has been turned on its head. Not only has the role of private association continued to expand, more importantly, political attitudes toward intermediacy have gone full circle: what Bull regarded with concern has now been accommodated as part of the modern condition. Today, the political emphasis is on finding ways of working *with* and *through* the large and influential areas of private intermediacy that now exist.

While globalisation presents many risks, for donor governments it is also regarded as opening up new opportunities for wealth creation and human emancipation (DFID, 2000). While regarded as a threat in the past, multinational companies have been rehabilitated and are now widely seen as the new agents of social development and international stability (Utting, 2000). Reflecting the growing influence of non-state actors in relation to humanitarian intervention, it is now commonplace – even within official circles – to assert that the time of unconditional international respect for sovereignty has passed (Boutros-Ghali, 1995). While causing some concern at first, this transition is now accepted as a keystone in the development of a more rational and humane international order. Perhaps the most fundamental change of all, however, relates to the idea of intermediacy. Rather than private intermediacy embodying a new medievalist threat – a grey zone of overlapping and competing private associations – it has been positively reconfigured as central to the dynamic public-private flows and networks of the informational society (Castells, 1996). Through the logic of privatisation, intermediacy has been transformed into a force for wealth creation, technological innovation and even security itself.

The main focus of this essay is on human security and the public-private networks of aid practice. That is, those contractual regimes, strategic frameworks and compacts that now regularly link metropolitan governments, multilateral agencies, UN organisations, NGOs and private companies in a political project we call development. Rather than a threat to state security, these contractual regimes are now central to a new vision of how order can be achieved in the world's conflict zones.

Reprising durable disorder

The work of Hedley Bull provides a benchmark for how far the concerns of a generation ago have now been *normalised* as part of the risks and opportunities of a globalising world. At the same time, it also continues to shape a view of security as remaining, essentially, state-based and, moreover, under threat from contemporary developments. This position remains detached and somewhat uncomprehending of the extent to which private associations – in this case the public-private networks and contractual regimes of aid practice – now provide states with a new vision of how to achieve security within the global margins.

In accepting that a new medievalism is already upon us, Philip Cerny (1998), for example, focuses on describing the implications for state-based security of the anarchic system of overlapping and competing authorities that he argues has replaced it. Borrowing the term from Minc (1993), he describes the political consequences of a secular medievalism as that of "durable disorder". This condition is seen as resulting from the synergy between several developments. Usually described as low-intensity, internal or ethnic conflict, since the 1970s, a new threat to international security has emerged. State-based security, centred on political alliance, nuclear deterrence and arms superiority is ill suited to confront this threat (van Creveld, 1991). At the same time, under the impact of globalisation, the increasing influence of private associations has undermined the state "from both above and below, inside and out, since the 1960s" (Cerny, 1998: 38). The fragmented international and transnational structures that have emerged, are either incapable or unwilling to defend the past gains of liberal democracy. The "hollowing-out" of the state has not been matched by a corresponding "filling-in" of the authority of any multilateral or regional governance systems (p. 49). The governance gap has grown. To use Bull's terminology, in the face a growing private intermediacy, rather than concerted action, a deepening international entropy and political paralysis has resulted. In these conditions, a durable disorder characterised by endemic regionalised cross-border wars has now taken shape.

This idea of durable disorder is based upon a view of sovereign power as a fixed quantity. The more private actors appropriate aspects of sovereignty or take over areas of state competence, the less there is for the state itself. Its ability to respond effectively to new security threats consequently decreases. While Hedley Bull was sceptical regarding the possibility of a new medievalism in the 1970s, he nevertheless envisaged such a prospect in terms of the enfeeblement of the state and its subordination to the agendas of outside agencies. Rather like body's life-blood, the more that is drained away the weaker the person becomes and more vulnerable to invasive malady. The explanatory power of the durable disorder thesis, as in much of political economy, rests upon a view of the state as weakened and enslaved by the agents of globalisation. Cerny (1998: 44) has argued, for example, that although faced with new threats, the state is now unable to develop a coherent response. It has become "increasingly incapable of generating effective, authoritative, multifunctional co-ordination and control mechanisms or government systems". Durable disorder emerges out of state paralysis in the face of non-conventional security dilemmas. It denotes a situation where, through constant crisis management, total systemic collapse is avoided but root problems are never effectively addressed.

Rather than a growing intermediacy of private associations weakening states, this essay argues something different. A new possibility for achieving security has emerged in which non-state organisations now provide innovative forms of mobilisation, means of intervention and systems of material reward in the interests of global governance; more specifically, in the interests of global *liberal* governance (Dillon and Reid, 2000). Rather than being enfeebled and enslaved by these new international public-private networks and contractual regimes, metropolitan states have situated themselves within them as active and formative partners.

If the notion of durable disorder can be reprised – especially the idea of *a regime of governance characterised by constant crisis management that avoids systemic collapse but cannot solve root problems* – ideas of state enfeeblement and paralysis do not take us very far. To the contrary, such durable disorder exists as a collateral effect of the manner in which metropolitan states are pro-actively attempting to address new security dilemmas and developing innovational public-private systems of power and authority. Durable disorder arises not out of paralysis, but of the will to govern. This essay focuses upon one aspect of this reprised durable disorder. That is, the collateral effects of the transformation of the public-private networks of aid practice into a strategic tool of international governance.

Conflict and the Failure of Modernity
Imagining the borderlands

Using the end of the Cold War as a rough divide, there has been a significant change in the international attitudes towards organised violence. The case of the National Union for the Total Independence of Angola (UNITA) is a good example. While seen by some sections of international opinion during the 1970s as the legitimate government in waiting, today it is generally regarded as a pariah movement marked down for containment and neutrali-sation. In rationalising this change, one could argue that without the dis-tracting rivalries of the Cold War, we now enjoy a more balanced view of so-called national liberation struggles.

Whatever the case, it should not hide the fact that private organised vio-lence was often condoned in the past. For several decades prior to the 1980s, international support was directed to local political actors engaged in inde-pendence, secessionist or revolutionary movements in what was then known as the Third World. In different ways, such movements contested the legiti-macy of existing states or wished to create new ones. Left and right metro-politan opinion variously supported or opposed them according to political persuasion and the international dynamics of the Cold War. They were re-garded, essentially, as competing forces of modernisation.

During the 1980s, metropolitan views of organised violence in the South changed decisively; movements and actors began to lose focus as if, with the waning of superpower rivalry, they ceased to have a coherent political mean-ing or clear legitimacy of their own. By the 1990s, the more robust exam-ples of this delegitimation began to emphasise the irrationality and volatil-ity of political movements in the global margins (Kaplan, 1994). This was complemented by more measured views, arguing that organised violence could no longer be supported under present conditions. Political violence in earlier times, often linked to nation-building or defending democratic rights, may have had some justification. With these battles won, however, conflict now takes on a more negative aspect (Anderson, 1996). It is now widely held that the economic opportunities for private enrichment that today's wars afford, are its main determinants; the silent force of greed rather than the froth of grievance is the real motivation for organised violence (Collier, 2000). Given this delegitimation, international support for organ-ised violence has radically changed its nature.

Rather than patronise Third World political entities, the trend today is joint metropolitan public-private humanitarian alliances and aid regimes, designed to contain and neutralise what is now interpreted as international instability. From support, the trend is towards containment, management and eradication: as Iraq, Bosnia, Kosovo and Sierra Leone have shown, even to the extent of using force if necessary.

It is now commonplace to claim that conflict today is different from the past. Not only has the international status accorded to sovereignty declined, the world is presented with "fierce new assertions of nationalism and sover-eignty" and "new assertions of discrimination and exclusion" (Boutros-Ghali, 1995: 41–42). Contrary to the inter-state norms of the past, the new wars are internal to states or weave back and forth across borders to form regionalised systems of instability; they are not state-based wars in the traditional sense.

Moreover, unlike the national-liberation struggles of yesterday, warring parties are now more likely to pursue narrow sectarian interests, including criminal ones, rather than popular or legitimate political causes (Carnegie Commission, 1997). In the course of such violence, the social fabric of society is destroyed and development gains reversed. Another often described feature of these new conflicts, is their effect on civilians. In contrast to the stipulations of the Geneva Conventions, civilians now find themselves the deliberate targets of organised violence and are killed, abused and robbed with impunity (International Alert, 1999: 74). As well as being victims, warring parties also cynically exploit their vulnerability. Displaced *en masse*, civilians become tools of regional destabilisation as well as providing bait to attract humanitarian assistance (UNDP, 1994). Widespread human rights abuse is consequently not a side effect of the new wars, it is organic to how they are fought and their aims realised.

Such sentiments on the nature of contemporary conflict can be found in countless UN reports, consultancy documents, NGO briefings and academic works. They reflect the mainstream or generic view of the new wars. While not doubting the reality of organised violence, it is important to examine such ideas critically. That is, how they make violence knowable to us through specific forms of appropriation and representation. As much as anything, it involves looking for what is suggested or implied rather than being said openly. Conventional descriptions of the new wars create a series of implicit "them" and "us" dichotomies. *Their* wars, for example, are internal, illegitimate, identity-based, characterised by unrestrained destruction, abuse civilians, lead to social regression, rely on privatised violence, and so on. *Our* wars, by unspoken suggestion, are between states, are legitimate and politically motivated, show restraint, respect civilians, lead to social advancement and are based upon accountable force. In describing their wars such ideas suggest a good deal about how we like to understand our own violence. They establish, for want of better terms, a formative contrast between *borderland* traits of barbarity, excess and irrationality and *metropolitan* characteristics of civility, restraint and rationality.

The failure of modernity and the will to govern

It should be emphasised that the borderland-metropolitan distinction is a metaphor for the opposing characteristics of anarchy and order. Rather than existing ethnographic realities, the distinction exists as a series of imagined geographical spaces. In those shifting zones of political instability where we may think the borderlands exist – Congo, Kosovo, Columbia, Liberia, Afghanistan, and so on – the situation on the ground invariably proves to be more complex and ambivalent than the imagery of irrationality suggests. When subject to close examination, the reflexive systems that support conflict have a tendency to fracture and reveal hidden and unexpected realities. The ethnography of organised violence, for example, frequently brings out its ambivalence and multileveled character (Keen, 1994; Richards, 1996).

However, the borderland-metropolitan distinction is not supposed to reflect an ethnographic reality. If it attempted to incorporate the complexity of the real world, it would loose the essential distancing and mobilising function it exists to perform. In creating a *them* and *us* division based on the opposing characteristics of irrationality and restraint, the conventional understanding of the new wars plays a distancing role. It draws an unwarranted veil of civility over the history of metropolitan inter-state warfare. Rather than seeing elements of similarity, for example, our shared capacity for genocide, the borderland-metropolitan metaphor acts to veil and separate. Any shared responsibilities are safely concealed.

In many respects, the borderland-metropolitan distinction reflects a much wider rationalisation of today's predicament. The conception of the borderlands is another example of the *failure of modernity* which itself is a recurring motif within liberal thought (Bauman, 2001). Since the beginning of the modern era, the varied and successive expressions of its failings, famine, pestilence, economic crisis, wars, ethnic cleansing – even a new medievalism – have mapped out the frailty and uncertain grip of modern institutions. Even with good intentions, they are not always able to resist contrary movements and opposing trends.

The failure of modernity is synonymous with a temporary loosening of civilisation's grip and reversing of the ameliorative effects of social organisation. Taking advantage of this frailty, various forms of regression, social collapse and irrationality are wont to break free. Out of the tendency for modernity to fail, however, emerges a powerful impetus for reform. To spare future generations from our predicament, each recurrent failure replenishes a reforming zeal to reconstruct social organisation anew and even better than before. If the failure of modernity is a recurring motif, it is because liberal society defends itself as being in a process of never-ending reform in response to its critics and detractors.

While the borderland-metropolitan metaphor is an oppositional construct, the relation of the latter to the former is essentially one of failure. The existence of the new wars is a contemporary example of the failure of modernity. Descriptions of borderland conflict destroying a nation's social fabric, laying the seeds of generations of hatred, abusing civilians, and so on, provide a *justification* for reform. At the same time, the veiling and separating of their regressive violence from the rationality of ours provides a *legitimation*. Together, such forms of justification and legitimation combine to establish a reforming *will to govern*. If the borderland-metropolitan distinction has a reality, it is not in terms of it being an ethnographic reality; it exists through a metropolitan will to govern the borderlands. That is, to reorder the relationship between things and people, including ourselves, to achieve desired outcomes (Dean, 1999; Rose, 2000). Such a reforming will to govern animates the public-private networks and contractual regimes of aid practice.

Network War
Globalisation and reflexive resistance

The critics of liberal globalisation often point out that its promise of order and prosperity has yet to be achieved. Indeed, they are wont to describe new patterns of exclusion and subordination within the international economy, the widening wealth gap between rich and poor countries, deepening poverty and the consequent growth of insecurity and disorder (Castells, 1998; Gray, 1998; Hoogvelt, 1997). While such arguments deserve attention, the paradox of globalisation does not lie in the juxtaposition of allusions to wealth and progress with narratives of poverty and conflict.

At the heart of the liberal interpretation of globalisation sits the open market as the archetypal self-regulating process. In its more triumphalist guise, liberal globalisation aspires to interconnect the peoples of the world using the market mechanism to automatically and rationally adjust labour, production and raw materials to secure the optimal benefit for all. The paradox of globalisation is not that deregulated markets produce poverty and disorder for some at the same time as creating wealth and stability for others; because of this tendency, capitalism has been reforming itself for the last two hundred years.

Liberal globalisation is conceived in terms of an irresistible and deepening process of international regulation through the power of superior forms of economic organisation and rational calculation. It is a dream of order through the management of non-territorial processes, flows and networks, of which the free market is the ultimate driving force. Rather than continuing poverty, the paradox of liberal globalisation is that instead of more effective and self-adjusting powers of regulation, the reforms and institutions necessary for its existence appear to be creating the conditions for widening systems of *autonomy* and *resistance*. It is the growing turn toward independence and rejection, in the face of a system that sincerely believes it has inherited and now dominates the world by virtue of its irresistible moral, economic and technological superiority, that is the paradox of globalisation.

While the end of the Cold War is seen as a triumph for liberal market values, it has also witnessed conflict zones in Latin America, Africa and Central Asia, effectively decoupling themselves from liberal forms of regulation and prediction. One response to this apparent aberration is to take refuge in the spurious imagery of a global borderland gripped by criminalised and regressive forms of violence. The view in this essay, however, is that the new wars – or rather, the economic, political and cultural systems that either directly or indirectly support them – are not an example of the failure of modernity, but are symptomatic of its inner possibilities and surprising capacities. Borrowing from Ulrich Beck, the new wars can be seen as the manifestation of various violent and ambiguous forms of "reflexive modernisation" (Beck, 1992). Reflexivity suggests the maturing of modernity as it becomes conscious of itself through recognition of its limitations and risks.

In metropolitan societies, reflexive modernisation is expressed in the activities of workers, consumers and protest groups who, on the basis of their predicament, critically interrogate the claims of official science and economic expertise. It establishes a form of resistive counter-modernity in relation to life-style, consumer boycotts, environmental protests, anti-globalisation campaigns, and so on.

In relation to the new wars, rather than a failure of modernity, they can be read as ambivalent forms of regionalised political struggle and resistance to the complex process of globalisation. Reflexivity is expressed in the innovative and critical ability to appropriate the opportunities afforded by liberal globalisation, and transform them into new and oppositional systems of autonomy, protection and social regulation. The reflexive modernity behind the new wars can exhibit impressive powers of adaptation and survival. In this respect, rather than a hierarchical *them* and *us* dichotomy reflected in the borderland-metropolitan metaphor, they become parts of a shared condition, and can be repositioned within the context of a globalisation that has produced a plurality of ambiguous and contrasting modernities and capitalisms (Pieterse, 2000).

Actually existing development

In understanding the new wars, a point on which commentators agree is that with the ending of Cold War patronage, if warring parties are to engage in organised violence they have to become self-supporting. Or at least, relatively more self-supporting than in the past. To the extent that funding and supplies are not provided by outside sponsors, then they have to be generated internally (Keen, 1998). Among other things, this can require the creation of systems to secure and exploit local resources or tax produce or services, the establishment and support of extensive transborder supply networks, and formation and maintenance regional and international political circuits and connections.

Transborder flows frequently intermesh with international commodity chains and social diaspora networks (Rubin, 2000). It also involves an ability to change and refashion such networks as conditions alter and political fortunes rise and fall. Each one of these networks and points of exchange constitutes a site at which new forms of legitimacy, identity and authority are continually reproduced (Roitman, 2000). It is in this creative and transformational sense that the multileveled systems associated with the new wars can be seen as ambiguous forms of reflexive modernity. As the remarkable UN report on Angolan "blood diamonds" suggests, in realising the possibilities of our shared global predicament, such networks are adept at exploiting the loopholes and blind-spots within the international economy and the ambiguous ethics of the business world (Fowler Report, 2000).

In the process of making local-global connections, networks have long transborder and transcontinental tails. Porous borders in a time of changing political authority have offered many social groups the opportunity to reposition and reinvent themselves as nodes in these interconnecting networks (MacGaffey and Bazenguissa-Ganga, 2000). Structural adjustment, for example, far from being part of the "lost decade" of the 1980s (see Cornia, *et al.*, 1987) has seen a massive redeployment of personnel from the decaying public bureaucracies of the developmental state to the informal networks of the dynamic shadow economy (Meagher, 1997). In parts of Central Africa and the Chad Basin, the long transborder supply chains of new wars have reversed the urban/rural bias of the previous period as the "economy of the bush" has come alive (Nordstrom, 2000; De Boeck, 1998; Roitman, 2000). The mining of diamonds and cutting of hardwoods (as with the growing of coca and poppy in other war zones) has provided small producers with an income in excess of that which legitimate commodities can provide (Goodhand, 1999).

Transregional supply and service chains require armies of drivers, fixers, porters and guards. At truck stops and cross-roads, the expanding shadow economy has revitalised old markets and created new ones, increasing demand for local produce and services. At border crossings and airports, legions of officials and compliant government staff are needed to fabricate documents, falsify origins and conceal destinations. Commodities, money and people are continuously circulated and laundered from the metropolitan heartland to furthest reaches of the bush. The shadow economy is an opaque and non-territorial phenomenon of impressive proportions.

A frequent lament in relation to the new wars is that conflict "destroys development". In this respect, one has to distinguish the local from the spatial modalities of organised violence. Rather than regression, the long transborder networks involved have had a contrary ethnographic impact. Extrapolating from Rudolph Bahro (1978), the same reflexive modernity that produces organised violence in one locality also encourages what could be called *actually existing development* in another. That is, within the distant networks, circuits and exchanges that directly and indirectly supports that violence. This is part of the ambiguity of the new wars. Actual development is embedded in those ethnographic outcomes that exist when stripped of the external gloss of developmental and social evolutionary assumptions; it is the wood rather than the trees.

Actually existing development is what keeps people alive and maintains social and political life in the face of adversity and an exclusionary international system. It includes the networks, flows and nodes of the shadow economy as well as the emerging and reflexive political complexes that are associated with it. It is an arena of survival in which the potentialities of modernity are exploited to the full and, in the process, identities and authorities are continually reproduced and changed. Actually existing development has not arisen because of "official" development: it has emerged despite it.

Ambivalence and reflexive violence

In attempting to counter the idea of social regression with that of reflexive modernisation and resistance, it is important to avoid the trap of simply setting up a counter-image of an alternative rationality; where aid policy claims social breakdown, the riposte becomes social transformation, and so on. As with the institutions and relations of metropolitan modernity, those associated with reflexive resistance and actually existing development are complex and ambivalent. Organised violence, for example, is real and devastating; it also has a fateful duality. While crushing for its victims, those groups or that cause in whose name it is being enacted tend to see things in a different light. For them, the perpetrators of terror campaigns, ethnic cleansing, and so on, rather than being criminals or manipulative elites, are often perceived as the protectors of what is essential for life and community existence.

The conventional understanding of the new wars tends to place an implicit horizontal division between elite "winners" and subaltern "losers" in borderland conflicts. This imagery, which asserts a simple connection between power and wealth, dominates aid policy. Through the emergence of war economies, power as wealth accrues to the few while the development opportunities of the many are blighted and destroyed. If there is a division between winners and losers, however, it is not horizontal but vertical. The new wars are not hierarchical class-like engagements that pitch the selfish interests of elites against the development requirements of subaltern groups. They often throw entire non-territorial networked social, ethnic or political systems against each other: in this sense, one can talk about *network war*. Such systems, have their own local and extended mix of leaders/led, rich/poor, men/women interconnections and dynamics that are affected in different and sometimes contrary ways by organised violence. This feature of organised violence gives network war its special characteristics. In this respect, its spatial association with shadow forms of actually existing development has already been mentioned.

Power within network war is not simply a matter of amassing wealth. If leaders are to survive they must establish claims to legitimacy, rights to wealth, a framework of social regulation and, importantly, provide protection across a range of networks (Keen, 1994; Verdery, 1996; Callaghy, *et al.*, 2000). While wealth is an advantage, power has to transcend multiple divisions and points of exchange. Although fear and intimidation are important, as the duality of violence suggests, also involved is friendship, trust, loyalty, devotion and group solidarity. This *social nature of power* means that mechanical developmental entreaties for subaltern groups to either enlighten themselves with conflict resolution training (Voutira and Brown, 1995) or ditch their oppressive elites via internationally sponsored elections frequently fail to deliver (Zakaria, 1997).

Another characteristic of network wars is their *longevity*. Conventional wars between states tend to go through stages of escalation, equilibrium and, if victory is not secured, exhaustion. Network war does not follow this trajectory and, importantly, it has great resilience. Rather than reaching exhaustion, rather like a living organism, as circumstances change networks mutate and draw in fresh dynamism from new regional players and international partners (Rubin, *et al.*, 2001). Since the 1960s, UNITA's regional networks have shifted direction from South Africa, the former Zaire to Zambia as it has organisationally mutated from a Cold War to a post-Cold War organisational system (Shaw, 2000). The network war in Afghanistan has also shown a remarkable ability to continually remake itself over the last two decades in a shifting pattern of regional and international alliances (Rubin, 2000). The longstanding conflict in Sudan also shows a similar pattern of shifting transborder networks and periodic rejuvenation. The latest in a succession of such mutations is the involvement of international oil companies on the government side (Verney, 1999). The longevity of network war is indicative of the remarkable and adaptive powers of reflexive modernity.

The necessity of massacres

When regionalised networked systems are pitched against each other in conflict, there is a tendency for organised violence to assume the characteristics of a "species war" in which social, ethnic and political groups will go to extremes, including genocide, to secure the conditions for their existence. In attempting to understand this phenomenon, since we occupy a shared space, it is worth considering the views of Foucault on metropolitan warfare; in particular, his claim that today "massacres have become vital" (Foucault, 1998: 137).

The twentieth century has proven the most calamitous, destructive and bloodstained in the long annals of human suffering (Hobsbawm, 1994). Rather than the warlords, failed-states and criminalised elites of the borderlands, however, it was metropolitan states that, in developing the technologies of total war, first dissolved the "trinitarian" distinctions between people, armies and government that had existed since the 18th century (van Creveld, 1991). Out of the hidden possibilities of modernity, total war developed in two contiguous ways. One of these was the Holocaust (Bauman, 2001). The other, also based upon capacities of bureaucratic rationality and scientific calculation, was the mass terror bombing of civilian populations on a scale previously undreamed, and culminating in the dropping of two atomic bombs on Japan. So far, we can only glimpse the nightmare possibilities of bio-genetic technology.

In many respects, the only thing that is "new" about today's wars is that the possibility of total war – its unrestrained brutality associated with the dissolving of the distinctions between people, armies and governments –

has been transferred from metropolitan areas to the global margins. The realisation of total war is now within the reach of many autonomous private, non-state and shadow state actors in the world's conflict zones. The more successfully external supply networks and political circuits can be mobilised, the greater the danger that internal relations of reciprocity and restraint are undermined. In pitching social systems against each other, network war has the ability to place on the line the right of one group or another to life itself. The interface of conflicting networks – the local site of organised violence – becomes an arena of total war.

Rather than the borderlands re-enacting primordial forms of tribal hatred and ethnic conflict, they have the hapless distinction of developing forms of warfare that are quintessentially modern. As Rwanda suggests, the potential for genocide has expanded beyond the institutional confines of techno-bureaucratic societies to embrace the willing associations of civil society armed with the more mundane but nonetheless effective Kalashnikov, club and machete. This has been understood as a failure of modernity, for example, the wrong type of development (Uvin, 1996). As the historian Gerard Prunier has reminded us, however, without the organising efficiency and professionalism of the civil administration, the scale of the Rwanda genocide would not have been possible (Prunier, 1995): actually existing development with a vengeance.

In relation to the new wars, the ambiguity of reflexive modernity exists in a fateful duality. The institutions and relations of actually existing development, through the extensive networks of the shadow economy, are able to keep millions of people alive. At the same time, they are just as capable of taking it away: in some cases, on genocidal proportions. Sustained by the opportunities for autonomy and resistance afforded by liberal globalisation, out of this paradox has emerged a new set of international risks and threats. In turn, they have underpinned a transformation in the way international security is viewed, including the emergence of ideas of human security, and the technologies that are being deployed to secure it.

The Securitisation of Aid

The contours of international governance

The modern idea of "development" first emerged in the troubled conditions of mid-19th century Europe. It furnished a principle for reconciling the disruption of industrial progress with the need for social order. With its in-built sense of design, development was imbued with an ability to bring stability to the chaos of progress then expressed in the rapid urbanisation, unemployment and poverty of capitalist expansion (Cowen and Shenton, 1995). In many respects, "development" has always represented forms of mobilisation associated with order and security. While different strategies and technologies have come and gone, the general aim has remained that of a reforming and modernising reconciliation of the inevitability of progress with the need for order. An objective that, since its inception, it has singularly failed to achieve. During the 1950s and 1960s, both development and security were inter-state affairs. Aid centred on strengthening Third World states as a means of promoting development and, at the same time, developmental states provided strategic partners in the Cold War balance of power. During the 1970s, however, this framework began to collapse and a new episode in the failure of modernity began to take shape. Apart from the emergence of neo-liberal policies, it was becoming evident that developmental states could not maintain security within their own borders. The growing refugee crisis of the time graphically illustrated that this weakness also had important international ramifications (Suhrke, 1994).

Over the past twenty-five years, donor governments, UN agencies, regional bodies, NGOs, commercial companies, and so on, have gained, albeit in an uneven fashion, new forms of economic, social and political influence in the world's conflict zones. Like the reflexive modernity it confronts, this influence is increasingly networked and non-territorial. To use Bull's terminology, it is found within the private intermediacy of the expanding public-private networks and contractual regimes of aid practice. Beginning at the end of the 1970s, intermediacy first embraced macro-economic policy through the reforming activities of the international financial institutions (IFIs). During the 1980s, helped by the rapid growth of NGOs, it enlarged to include development, social welfare and relief (Korten, 1990; Clark, 1991).

In the 1990s, through the emergence of UN system-wide humanitarian interventions and new patterns of aid subcontracting, the remit of non-state associations grew to embrace humanitarian, governance and security responsibilities (Duffield, 1997). From the Gulf War, through Bosnia to Kosovo, a new civilian/military interface has broadened its scope with each successive round of conflict (Williams, 1998). Multinational companies, including private security companies, have also become part of a proliferating system of public-private compacts and inter-action. The presence of these networks moreover now means that large areas of economic, social and political planning have either been decoupled from weak states or have become areas of rivalry and resistance.

This evolving North-South relationship has deepened as international non-state and private associations have assumed responsibility for widening areas of public competence. At the same time, it has begun to take on an appearance of permanence. While the broad aim remains that of achieving stability and sustainable development, there is a tendency within the public-private networks of aid practice to redefine what were initial short-term remedial interventions as indefinite and open-ended commitments (Karim, *et al.*, 1996; Chandler, 1999). At the same time, there are increasing calls for comprehensive aid planning in the interests of stability (OECD,

1998). This includes a desire for more coherence and "joined up government" linking aid and political actors (Macrae and Leader, 2000). The trend toward permanence and coherence within the networks of aid practice is independent of any unequivocal demonstration of their effectiveness. If anything, the reverse is true. In what has been a significant internationalisation of public policy since the 1970s, the growing economic, social and political role of non-state and private associations has been a central aspect of this deepening engagement. Indeed, without a significant privatisation of the technologies of aid, the internationalisation of public policy would not have been possible.

According to the new medievalist thesis, this growth of intermediacy should be reflected in a corresponding hollowing-out of metropolitan states resulting in paralysis. This condition, however, seems far from the case. The effectiveness and consequences of the internationalisation of public policy can certainly be questioned. To assume, however, that it has developed at the expense of metropolitan states does not square with the evidence. While dependent upon private associations assuming operational responsibilities, metropolitan states are playing a vital contractual, regulatory and reforming role in this process. Through the development of public-private contractual regimes linking state and non-state actors, metropolitan authorities are developing the technologies and regulatory tools that embody a vision of how to govern the borderlands in new ways. Since the borderlands are an imagined space, these technologies embody new ways of *thinking* and *possibilities* of control. While having an uneven and equivocal ethnographic impact, coherence has, at least, been achieved as a system of thought and direction of action.

Human security and the securitisation of aid

If one steps back from the raft of conflict related literature and policy reports that emerged during the 1990s (Gundel, 1999), it is possible to form the impression that development itself has been rediscovered in the encounter with the violence of the post-Cold War period. An essential part of this reprise concerns the representation of the new wars in the imagery of the borderlands. That is, not as an ambivalent form of reflexive modernisation but as a failure of modernity and the collapse into social regression.

From this perspective, the new wars have provided an opportunity to rediscover and reposition development *as a second chance* to make modernity work. Despite earlier criticisms of the development project (Escobar, 1995), in the encounter with resistance it has been reinvigorated and come to acquire a new strategic role. By being vested with the ability to alter the balance of power between competing groups and promote social harmony, it is now seen as capable of conflict resolution, post-war reconstruction and the promotion of plural civil society (Carnegie Commission, 1997; OECD,

1998): aid has been *securitised*. The securitisation of aid embodies one of the main responses to the resistant and reflexive modernity of the new wars. In response to this challenge, development actors have shown willing to reform and reapply their skills with a renewed sense of purpose.

During the 1980s, a view of state failure in the South leading to a breakdown in development, conflict and international insecurity began to take shape among metropolitan actors. A metropolitan consensus has emerged that holds that conflict is the result of a developmental malaise in which poverty, resource competition, environmental collapse, population growth, and so on, in the context of failed or predatory state institutions is fomenting non-conventional and criminalised forms of conflict (IDC, 1999).

Instead of seeing a Third World as a series of states constituting a site of strategic alliance and competition, the world's conflict zones have been remapped in the representational form of the borderlands. The topography of these new maps is informed by a concern that underdevelopment is now dangerous, not only for the people concerned but for us as well. Under the rubric of human security, the stability concerns of metropolitan states have merged with the social agenda of aid agencies; they have become different expressions of the same thing. If poverty and underdevelopment encourages conflict and instability, then sustainable development with its intention of eliminating these maladies can also play a security role. The link between development and security is now a declaratory position within mainstream aid policy (DFID, 1997). In the transition to a post-Cold War international system, aid and politics have been brought together in a new way. During the Cold War, they were (OECD, 1998; IDC, 1999) state-based affairs, with the post-Cold War securitisation of aid they have been reunited in the public-private networks of aid practice.

The changing perception of security has profound implications for the nature of international governance. Within a development-security framework, except as things to be "reformed" or "reconstructed", states in what are now borderland areas have lost much of their relevance. Sovereignty is widely argued by donor governments and multilateral agencies to be a conditional status. The nature and quality of the domestic relations has taken the place of sovereignty as the locus of security. The types of economic and social policies being pursued, levels of poverty, the extent of corruption, the role of women, the status of the media, psychological well-being, and so on, have all become areas in which the borderlands *as a social body* have been opened up to levels of metropolitan monitoring, intervention and regulation unprecedented since the colonial period. The transformation of the borderlands from a series of strategic states into a potentially dangerous social body forms the basis of current understandings of human security (Boutros-Ghali, 1995).

The social diagnostics associated with human security constitute the points of intervention where metropolitan actors attempt to change the behaviour of the populations involved. Rather than build things or redistribute resources, development is now concerned with promoting self-reliance through trying to change the way people think and what they do (World Bank and Carter Centre, 1997). Because such interventions are relatively cheap – they relate to software rather than hardware – paradoxically, the securitisation of aid is consistent with falling levels of total overseas development spending.

The securitisation of aid has played an important role in encouraging the emergence of public-private networks linking metropolitan governments, NGOs, UN agencies, militaries and private companies. To put it another way, the movement of security into the ambit of aid has legitimised the growing involvement of non-state actors. Human security does not tackle political problems directly; it addresses the social background to them. At the same time, changing the behaviour of borderland populations, while vital for international security, is beyond the capacity, remit or legitimacy of metropolitan states. Despite the increasing conditionality of sovereignty, apart from a few strategic exceptions, metropolitan governments are usually unwilling or unable to intervene directly in the internal affairs of troubled countries. The involvement of private associations in addressing human security has become necessary. At the same time, mobilising around the imagery of a potentially dangerous social body makes this a possibility. Security has been redefined as a social problem, that is, as reducible to a series of developmental or psychological imbalances relating to the economy, health, gender, education, and so on. As a result, it is possible to divide the social body of the borderlands into sectors and parcel it out to the care and guidance of specialist non-governmental organisations.

Governing at a Distance
Aid as a technology of control

As a technology of governance, that is, a way of ordering the relationship between people and things to produce desired outcomes, development is different from colonialism. The latter was based on disciplinary technologies located within institutions and the boundaries of territorial authority. With the exception of the economy, which was an important site of colonial intervention and reconfiguration, such technologies usually left indigenous social and cultural forms relatively intact; in many cases the "tribe" or "caste" was preserved after a fashion as the most appropriate unit of administration. Feelings of racial superiority helped foster this cultural apartheid. The radicalism of development, especially those technologies associated with the securitisation of aid, lies in the attempt – fostered by sentiments that we are now all the same – to instigate a wide-ranging cultural revolution that transforms societies as a whole and makes behaviour consistent with liberal norms of modernity (Stiglitz, 1998).

In attempting to achieve this radical aim, development has adopted and extended the regulatory techniques of social control now found in metropolitan countries (Deleuze, 1995: 177–182). This is not just a simple extension however; it has a history. The centre and periphery of the modern world have always shared similar techniques and strategies of governance. Forms of central discipline and control have shaped approaches to the periphery; experience there has informed the evolution of central governance, and so on (Cohn, 1996). Within this inter-relationship, by its nature, the periphery has often allowed an idealised and more unfettered environment for the experimental application of emerging systems of governance. The securitisation of aid is an example of this wider dialectic.

During the 19th century, the development of institution-based disciplinary technologies (in families, schools, factories, hospitals, prisons, asylums, etc.) was helped by the scope for experimentation afforded by the colonies (Rose, 2000: 107–111). Excursions into centralised political administration, public dispensaries, unified police forces, town planning, elementary schools, asylums, the care and discipline of the poor, ordinances for road and bridge repair, model rural villages, prisons as a site for medical observation, and so on, were regularly undertaken. Today, something similar occurs in relation to the development of regulatory technologies of social control that now complement and supplant those of institutional discipline. Regulatory techniques create the possibility of modulating the behaviour of populations through controlling processes and networks rather than disciplining individuals *per se*. The history of structural adjustment and market deregulation in the South is a good example of unaccountable experimentation with an emerging set of liberal technologies of social control. This was a programme of privatisation far more radical, for its time at least, than would have been possible in any northern country.

Control technologies, whether applied in metropolitan areas or in zones of insecurity, share a number of characteristics. Disciplinary systems attempt to alter the conduct of individuals within the confines of institutions and juridical relations. Control systems, however, as embedded in the public-private networks of aid practice, attempt to alter the wider social context, the web of interactions and the pattern of rewards and sanctions in which social groups operate (Castel, 1991). In relation to international governance, reflecting its idealised nature, one difference between metropolitan and borderland regulation is that the latter is conceived as applying to political regimes as a whole, as well as to non-territorial units of population that cut across them (the poor, women, migrants, AIDS victims, child soldiers, etc.). Within control systems, groups and regimes are not seen as having fixed and unchanging capacities; they are aggregates of different potentialities and choices that can be nurtured or discouraged by the power of aid to shape the networks and systems of opportunity within which they operate. Rather than the unfolding of an immutable essence, through lifetime learning and endless need to chose, the future is one of self-realisation and constant becoming. Control is not centralised but dispersed, "it flows through a network of open circuits that are rhizomatic and not hierarchical" (Rose, 2000: 234). Conduct is continually monitored and shaped by the governmental logic that is consciously designed into the networks of aid practice involved.

A good example of securitised aid as a technology of control is the UN's Strategic Framework for Afghanistan (SFA). The SFA emerged in 1998 with the primary aim of bringing coherence to the relations between the UN's political mission and its aid community in order to encourage a transition to peace in Afghanistan (UN, 1998). Objectively, the SFA was a tool to confront the reflexive modernity and resistance of the Taliban. However, it saw the Taliban regime as representing a failure of modernity (in this case as a failed state). In response to the perceived borderland conditions of fragmentation and collapse, the SFA situated itself as a competing "surrogate government" (UNCO, 2000: 1). Since the Taliban were international pariahs, one task of the SFA was to establish a system of "principled engagement", which met humanitarian needs but avoided legitimating the regressive characteristics of Taliban administration. The SFA tried to do this by dividing the administration into good and bad parts; the former are those sections that "provide essential services to the civilian population in a non-discriminatory manner" (UNOCHA, 1999). To encourage good behaviour, the SFA envisaged that specific leverage points would "be identified so that 'sanctions' or 'rewards' can be targeted and effective" (OCHA, 1998: 4). To activate such levers, the SFA called for a graded list of non-life saving activities on which conditionalities can be applied, such as suspending or increasing valued aid activities. In this way, the SFA provided a measured response to Taliban behaviour giving the UN the means to encourage positive developments while defining "the benchmarks and indicators to measure [. . .] progress and adjust its presence inside the country accordingly" (p. 3). However, the SFA failed to mollify Taliban behaviour; if anything, resistance grew.

Trying to modulate behaviour in conflict zones through aid practice represents a special case of the liberal problem of "governing at a distance" (Rose, 2000: 48–49). That is, given that a multitude of private and non-state actors intervenes, how can the calculations of donor governments be translated into actions in the global margins? Before this is discussed, a related issue needs brief examination. That is, what particular "way of knowing" is best suited for aid actors wishing to change the conduct of populations? While the imagery of the borderlands legitimates intervention, it does not tell us how technologies of control are operationalised.

Actuarial and risk analysis

The borderlands are understood through a mixture of the actuarial mapping of conduct and the calculable assessment of risk. These complimentary ways of knowing have been extended to the borderlands in numerous and inter-connected ways. Actuarial analysis attempts to map zones of insecurity in terms of the behaviour of the regimes concerned. For example, representing a clear break with Cold War logic, the US State Department has recently developed a new way of categorising all the 190 states of the world. They have been classified and placed in several categories of "concern" according to their possession of missile technology and weapons of mass destruction, together with their actual or potential ability to destabilise the international system (Berry, 2000). A new Bureau of States has been established to monitor the global scene and annually update the list.

By mapping conduct, the aim of actuarial systems is to help decision-makers encourage useful trends while discouraging the harmful. In relation to the US State Department, the position of a country within the ranked categories of concern, provides a guide to the operation of US trade and sanctions policy. The actuarial mapping of conduct is also reflected in the growing tendency for donor governments to concentrate bilateral assistance in those countries believed to better reflect liberal values and practices (Macrae and Leader, 2000). Since aid is now an investment, it makes sense to concentrate it where returns are more likely.

Risk analysis disaggregates conflict zones into various factors of threat and vulnerability. Risk is a way of ordering reality by presenting it in a calculable form, thereby allowing it to be governed (Dean, 1999). Apart from providing a calculative rationality that shapes the conduct of individuals, risk analysis provides the tools to manage the public-private networks of aid practice. Risk requires particular forms of knowledge in order to make it thinkable – statistics, sociology, epidemiology, management and accounting. Such forms of knowledge are embedded in the relations of international governance in many different ways. It is argued, for example, that poverty does not automatically give rise to conflict. However, it is nonetheless the case that poor countries are more likely to endure war (Saferworld, 1999). In other words, the relationship between poverty and violence is one of probability.

The works of the World Bank's research programme on The Economics of Civil Wars, Crime and Violence, for example, seeks to understand the origins of organised violence. It has compared borderland countries "greed" factors such as reliance on a primary products, the proportion of young men and its educational endowment with "grievance" factors such as the degree of factionalism, lack of political rights and economic inequality and has concluded that greed outweighs grievance (Collier, 2000). This is not an ethnographic finding but a statistical one. A country endowed with natural resources, many young men and few opportunities for the educated, is more at risk of conflict that one that is not. In this way, risk analysis turns countries and regions into areas of calculable space that can be used to guide policy. NGOs such as International Alert and Saferworld, for example, have made a cottage industry out of attempting to rank the borderlands in terms of risk factors (Leonhardt, 2000). Understanding of conflict from a risk perspective also underpins the expansion of new surveillance techniques, early warning systems and fora for information exchange.

The technologies of control associated with risk also extend to the management of the project and the ethical comportment of the aid worker. During the mid-1990s, as part of the reforming turn associated with the securitisation of aid, humanitarian action became problematised. It was capable of promoting dependency among recipients and, worse still, actually fuelling conflict (Anderson, 1996). Consequently, humanitarian action has become ambiguous and risk analysis has taken root in project management. Projects and programmes have been transformed into areas of calculable space. For example, using such techniques as Peace and Conflict Impact Assessment (PCIA), since socio-economic disparities are seen as a source of conflict, depending on how it is managed, aid can either entrench existing divisions or encourage collaboration and social cohesion (Leonhardt, 2000). Project management has become a system of harm-benefit analysis whereby decisions are shaped by the consequences actions are presumed to have (O'Brien, 1998). In relation to humanitarian action, there has been a shift from an earlier prevalence of duty-based (deontological) ethics based on the assumption that right actions are right in themselves, to a consequentialist (teleological) ethics that subordinates actions to attempts to calculate future outcomes (Slim, 1997).

Since the mid-1990s, the emergence of a consequentialist ethics associated with risk analysis has led to a growing number of cases where humanitarian inaction has been decided the best, albeit tough, decision (Leader, 1999). This reflects what is known in Britain as the "new humanitarianism", the sentiments of which are also supported by a number of other European governments. As part of the securitisation of aid, humanitarian action is no longer sufficient on its own; it must also contribute to, or at least not contradict, conflict-resolution and peace building efforts. This implies that humanitarian assistance can be conditional on such expectations being met (Short, 1998). The new humanitarianism, while informing donor decision-making, also operates at the level of the project. In numerous micro-locations, consequential calculations of risk result in a continually changing pattern of social inclusion and exclusion within the circuits of aid practice, a pattern that combines control with elements of discipline.

Governing the borderlands

Rather than metropolitan states being enfeebled by globalisation, they have repositioned themselves within the collective and, helped by actuarial and risk analysis, are learning to govern at a distance through new and more indirect means. This repositioning involves an institutional and a technical problem. The institutional problem relates to the halting process of organisational reform that the post-Cold War reuniting of aid and politics has initiated. Operationalising the new security paradigm has involved changes in the division of labour within and between "aid" and "political" departments in metropolitan states and multilateral organisations. The technical aspect relates to how metropolitan calculation can be translated into action in the borderlands when a multiplicity of non-state and private associations intervenes. New techniques of public management and performance auditing have emerged that provide one way of attempting to manage the public-private networks of aid practice.

Governing institutionally

A key concept underlying the securitisation of aid is reflected in the term "coherence". That is, in relation to conflict the different tools of aid and politics, trade and diplomacy, civilian and military actors, and so on, should work together in the interests of stability and development. The demand for coherence – which now defines the consensus within mainstream aid policy – emerged from the mid-1990s critique of aid and conflict. In countering the ambiguity of humanitarian assistance, it is now required that relief should link with development activities. Since development itself has also been imbued with strategic peace-building powers, the collapse of relief-development distinctions quickly fed into the more general securitisation of aid. Aid became redefined as part of a coherent or strategic framework bringing together humanitarian action, development, diplomacy, military assistance, private investment, and so on, into one functioning whole. While most commentaries have focused on the broad descriptions of coherence (e.g., OECD, 1998), Macrae and Leader (2000) have analysed the institutional reforms that are taking place to make coherence a reality.

The reuniting of aid and politics has set in motion a wide-ranging if contested process of institutional metropolitan reform. Cold War barriers between aid and political departments have tended to blur and become more equivocal. If Boutros-Ghali's Agenda for Peace (1992) was an early articulation of human security made possible by the securitisation of aid, then the 1997 UN reforms were an attempt to realise this vision institutionally (Macrae and Leader, 2000: 33–35). The American, British and Dutch governments, for example, have also undertaken institutional reforms to bring aid and politics closer together. At the same time, however, a new division of labour is also emerging between these categories. Foreign and defence ministries are tending to retain or develop their authority in those zones of insecurity that retain economic or strategic interest, while aid departments, especially humanitarian departments, have become important players in shaping international policy in the remaining non-strategic areas. Countering the criticism that aid has become a substitute for political action (Higgins, 1993), as Macrae and Leader (2000: 30–31) have argued within this two-tier system "aid is no longer a *substitute* for political action, it is the primary *form* of international policy at the geo-political periphery".

Governing technically

While institutional reform is attempting to give organisational substance to the securitisation of aid, the technical problem of linking central calculation with distant application through a multiplicity of private associations remains. This aspect of governing at a distance involves the introduction of "new public management", initially developed in relation to the bureaucracies of Northern welfare states, to the public-private networks of aid practice. New public management is associated with accountability, performance indicators, contracts, competition and budgetary parsimony (Rose, 2000: 150). The marketisation of public bodies denotes a shift from the ethics of bureaucracy and public service to that of business and private management. Beginning in the 1980s, Northern governments have reorganised the social state, repackaging much of its bureaucracy into quasi-independent cost-centres, agencies and authorities, privatising and contracting them out to leave a marketised core. These new entities no longer authorise themselves through the ethical claims of bureaucracy but on the delivery of services and the production of results. They are governed through contracts, targets, performance measures, quality assessments and the regular auditing of conduct.

The fulcrum of governance within new public management is financial. Modes of financial calculation now extend into areas previously accorded professional independence. Public accounting has developed a number of powerful technologies for governing at a distance. Complementing the trend toward the calculation of risk as a means of operationalising aid, accounting has transformed institutions themselves and the performance of people within them into aggregates of accountable space. The aim has been to make the actions of erstwhile independent professionals calculable in financial and performance terms. Rather than their own discrete vocabularies, experts now speak the universal language of accounting. While globalisation may have entailed a loosening of the political control of the economy, in the social sphere at least – through the ability to breach professional enclaves in the name of accountability, transparency and quality – Northern states have centralised authority. Government increasingly occurs in new and indirect ways through technologies of performance auditing across private and non-state bodies (Dean, 1999). Social and public accounting has enabled states to "put in place new techniques of control, strengthening the powers of centres of calculation who set the budgeting regimes, the output targets and the like, reinstating the state in the collective body in a new way and limiting the forms of possible resistance" (Rose, 2000: 147).

Governing the public-private networks of aid practice through performance technologies is somewhat distinct to the privatisation and marketisation of the social state. Aid agencies and NGOs, for example, were never an organic part of the social state. In many respects, while the result is similar, governing at a distance has involved *bringing them in* to the orbit of central calculation rather than farming them out. The critique of humanitarian aid as capable of doing harm as well as good has played a pivotal role in this reforming process of reeling in. The transformation of organisations into areas of calculable space is a double process. It involves the presentation of performance in ways that are measurable by external audit and, at the same time, it needs practitioners that are willing to measure their own conduct in this way. Regarding the latter, part of the process of bringing aid agencies into the remit of central calculation has, paradoxically, been the attempt by NGOs to professionalise themselves by developing their own voluntary codes of conduct, performance indicators and the standardisation of humanitarian provision (Leader, 1998). The Sphere Project, launched in 1997 by a several international NGO networks, to develop a set of universal minimum standards in core areas of humanitarian assistance is a good example of internal audit (Sphere, 2000).

Performance auditing has not only been developing within aid agencies; more significantly, it has also been developing between them and metropolitan governments and multilateral organisations in the form of new contractual regimes and strategic frameworks. An important innovation has been the emergence of Project Cycle Management (PCM). This affords one way to manage the public-private networks of aid practice. It is a means of translating central calculation into coherent distant actions across a multiplicity of private actors. Through negotiation, the basic aims and project objectives are established at the outset. Using a series of intermediary stages involving close collaboration between donors and the implementing agency, the project or programme is designed and eventually commissioned. Actions are monitored against a consequentialist log-frame of aims and expectations. A final evaluation usually examines impacts, lessons learnt, and so on (Leonhardt, 2000: 8).

PCM emerged first in relation to development work but, with the rise of the consequentialist ethics of the new humanitarianism, PCM auditing techniques for humanitarian action began to develop during the mid-1990s. By the end of the decade, the European Commission Humanitarian Office (ECHO), one of the largest donors of humanitarian assistance, had augmented its growing range of managerial tools with the introduction of performance indicators (EC, 1999). Compared to the arms length subcontracting that characterised the relationship between donors and NGOs during the 1980s, PCM technologies entail a much closer partnership.

Conclusion: The Limits of Aid Securitisation

A widening range of contractual tools, performance indicators, partnership frameworks and auditing techniques interconnect metropolitan states and multilateral agencies, as donor organisations, to a growing number of operational non-state associations including NGOs, welfare agencies and private companies. As a means of governing at a distance, the techniques of new public management have made it possible for novel and flexible forms of strategic alliance to emerge that cut across traditional political, institutional and sector boundaries. Such techniques operationalise the post-Cold War securitisation of aid. In the interests of international order, they bring coherence to the public-private networks of aid practice. Rather than the authority of metropolitan states being eroded by the proliferation of non-state associations and the emergence of a new medievalism, these technologies hold the possibility of projecting international power through non-territorial networks and systems of private calculation. Despite the trend toward the decentralisation of aid work, often rationalised through the dubious equation of authenticity with proximity, decision-making is increasingly centralised. The transformation of the Third World from a series of strategic states into the potentially dangerous social body of the borderlands has provided the justification and urgency for this strategic centralisation.

The intention of this essay has been to reprise the idea of durable disorder as a system of international governance where, through constant crisis management, systemic collapse is avoided but root problems are never solved. Rather than resulting from state enfeeblement, however, this reprise is located in the collateral effects of the innovative response and engagement of metropolitan states with the non-conventional security threats they face. Durable disorder is located in the structural contradictions, limitations and unintended consequences of the encounter between the securitisation of aid and the network wars associated with the reflexive modernity of actually existing development.

Of central concern is the continuing interpretation of the new wars as a failure of modernity rather than reflexive forms of resistance to the process of globalisation. Not only does this conceal our shared predicament; it transforms political resistance into forms of social regression that are amenable to technical remedy. Rather than seeking political solutions, the securitisation of aid holds out the illusory promise that, through aid based control technologies, organised violence can be mollified and massaged away.

Unevenness of intervention and response

The use of sanctions, conditionalities and other forms of exclusion, has resulted in a marked unevenness in the international density of public-private aid networks. While this unevenness crudely reflects differences between strategic and non-strategic areas, even within relatively favoured regions like the Balkans, there are marked variations (Skuric-Prodanovic, 2001). This situation is represented in the wide range and selectivity of responses by metropolitan governments to appeals for international assistance (Forman and Patrick, 2000). Regional differentiation and unevenness, however, is not a fault within the aid system. It is consistent with technologies of control that are governed by consequentialist perceptions of risk and opportunity. Many regimes are now either unfit for assistance or lacking the social comportment that would make aid a success. Because aid is now ambiguous and can harm as well as empower, non-conventional security threats do not automatically imply that metropolitan states are going to spend money confronting them.

Reflexive resistance and mechanical predictability

The securitisation of aid embodies a dream of the technocratic control of the accidental through continuous monitoring and pre-emptive risk management. As well as defining the borderlands metaphor in terms of failure and excess, zones of insecurity have been transformed into a mechanical universe where social groups and political actors are amenable to the superior rationality of aid practice. If badly managed humanitarian assistance can fuel war and create dependency, it follows that in safe hands it can promote peace and self-sufficiency. Actually existing development consequently loses its reflexive and unpredictable characteristics. Indeed, the technologies of risk, performance and auditing through which the securitisation of aid is operationalised require machine like prediction for their success.

Network war, however, is more like an organism than a machine. Change the environment of an organism and the will to live causes it to mutate; press a button on a machine and it will execute a predicable function. There is a serious gap between metropolitan technologies of control and the ethnographic reality of the new wars. For this reason, despite the unevenness mentioned above, even in regions where the public-private networks of aid practice are relatively dense, results are equivocal. In Bosnia for example, at a cost of billions of dollars, every known technique of conflict resolution and social reconstruction has being tried to uncertain effect (Griffiths, 1999).

The uncertainty of knowledge

As a means of governing at a distance, new public management techniques have opened up the enclaves of professional conduct to external scrutiny. While they allow centralised decision-making in the interests of coherence, they have changed the nature of knowledge itself. In the process of setting budgets and performance targets, authority is transferred outwards to administrators and managers. Within the networks of aid practice, technologies of performance operate in a context of a high turnover of expatriate field personnel that, in general, have few language skills and little knowledge of the countries where they work.

While a lack of institutional memory is often lamented, performance technologies are not reliant upon institutional memory. It has the troublesome ability to support independent claims to authority. In its attempt to colonise the future, risk management demotes tradition in favour of an endless search for fresh faces and new ways of doing things. As Nikolas Rose has argued in relation to liberal technologies of control generally, the transfer of authority from experts to managers " masks the somewhat weak knowledge base – the uncertain status, inescapably partial vision, lack of evidential support, history of failure, [and] vulnerability to changes in fashion" (Rose, 2000: 153). In the ethnographic context of the new wars, the uncertainty of knowledge within the public-private networks of aid practice is their hallmark.

Bringing politics back in

In finding a way out of this impasse, the fundamental weakness in the securitisation of aid needs to be addressed. That is, a political vision needs to replace the social claims of aid discourse. At the same time, aid should be 'de-securitised' and, in conflict zones, returned to its more modest but no less important role of impartial humanitarian assistance. In order to bring politics back in, however, it is clear that the nature of contemporary conflict, especially as sites of total war, has problematised political leadership in areas of conflict. Politics requires reform to address the wider conditions of network war and the nature of the non-territorial political entities associated with it. Apart from leading governments having to settle their own differences and bilateral leanings, informed by public debate, they would have to be prepared to take a regional view of insecurity and, especially, to pool decision-making in relation to specific emerging political complexes.

At the same time, the field of diplomacy and negotiation should expand. Apart from dealing with state entities or aspiring entities, political actors need to address the multileveled and transborder nature of network war. In order to add ethnographic depth, the modalities of organised violence, together with the long-transborder networks and regional political and cultural circuits of reflexive modernity, should be analysed over time by people with area and language skills. As the object of collective political engagement, a more nuanced, ethnographically located and networked interpretation of emerging political complexes should replace the generalised and mechanical aid based imagery of the borderlands. Finally, in recognition of our shared predicament, there should be a political willingness to negotiate between different regimes of truth and systems of cultural interpretation. In so doing, political actors should be prepared to establish their own moral identities and social agendas as well as the responsibilities that bind us all. Unless we are able to bring politics back in, durable disorder is likely to continue.

References

Anderson, M.B., 1996, *Do No Harm: Supporting Local Capacities for Peace Through Aid*, Local Capacities for Peace Project, The Collaborative for Development Action, Inc., Cambridge, MA.

Bahro, R., 1978, *The Alternative in Eastern Europe*, London: Verso.

Bauman, Z., 2001, "Sociology After the Holocaust [1989]" in Beilharz, P. (ed.), *The Bauman Reader*, Oxford: Blackwell Publishers.

Beck, U., 1992 (1986), *Risk Society: Towards a New Modernity*, London: Sage Publications.

Berry, N., "State Department Classifies Foreign States: 'States of Concern' Only One of the Categories", *The Weekly Defence Monitor*, no. 10–11, 2000, Washington DC: The Center for Defence Information.

Boutros-Ghali, B., 1995 (1992), *An Agenda for Peace*, United Nations, New York.

Bull, H., 1977, *The Anarchical Society: A Study in Order in World Politics*, London: Macmillan Press Ltd.

Callaghy, T., Kassimir, R., and R. Letham (eds.), 2000, *Transboundary Formations: Global/Local Constructions of Authority and Violence in Africa*, Cambridge: Cambridge University Press.

Carnegie Commission, 1997, *Preventing Deadly Conflict: Executive Summary of the Final Report*, Carnegie Commission on Preventing Deadly Conflict, Washington DC.

Castel, R., 1991, "From Dangerousness to Risk", in Burchell, G., Gordon, C. and P. Miller (eds.), *The Foucault Effect: Studies in Governmentality*, London: Harvester Wheatsheaf.

Castells, M., 1996, *The Rise of the Network Society*, Oxford: Blackwell Publishers Ltd.

Castells, M., 1998, *End of Millennium*, Oxford: Blackwell Publishers Ltd.

Chandler, D., "The Bosnian Protectorate and the Implications for Kosovo", *New Left Review*, no. 235, 1999, pp. 124–34.

Clark, J., 1991, *Democratizing Development: The Role of Voluntary Organizations*, London: Earthscan Publications.

Cohn, B.S., 1996, *Colonialism and Its Forms of Knowledge: The British in India*, Princeton, NJ: Princeton University Press.

Collier, P., 2000, "Doing Well Out of War: An Economic Perspective", in Berdal, M. and D.M. Malone (eds.), *Greed and Grievance: Economic Agendas in Civil Wars*, Boulder and London: Lynne Rienner.

Cornia, G.A., Jolly, R. and F. Stewart (eds.), 1987, *Adjustment with a Human Face: Volume 1*, Oxford: Clarendon Press.

Cowen, M. and R. Shenton, 1995, "The Invention of Development" in Crush, J. (ed.), *The Power of Development*, London: Routledge.

De Boeck, F., "Domesticating Diamonds and Dollars: Identity, Expenditure and Sharing in Southwestern Zaire (1984–1997)", *Development and Change*, no. 29, 1998, pp. 777–810.

Dean, M., 1999, *Governmentality: Power and Rule in Modern Society*, London: Sage Publications Ltd.

Deleuze, G., 1995, *Negotiations: 1972–1990*, New York: Colombia University Press.

Derlugian, G.M., 1996, "The Social Cohesion of the States.", in Hopkins, T.K. and I. Wallerstein (eds.), *The Age of Transition: Trajectory of the World-System, 1945–2025*, London: Zed Books.

DFID, 1997, *Eliminating World Poverty: A Challenge for the 21st Century*, White Paper on International Development, The Stationary Office for International Development Department, London.

DFID, 2000, *Eliminating World Poverty: Making Globalisation Work for the Poor*, White Paper on International Development, The Stationary Office for the Department for International Development, London.

Dillon, M. and J. Reid, "Global Governance, Liberal Peace and Complex Emergency", *Alternatives*, vol. 30, no.1, 2001, pp. 41–66.

Duffield, M., "NGO Relief in War Zones: Toward an Analysis of the New Aid Paradigm", *Third World Quarterly*, vol. 18, no. 3, 1997, pp. 527–42.

EC, *Assessment and Future of Community Humanitarian Activities*, Communication From the Commission of 26 October 1999, European Commission, Brussels, 26 Oct 1999.

Escobar, A., 1995, *Encountering Development: The Making and Unmaking of the Third World*, New Jersey: Princeton University Press.

Forman, S. and S. Patrick (eds.), 2000, *Good Intentions: Pledges of Aid for Post-Conflict Recovery*, Boulder: Lynne Rienner.

Foucault, M., 1998, *The Will to Knowledge: The History of Sexuality Volume 1*. London: Penguin Books.

Fowler Report, 2000, *Report of Sanctions Committee on Violation of Security Council Sanctions Against UNITA*, Robert Fowler, Chair, United Nations, New York.

Goodhand, J., *From Holy War to Opium War? A Case Study of the Opium Economy in North Eastern Afghanistan*, IDPM, University of Manchester, Oct 1999.

Gray, J., 1998, *False Dawn: The Delusions of Global Capitalism*. London: Granta Books.

Griffiths, H., 1998, "A Political Economy of Ethnic Conflict – Ethnonationalism and Organised Crime", Unpublished manuscript.

Gundel, J., 1999, *Humanitarian Assistance: Breaking the Waves of Complex Political Emergencies – A Literature Survey*, CDR Working Paper, No 99.5, Copenhagen: Centre for Development Research.

Held, D., McGrew, A., Goldblast, D. and J. Perraton, 1999, *Global Transformations: Politics, Economics and Culture*, Cambridge: Polity Press.

Higgins, R, 1993, "The New United Nations and the Former Yugoslavia.", *International Affairs*, vol. 69, no. 3, pp. 465–83.

Hirst, P. and G. Thompson, 1996, *Globalisation in Question*, Cambridge: Polity Press.

Hobsbawm, E., 1994, *The Age of Extremes: The Short Twentieth Century*, London: Michael Joseph.

Hoogvelt, A., 1997, *Globalization and the Postcolonial World*, Baltimore, Maryland: The John Hopkins University Press.

IDC, *Conflict Prevention and Post-Conflict Reconstruction, Volume I, Report and Proceeding to the Committee*, International Development Committee, London, The Stationary Office, 28 July 1999.

International Alert, "Memorandum From International Alert: 6 March 1998", Sixth Report of the International Development Committee, *Conflict Prevention and Post-Conflict Reconstruction, Vol II, Minutes of Evidence and Appendices*, 73–79, London: The Stationary Office, 28 July 1999.

Kaldor, M., 1999, *New and Old Wars: Organised Violence in a Global Era*, Cambridge: Polity Press.

Kaplan, R.D., 1994, "The Coming Anarchy: How Scarcity, Crime, Overpopulation, and Disease Are Rapidly Destroying the Social Fabric of Our Planet", *Atlantic Monthly*, February, pp. 44–76.

Karim, A., Duffield, M., Jaspars, S., Benini, A., Macrae, J., Bradbury, M., Johnson, D. and G. Larbi, *Operation Lifeline Sudan (OLS): A Review*, Department of Humanitarian Affairs, Geneva, July 1996.

Keen, D., 1994, *The Benefits of Famine: A Political Economy of Famine and Relief in South-western Sudan, 1983–1989*, Princeton NJ: Princeton University Press.

Keen, D., 1998, "The Economic Functions of Violence in Civil Wars", *Adelphi Paper 320*, pp. 1–88, London: International Institute of Strategic Studies.

Korten, D C., 1990, *Getting to the 21st Century: Volutary Action and the Global Agenda*, Connecticut: Kumarian Press.

Leader, N., "Proliferating Principles; Or How to Sup With the Devil Without Getting Eaten", *Disasters*, vol. 22, no. 4, 1998, pp. 288–308.

Leader, N., 1999, *Humanitarian Principles in Practice: A Critical Review*, Relief and Rehabilitation Network (RRN) Discussion Paper, Overseas Development Institute, London.

Leonhardt, M., 2000, *Conflict Impact Assessment of EU Development Co-Operation With ACP Countries: A Review of Literature and Practices*, International Alert and Saferworld, London.

MacGaffey, J. and R. Bazenguissa-Ganga, 2000, *Congo-Paris: Transnational Traders on the Margins of the Law*, Bloomington/Oxford: International African Institute/James Currey.

Macrae, J., and N. Leader, 2000, *Shifting Sands: The Search for 'Coherence' Between Political and Humanitarian Responses to Complex Emergencies*, Humanitarian Policy Group (HPG) Report 8, Overseas Development Institute, London.

Meagher, K., 1997, "Informal Integration or Economic Subversion? Parallel Trade in West Africa", in Lavergne, R. (ed.), *Regional Intergration and Cooperation in West Africa*, Trenton NJ: Africa World Press, Inc with International Development Research Centre, Ottowa.

Nederveen Pieterse, J., 2000, "Globalization North and South: Representations of Uneven Development and the Interaction of Modernities", *Theory, Culture and Society*, vol. 17, no. 1, pp. 129–37.

Nordstrom, C., 2000, "Out of the Shadows.", in Callaghy, T., Kassimir, R. and R. Letham (eds.), *Transborder Formations: Global/Local Constructions of Authority and Violence in Africa*, Cambridge: Cambridge University Press.

O'Brien, P., 1998, *Sudan Case Study for CARE International*, Human Rights and Humanitarian Principles, Kampala.

OCHA, *Next Steps for the United Nations in Afghanistan*, UN Office for the Coordination of Humanitarian Affairs, New York, 24 Sept 1998.

OECD, 1998, *Conflict, Peace and Development Co-Operation on the Threshold of the 21st Century*, Paris: Organisation for Economic Co-operation and Development.

Prunier, G., 1995, *The Rwanda Crisis*. London: C. Hurst and Co. Publishers.

Richards, P., 1996, *Fighting For the Rain Forest: War, Youth and Resources in Sierra Leone*, London: James Currey.

Roitman, J., 2000, "New Sovereigns? The Frontiers of Wealth Creation and Regulatory Authority in the Chad Basin" in Callaghy, T., Kassimir, R. and R. Letham (eds.), *Transboundry Formations: Global/Local Constructions of Authority and Violence in Africa*, Cambridge: Cambridge University Press.

Rose, N., 2000, *Powers of Freedom: Reframing Political Thought*, Cambridge: Cambridge University Press.

Rubin, B.R., 2000, "The Political Economy of War and Peace in Afghanistan", *World Development*, vol. 28, no.10, pp. 1789–1803.

Rubin, B.R, Ghani, A., Maley, W., Rashid, A. and O. Roy, 2001, *Afghanistan: Reconstruction and Peacebuilding in a Regional Framework*, KOFF Peace building Reports 1/2001, Centre for Peace building (KOFF)/Swiss Peace Foundation (SPF), Bern.

Saferworld, 1999, "Memorandum From Saferworld: February 1998", Sixth Report of the International Development Committee, *Conflict Prevention and Post-Conflict Reconstruction, Vol II, Minutes of Evidence and Appendicies*, 68–73, London: The Stationary Office.

Shaw, M., 2000, *War Without End? The Political Economy of Internal Conflict in Angola*, Paper presented at the Seminar on Political Economy of Internal Conflict, The Hague: Netherlands Institute of International Relations (Clingendael), 22 Nov 2000.

Short, C. (Secretary of State for International Development, DFID), "Principles for a New Humanitarianism", Paper presented at *Principled Aid in an Unprincipled World*, London: Church House, 7 April 1998.

Skuric-Prodanovic, M., "Serbia: Exclusion and Its Consequences", Paper presented at *Semi-*

nar on Aid and Politics: Debates, Dilemmas and Dissention, London, Commonwealth House: CAFOD, ODI and Leeds University, 1 Feb 2001.

Slim, H., 1997, "Doing the Right Thing: Relief Agencies, Moral Dilemmas and Moral Responsibility in Political Emergencies and War", Studies on Emergencies and Disaster Relief, Report No. 6, Uppsala, Sweden: The Nordic Africa Institute.

Sphere, 2000, The Sphere Project: Humanitarian Charter and Minimum Standards in Disaster Response, Geneva and Oxford: The Sphere Project and Oxfam Publishing.

Stiglitz, J.E., "Towards a New Paradigm for Development: Strategies, Policies, and Processes", Paper given at 1998 Prebisch Lecture, Geneva: UNCTAD, 19 Oct 1998.

Suhrke, A., 1994, "Towards a Comprehensive Refugee Policy: Conflict and Refugees in the Post-Cold War World", in Bohning, W.R. and M. L. Schloeter-Paredes (eds.), Aid in Place of Migration?, Geneva: International Labour Office.

UN, Strategic Framework for Afghanistan: Towards a Principled Approach to Peace and Reconstruction, United Nations, 15 Sept 1998.

UNCO, The Three Pillars: Strengthening the Foundations, UN Co-ordinator's Office , Islamabad, 31 May 2000.

UNDP, Position Paper of the Working Group on Operational Aspects of the Relief to Development Continuum, UNDP, New York, 12 January 1994.

UNOCHA, Next Steps in Afghanistan: March to June 1999, UNOCHA, Islamabad, 26 Feb., 1999.

Utting, P., 2000, "Business Responsibility for Sustainable Development", OPG No. 2 UNRISD, Geneva.

Uvin, P., "Development, Aid and Conflict: Reflections on the Case of Rwanda", Research for Action, vol. 24, 1996, pp. 1–41. Helsinki: United Nations University, World Institute for Development Economics Research (UNU/WIDER).

van Creveld, M., 1991, The Transformation of War, New York: Free Press.

Verdery, K., 1996, What Was Socialism, And What Comes Next?, Princeton, New Jersey: Princeton University Press.

Verney, P., 1999, "Raising the Stakes: Oil and Conflict in Sudan", Sudan Update, London.

Voutira, E. and S.W. Brown, 1995, "Conflict Resolution: A Review of Some Non-Governmental Practices – 'A Cautionary Tale'", Studies on Emergencies and Disaster Relief - Report No 4., University of Oxford: Refugee Studies Programme, Queen Elizabeth House.

Waters, M., 1995, Globalization, London: Routledge.

Williams, M.C., 1998, "Civil-Military Relations in Peacekeeping", Adelhi Paper (International Institute for Strategic Studies), no. 321, pp. 1–93.

World Bank and Carter Centre, 1997, From Civil War to Civil Society: The Transition From War to Peace in Guatemala and Liberia, World Bank and Carter Center, Washington DC and Atlanta.

Zakaria, F., "Democratic Tyranny", Prospect, no. 25, 1997, pp. 20–25.

4. Reforming the World Order: Multi- and Plurilateral Approaches

Raimo Väyrynen

Introduction

Do we need global governance and, if so, why, and of what kind? The simplest answer to these questions is twofold; both the emerging structural conditions in the international system and several practical needs created by this transition require new and more effective governance strategies. The aim of these strategies is to assure the stability of international economic relations and advance other desirable goals, but, as a kind of side-product, also to promote specific social interests and values. Thus, global governance is not a neutral set of policies, but it is necessarily also a battleground between the advocates of different ideologies and policies.

Globalisation and other international structural changes have created new demands on institutions, norms and policies to cope with their multiple consequences. These effects may concern the entire international system or its specific regions, economic sectors or social strata. At present, compared with the demand, institutions and instruments of global governance are under-supplied by national and international actors. It is this discrepancy that creates the current *governance dilemma*. A solution to this dilemma could be the provision of new institutions and norms that create "a new balance between politics and market" and "rules of game creating just conditions" as a recent Swedish government report puts the matter (Regeringskansliet, 2001).

As a rule, global governance is viewed as a positive endeavour to stabilise the process of economic globalisation and ameliorate its adverse effects by incorporating some basic values to guide the operation of the market. Seen from another perspective, global governance can be perceived as a political effort to prop up economic practices that increase inequality, harm the environment, and violate human and labour rights. In between these two opposing arguments, there is the more detached view that global governance is one way of living a global life and trying to make it, under existing constraints, as decent as possible for the majority of the world's population. These three perspectives can be identified as market liberal, critical and reformist approaches to global governance, respectively. While they overlap, they manifest three different ways of defining the relationship between politics and global capitalism. *Market liberalism* accepts the participation of the state in the market, but only to the extent that its basic mechanisms (in particular property rights) are not violated. The *critical approach* aims, in turn, to restructure the foundations of economic action, not necessarily by means of central political control, but by affording a stronger economic role to popular movements and human communities. Finally, the *reformist model* supports governmental intervention in the market, especially to promote equality and stability, but without leading to its political control.

Historically, the rise of the nation state and capitalism have taken place in tandem. In this process, the state often had the leading role as it created a legal and political framework in which the extraction and accumulation of economic assets could take place. The state acquired and, ultimately, monopolised the control of physical force on the territory and used it, among other things, to expand its international influence and protect the country against external threats. In major powers, economic resources and military instruments were integrated in a national grand strategy that they pursued either alone or in alliance with other countries.

Thus, the involvement of the state in national economic development is nothing new. However, early on, capitalism started to reach beyond state borders, in which process it needed the political and military support of the state. The establishment and activities of the British and Dutch trading companies for East Asia are examples of how imperial and capitalist interests interacted with each other. Over time, these trading companies turned out to be inadequate to manage the world economy and the states had to step in to create a framework for a more liberal form of capitalism.

However, the power of the state has its own cycle too and according to a rather common view, it is currently declining. This augurs the continuing denationalisation of the economy, leading to both its regionalisation and globalisation – tendencies that are complementary rather than contradictory. This stems from the fact that the material resources and physical reach of most states have turned out to be inadequate. As a result, global capitalism has had to expand on its own. However, such a solo flight is necessarily unsteady and even unpredictable.

For all these reasons, the expansion of global capitalism has been closely intertwined with, and sometimes contradicted by, the patterns of international political hegemony, its historical cycles, and the competition between the hegemons and their challengers. In the present circumstances, economic globalisation takes place under the auspices of the leading power of the system and, at a minimum, the existing states system. From different intellectual points of view, it has been argued that the process of globalisation cannot succeed over the long term without the support of (hegemonic) states (for further discussion, see Arrighi, 1994; Gilpin, 2000; Schwartz, 2000).

Also in a more practical vein, the global economy and environment have needed the visible hand of the state. This has been the case for two reasons; without societal guidance, the autonomous market system easily becomes self-destructive and suffers from various problems of stability and legitimacy. Therefore, global governance is needed to fill the twin deficits of efficiency and democracy. In other words, the stability and legitimacy of global capitalism require the extension of political institutions and norms to a transnational level. Fred Halliday (2001: 63–67), among others, has stressed that globalisation is inherently an unequal and destabilising process and calls for countervailing measures.

In the transnationalisation of political relations, the cooperative link between the nation state and capitalism is reproduced at the regional and global levels to counter the risks and critics of globalisation. It is indeed appropriate to stress that globalisation is a risky and unstable process as it can lead to periodic crises and other disruptions. Ultimately, these risks may threaten capitalism itself. On a more tactical level, the opponents of globalisation can drive a wedge between governments and companies by using both domestic and transnational channels of influence that are outside the effective control of governments.

To sum up, global governance is a new mode of problem-solving cooperation between private economic interests and public politics for coping with new international challenges. This means that much of global governance essentially boils down to a reformist strategy, leavened with market liberalism, in which states still have a key, but precarious role. However, this new form of national, but increasingly private-public relationship is constantly challenged by social non-state actors which tend to consider it detrimental to democracy, equity and other social values. This introduces a critical political element in the debate on and practices of global governance. It would be too limiting, however, to view non-governmental organisations (NGOs) and other social actors merely as critics of the state-business relationship – a monkey-wrench in the wheel of global capitalism. NGOs are also social agencies, representing organised social forces with their own interests, ideologies, goals and strategies. In addition to expressing dissent, these agencies may try to redistribute power in society, shape public opinion and influence governmental policies. For these purposes they raise funds, mobilise people for collective action, and establish national and transnational advocacy networks. In other words, civil society is not just a collection of groups, but, especially in democracies, an organised system of social actors which often have a transational dimension in their activities (for more sophisticated discussions, see Keck and Sikkink, 1998; della Porta and Diani, 1999; Schechter, 2000; Bleiker, 2000).

Furthermore, environmental, development and human rights NGOs not only have a long history of opposition to, but also of cooperation with, the World Bank and other international agencies. This collaboration has forced NGOs to specify their goals and strategies to be able to wield practical influence. It has also prompted associations with particular agendas – focusing, for instance, on poverty, structural adjustment and human rights – to coordinate their positions. This, in turn, has increased convergence in the NGO community. It has been argued that civil society organisations have, in several ways, shaped the activities of the World Bank. On the other hand, it is also asserted that links with NGOs have expanded the Bank's influence over them, not only by the virtue of funds allocated to their activities, but also by selecting participating organisations and shaping their agendas (Nelson, 2000; O'Brien, et al., 2000).

In concrete terms, global political governance is needed for at least the following three reasons:

a. international society needs means by which to cope with the negative and positive *externalities* which each country produces. Obviously, governance is most needed when a big and risky state produces major negative externalities, such as ecological damage, organised crime or military threats (Väyrynen, 1997).[1] Many of these externalities can be managed by unilateral and bilateral means available to national governments, but multilateral approaches are often also needed;

b. states experience, in their political, economic and security relations, various *problems of collective action*. In the absence of mutual cooperation, regulation and confidence, the outcomes of these actions can be suboptimal rather than Pareto-improving. Therefore, states have an incentive to overcome the problems by embarking upon reciprocal collaboration;

c. some of the challenges and their effects, especially ecological ones (such as global warming), cannot be apportioned between the individual actors and are, thus, of a contextual nature. National responses to *contextual problems* tend to be inadequate and governments have to develop multilateral means to reach common solutions, including the production of collective goods.

The reasons for global governance and the models for its management can be correlated with each other in the following, very tentative manner:

Table 1. Reasons and models for global governance

	Market liberalism	Critical approach	Reformist model
Externalities	Externalities are internalised by market incentives	Social forces demand the cutback of harmful activities	Legislation and treaties to deal with harmful activities
Collective action problems	Restructure market incentives to promote cooperation	Demand that companies and governments cooperate	Bind parties to agreements and enforce them
Contextual problems	No permanent or viable solutions	Change in the source of problems, e.g. economic restructuring	Regulatory agreements, e.g. pollution quotas

[1] Although economic and sometimes environmental issues have dominated debates on global governance, it is well to remember that there is also a school of thought that sees the problems mostly in political and military terms. Thus, Bill Emmott, Editor of *The Economist*, listed the diffusion of economic and military power, nuclear proliferation, and political instability in China and Russia as key challenges to global governance. On the other hand, he foresaw, correctly, the rising backlash to "global liberalism" and the ensuing need to deal with poverty in industrial societies; see Emmott (1997).

This outline suggests that the three approaches to global governance all have their specific remedies to the problem. Market liberalism stresses the need to redefine incentives, for instance through the price system, so that companies find it attractive to cooperate in order to reduce externalities, overcome the collective action problem and work on contextual problems. The critical approach, usually pursued by scholars and social movements, calls for more fundamental changes, for instance, in the structure of the economic system and its principles of operation. The reformists believe in the power of legislation, agreements and other regulatory approaches which define the limits of what is and what is not permitted. Once the rules have been established, the state has the primary responsibility for monitoring that they are followed, and enforced in the case of non-compliance.

This paper is biased towards the reformist model, although this does not mean that alternative approaches are considered unimportant or even secondary. The paper also adopts a multi- and plurilateralist, i.e. an international, perspective devoting less attention to domestic or even bilateral problems. In defining the concept of *multilateralism*, I am following the lead of Ruggie, who uses it to refer to "coordinating relations among three or more states in accordance with certain principles". These principles are expected to be general rather than specific in nature. They "specify appropriate conduct for classes of actions, without regard to the particularist interests of the parties" (Ruggie, 1998: 107–110). Most-favoured nation (MFN) treatment in international trade treaties, or a ban on anti-ballistic missiles in arms-control agreements, are examples of generalised principles which, in turn, have various specific implications.

According to the standard formulation, multilateralism considers states to be the central actors in international cooperation, although other actors do of course exist in the system. The situation may be changing, however. The end of the cold war has ushered a process of "structural differentiation", to use Philip Cerny's term. In this process, different levels of the system are separated from each other, and, at the same time, various functional structures – for instance, security, economy, politics and culture – become more distinct.

In *plurilateralism*, the international system structure is complex and volatile because it is not stabilised by any hierarchical system, be it unipolar or bipolar. The system has indeterminate and unpredictable characteristics. In the plurilateral model, various crosscutting links and actions occur across both levels and structures. Each actor has a combination of characteristics and overlapping memberships; therefore, the system is pluralistic in nature (Cerny, 1993).[2] The advantage of the plurilateral model is precisely its plu-

---

[2] I am using "plurilateralism" here in a different sense from Björn Hettne in his lead article, in which it refers to the transatlantic alliance. In my view, the main characteristic of plurilateralism is the existence and combination of multiple types of actors that make it a hybrid constellation.

ralism; it takes all kinds of actors seriously – not just states – and explores how they operate across different levels and functional structures. For instance, the previous clear-cut separation of the public and private spheres has broken down, and new types of public/private combinations have emerged at both the domestic and the international level.

Multilateralism and plurilateralism do not exclude each other. Rather, multilateralism is a state-based subcategory of organisational forms and actions within a broader plurilateral world. Neither are multilateralism or plurilateralism, in themselves, good or bad. Multilateral forms of organisation can be used in military interventions, but also in international treaties to protect the environment. According to traditional sociological theories, for example those of Lewis Coser, a plurilateral structure is expected to be peaceful because of its flexibility and capacity to absorb shocks. On the other hand, Cerny (1993: 49–50) refers to the possibility that inequality can be quite pervasive and conflicts can spread more easily in a plurilateral structure than in a more hierarchical system. Nevertheless, a plurilateral structure is probably not as prone to a breakdown as a hierarchical system, which can be badly damaged, for instance, by the collision of great powers

Collective and Contextual Aspects

This paper deals primarily with the third category of governance problems, i.e., the contextual ones. This does not mean that the management of negative externalities or collective-action problems are unimportant. In fact, these kinds of market failures are key items on the global governance agenda as they have a direct, and often deep, impact on individuals, governments and companies. Therefore, considerable political attention has been paid to risks emanating, for instance, from the spread of weapons of mass destruction, the operation of terrorist networks, protectionism encumbering free trade, unregulated or illegal immigration and the pollution of regional seas. The practical need to manage negative externalities and collective-action problems has also inspired a wealth of quickly growing scholarly literature, both theoretical and empirical, on the externalities problem (Sandler, 1997; Cable, 1999; Young, 2000).

A common feature in the management of contextual problems is that it cannot normally be left solely to the market, but that ameliorative public action is needed. Contextual global challenges appear in a number of guises and cannot, therefore, be squeezed into any single category. Even the most contextual of these issues, such as global warming and the thinning ozone layer, have somewhat different physical and climatic effects in different parts of the world – the Maldives and Mongolia face rather different problems as a result of global warming. In most cases, the contextual (indivisible) and divisible effects exist side by side, and their management calls, depending on the situation, for a suitable combination of multilateral, unilateral and bilateral actions.

There are three alternatives to market-based solutions in collective-action problems: contract, community and hierarchy (McGinnis, 1999). In international relations, which are decentralised in nature, a hierarchical organisation to decide and enforce rules is seldom a feasible option. After the end of the Cold War and the onset of globalisation, this has become even less likely. A transition is taking place towards an international society in which members agree on some basic institutions and rules, but not all. In essence, such a society contains basic rules for the management of conflicts and cooperation between the key units.

In the established version, international society exists among the state actors. However, the scenario is currently changing towards more hybrid, plurilateral manifestations of the international society. Still, this does not mean that a communitarian approach is the best, let alone the only, way to provide a basis for global governance.

This leaves, in international relations, contract-based approaches as the main alternative to purely market-based solutions. In terms of definition, a contract is the result of a bargaining process over a set of issues between key actors. Contracting leads to formal or informal agreements among such actors on how the rules of the bargain are specified, monitored and enforced, and their costs divided. Krasner adds that contracts must also be "Pareto-improving and contingent", i.e. they must be mutually beneficial and acceptable as they cannot be imposed on other actors (Krasner, 1999: 33–36).

In other words, a contract is a voluntary agreement that the parties, usually governments, respect as long it serves their interests. Although global governance relies mostly on a state-centric, contractual approach, it would be inappropriate to entirely dismiss hierarchy and community as structural approaches to markets. The effective conduct of global governance often requires multiple solutions and agents which may, for instance, pool their resources or create a division of labour among various actors and sectors of activity (McGinnis, 1999: 62–64). Multiple agents and their complex mutual relations have played an important role in, for instance, international campaigns to relieve the debt burden of poor countries or to ban landmines. As a result, globalisation, sovereignty and transnational social movements are becoming intertwined with each other in novel ways (Väyrynen, 2001).

National governments can try to tackle debt relief, poverty reduction and other similar problems through unilateral actions and various forms of bilateral cooperation. The problem is that governments are often unwilling and, ultimately, unable to offer a solution to these deep-seated problems. Therefore, unless one admits that social, economic and political inequality are a common denominator of these troubles, success in such efforts will be minimal. While poverty and indebtedness are individual or group problems, inequality is a systemic condition which cannot be divided between individual actors. Depending on the perspective chosen, the increasing distributional inequity can be treated either as a political failure or as a market failure.

Inequality and Governance

According to this perspective, income equality is a particular kind of public good which is extremely difficult to achieve. This is all the more likely for the reason that the developed countries, especially the United States, have refused to consider the reduction of poverty and inequality to be legally or morally obligating goals (Pogge, 2001: 11; Hurrell, 2001: 51–53). However, even if there were serious political efforts to promote greater equality, their "distributional outcome might still be socially and ethically inadequate". Moreover, even if such efforts were superficially successful, it cannot be taken for granted that non-market solutions to distributional inequity necessarily produce socially optimal outcomes, as public authorities can also fail (Wolf, 1979: 110–12, 128–31).

The contextual nature of inequality means that its effects spread and permeate the entire system; as it is not actor-specific, it is difficult to trace social inequality to its original sources. In the same spirit, Robert Wade compares inequality with global warming, another contextual phenomenon; "its effects are diffuse and long-term, and there is always something more pressing to deal with (Wade, 2001: 74). Moreover, inequality cannot be tackled by means of undifferentiated collective actions; those concerned with it must find a conceptual or political entry point that permits efforts through individual actors and their communities.

Inequality should not be considered a unidimensional phenomenon, such as income inequality, but one has to recognise its roots in the multidimensional "capability poverty". As Amartya Sen notes, the "relation between low income and low capability is variable between different communities". *Capability poverty* is a more serious condition than, for instance, low income alone as the latter can be compensated by various economic and social mechanisms. Thus, there is good reason to consider poverty broadly as "the deprivation of basic capabilities" (Sen, 2000: 87–110). Thus, Sen rejects not only the utilitarian, but also the income-egalitarian approach to social well-being. Instead, he favours the enhancement of human capabilities, and the *freedom* to achieve them, as the key goal and strategy of development (cf. Margalit, 2000).

The World Bank has adopted a somewhat different approach to the definition of poverty, and seems to put a greater emphasis on the *vulnerability* and powerlessness of the poor (World Development Report, 2000/2001: 15–21). While an emphasis on freedom on the one hand and vulnerability on the other can lead to similar policy prescriptions, they spring from different political roots. Freedom is associated with the nature of the political society, while vulnerability results more from social and economic conditions, especially inequality and poverty. Poverty, and thus vulnerability, cannot be addressed separately from inequality. In the real world, as the income share of the richest people in the world grows, the number of poor people remains stubbornly high. Globalisation may not cause poverty, but the two continue to persist in parallel, which means that globalisation has been unable to alleviate distress and misery (Wade, 2001; Pogge, 2001).

If the aim is to mitigate the systemic condition of inequality, the focus has to be both on the high and low ends of global income distribution. This requires, among other things, the taxation of the income of the rich and the transfer of some of these resources to improve the basic capabilities of the poor, as well as their access to education and other social services. To put it simply, the freedom of the poor has to be made real by means of a workable political strategy and social reform.

Although economic globalisation generates new resources, many do not believe it to be capable of redistributing them. Instead, globalisation will encourage the displacement of labour in developing countries and the creation there of a permanent and growing pool of surplus labour, whose relative, and even absolute standard of living will decline. In general, it has been suggested that the factors that boost living standards may decline all over the world. If this is the case, one can justifiably ask "why globalisation did not deliver the goods?" (Kaplinsky, 2001).

Various popular gaps, such as the "digital divide", are not, primarily, technological problems, but a result of general poverty due to inadequate capabilities and freedoms. Their common denominator seems to be the *lack of access* by the common people to material resources and political influence. This theme is reflected, somewhat surprisingly, in Jeffrey Sachs' recent writings and political activities, in which the main emphasis has been on the need to create opportunities for the two billion people who are excluded from education, health care and communications (Sachs, 2000). He does not, however, consider adequately the fact that in access, the pivotal issue is *power*; i.e., the capacity to restrict and control access to resources that are deemed valuable.

These problems can be solved only if appropriate universal standards are developed for the redistribution of resources and power relations are restructured. This suggestion can be criticised on two grounds; first, the roots of the problem are often domestic rather than international and second, universal criteria may be too rigid in a diverse world. Charles Beitz (1999) does not see any contradiction in the combination of universal standards, which he calls "cosmopolitan liberalism", and the recognition of the fact that the biggest impediments to their realisation are often domestic in nature. There is "a reason for concern about the justice of [the global] structure even after the influence of the local factors is conceded". This implies that the state is no solution to the problem of international inequality (Beitz, 1999: 525).

On the other hand, a need can often arise to apply relativistic criteria of equity, instead of universal ones, to specific regional and national conditions. Obviously, the division of the world into several categories of rights can be criticised both on ethical and practical grounds. However, according to one view, inequality on a global scale becomes an important political issue only when its "production" leads to social deprivation and becomes politically visible. From this perspective, it has been suggested that global inequalities are unjust only if they "entail that some people's basic rights are being violated" and arise because of "exploitative economic processes" (Miller, 1999).

This solution reflects a form of minimal liberalism as it takes seriously only explicit violations of universal rights. This case is undermined by the fact that, while the causes of explicit violations of rights can be traced with relative ease, social inequities are produced by complex processes whose effects are indirect, delayed, and often unpredictable. This is due to the institutional mediation between the original causes of inequality and poverty and their various individual and collective effects.

The institutional or, as some say, comprehensive liberal approach to justice argues that we have a moral duty not to impose unjust institutions on others, and perhaps even an obligation to participate in efforts to dismantle them and promote alternative solutions. People may be regarded as morally responsible even if they do not commit discriminating acts, but participate in or condone institutions that do so. Ultimately, the restoration of justice may require positive discrimination or affirmative action; i.e., the extension of special rights to the disadvantaged by the appropriate institutions and rules (Mandle, 2000; Tan, 2000).

The comprehensive liberal approach goes some way towards responding to the contextual nature of international inequality as it tries to redistribute resources on a global scale and not just redivide them between states (as, for instance, the New International Economic Order in the 1970s demanded). The comprehensive approach rejects any absolute notion of national sovereignty and the ontological or political prioritisation of the nation state. On the other hand, one has to recognise that any universal scheme to accord the same rights to all people of the world is not a feasible proposition in any foreseeable future. Therefore, the only tenable solution may be what Sen (1999) calls "plural affiliation"; i.e., one has to recognise that people belong to various national and transnational communities in which somewhat different standards of justice and fairness may apply.

It can be argued that there is currently a slow, but gradual movement towards a common global ethic. This can be witnessed, for instance, in the emphasis on *Weltethik* by Hans Küng, the revival of interest among political philosophers in the topic and recent statements by many a political leader. However, this change is necessarily limited and even contradictory in nature; ethical standards are probably taken more seriously than before, but they bind individual and collective actions only to a partial and variable degree. Moreover, so far, no governments either in industrial or in developing countries have formulated any consistent or effective response to the growing demands for greater international equity (Doyle, 1999; Hurrell, 2001).

Another contextual aspect of inequality and poverty is practical; the economic and social polarisation of the international system and its domestic manifestations can have adverse political consequences such as instability and violence. Both domestic and international polarisation are systemic properties which cannot be divided between individual actors; therefore, inequality affects everyone, though this may not be easy to admit (especially by the rich).

The interdependence created by inequality is explicitly pointed out by David Landes: "wealth is an irresistible magnet; and poverty is potentially raging contaminant; it cannot be segregated, and our peace and prosperity depend in the long run on the well-being of others" (Landes, 1998: xx). In a global world, economic motives of profit and greed are the seedbeds of organised crime, drug trafficking, illegal immigration and other similar problems. On the other hand, organised crime always benefits someone; otherwise it would not exist. This also concerns inequality; for instance, demography and poverty create a pool of labour from which less skilled, but mobile workers needed in various business sectors are recruited.

Empirical evidence indicates that since 1960, developed countries have converged towards a common level of per capita income, but that most developing countries have diverged from this level. The statistical findings on the continuing and, in many cases, *growing income inequalities* among nations are striking. Evidence contradicting the growing divergence of income levels can be provided only by weighting national economies by the size of their populations and using purchasing power parity (PPP) exchange rates. This brings China (and India) into the picture.

In this case, the rapid economic growth of populous China since the 1980s conceals the relative decline of most developing countries, especially in Africa. On the other hand, a closer look at China reveals rapidly growing inequalities, especially between rural and urban populations, amidst the rising average income. Yet a particularly stark picture of the escalating inequality is obtained when market exchange rates are used and the countries are not weighted by population (Jones, 1997; Firebaugh, 1999; Sarkar, 2000; Wade, 2001; Kaplinsky, 2001: 48–49, 56–60).

It is often suggested that most global inequality is due to international differences in national income levels and that domestic income distribution is of little significance. On the other hand, there is evidence that intranational income disparities are growing in most developed countries as well as in less developed countries, including China. This tendency cannot but be linked to economic globalisation, which by itself does not actually cause so much poverty, but rather tends, especially if combined with neoliberal economic policies, to leave the weakest and poorest behind. The trickle-down theory of development simply does not work. In the absence of resources, such social groups do not usually rebel openly, but express their discontent by latent and indirect means (Chin and Mittelman, 1997).

Actors of Global Governance
The role of the state

Much of the literature dealing with the management and governance of international relations is, in its basic orientation, very state-centric. Actions by national governments, as well as their mutual cooperation, are considered keys for solving the problems created by negative externalities, suboptimal collaboration and even systemic challenges. This view has its justification, especially in areas in which major financial resources are needed to strengthen multilateral arrangements and the effective monitoring, and enforcement of international rules require their incorporation in domestic legislation. In such areas there is simply no alternative to the state as the key actor in the implementation of global governance (Lentner, 2000).

On the other hand, states cannot deal effectively with all international problems, either because they become victims of their own self-centred nature and hence of collective-action problems, or because they are inappropriate actors to address a particular issue. As discussed by liberal institutionalists, collective-action problems can be solved by various means available to state actors. They include, for instance, the mutual commitment of governments to the norm of reciprocity (a tit-for-tat strategy) and the integration of the issue under dispute in a more comprehensive political framework (Axelrod and Keohane, 1985). However, the success of these cooperative efforts is by no means guaranteed and states may continue to disagree.

Another limitation of the state-centric strategies of global governance concerns the "politics of contested institutions", to use Peter Gourevitch's (1999) expression. It differs from the neorealist argument that international institutions are, most of the time, due to the unilateral interests of their state members, ineffectual in monitoring and enforcing international cooperation and, therefore, unreliable guarantors of the world order (Mearsheimer, 1995). Instead, the reference to the contested nature of institutions means that governments perceive them to have real power. Where international institutions matter and governments invest resources in them, they can also easily have different views and even disputes about their internal arrangements, organisational goals and external strategies (Gourevitch, 1999).

Such a utilitarian interpretation of global governance problems helps to account, for instance, for different governmental preferences concerning the structure and actions of the World Trade Organisation (WTO) and the International Monetary Fund (IMF). If these organisations were unimportant, there would not be as much pressure to restructure, or even abolish them as we are witnessing today. One possible way to understand the political urge to redesign international organisations is that they have developed dysfunctional features. This point is developed by Barnett and Finnemore (1999), who underline that one should not underestimate the bureaucratic influence of such organisations. They deploy resources, create and implement rules, identify new interests and actors, and develop social knowledge. Equipped with these resources, international agencies may become unresponsive to their environments and even develop pathological traits.

This interpretation deviates from the standard view that governments are strong enough to cope with intergovernmental agencies or that their basic nature is benevolent. Governments are expected to shun strong institutional forms that would restrict their sovereignty and freedom of action. Therefore, the first step taken by states is, as a rule, mutual recognition of national practices, followed by an attempt to reach a negotiated consensus on issues in which disagreements exist and finally the delegation of policies to international institutions, while retaining the final authority to make decisions (Coglianese, 2000).

These views of international institutions as real, but contested arenas for debate and decisions departs in a useful manner from the common view that globalisation is leading to an irreparable erosion of state power. However, the scope of effective state power may diminish as a result of globalisation for two reasons. First, since the 1980s, there has been a strong convergence towards common rules regarding foreign direct investment, capital taxation and intellectual property rights. Second, partly as a result of this convergence, some issues, such as monetary policy, are increasingly removed from national decision-making.

There is some evidence that globalisation and international institutions promote convergence in policy areas such as the protection of the ozone layer, in which state actions are affected by significant externalities and problems of collective action. Governments are rational actors in the sense that they usually cooperate in areas where it is necessary and useful. On the other hand, the absence of such externalities, and the access of private interests to decision-making, seem to permit a divergence of national policies (Botcheva and Martin, 2001). This suggests that a homogenisation of national policies does not necessarily follow from globalisation, but may rather result from domestic political choices.

Several empirical studies show that industrialised states, even small ones, are capable of protecting their domestic structures and remaining viable international actors. In fact, globalisation may even encourage such states to protect their people and project their liberal/social democratic values on the world scene (Garrett, 1998; Schultze and Ursprung, 1999). Moreover, it has to be recognised that even when governments decide to give up, say, their autonomy in monetary policy, this happens through their own voluntary decisions. Globalisation and other external factors may create pressures and incentives to opt for a certain policy, but ultimately it is the governments that decide to self-limit their freedom of action. The existence of a freedom to choose is witnessed by the EMU which most EU members have joined, although some key governments have decided not to.

The problem of "stateness" is much more complicated in developing countries, of which only a few have an adequate record of political stability and economic development to sustain their autonomy. In reality, their independence has only been "quasi-sovereign" in nature. In the process of decolonisation, major powers decided to extricate themselves from their commitments and grant independence to the former colonies. Until recently, national sovereignty in the South has depended on the external political and material support, which the governments have utilised to control their own people and, in general, legitimise their rule both internally and externally (Jackson, 1990; Clapham, 1996).

Private actors

Despite their continuing centrality, it is clear that states are not able to provide effective governance for international economic, social and environmental relations alone. States may be pivotal for the stability of the world economy, but once stability has been assured, they are unable to attain all specific goals. The marketisation and privatisation of the world economy generate a governance agenda that is both more extensive and complex than it used to be in the system of state-based interdependence. Together, the relative rise of corporate influence and the shrinking scope of effective state action mean that there has to be a shift towards greater self-regulation among market actors. Thus, the need to privatise some aspects of global governance arises from the structural shifts of power between the state and the market, and their new integration with each other.

Private self-regulation among corporate actors is an interesting game; on the one hand, corporations have to agree on how to cooperate in matters of common interest, but, on the other hand, they continue to compete for market shares and technological leadership. Private self-regulation is used, in particular, to coordinate technical standards and business practices that reduce transaction costs in the market. Cooperation can, of course, also be informal and even border on cartel-like behaviour, which is often illegal in nature. As soon as the need for legal regulation and its political demands walk in the door, states have to enter the governance game.

As mentioned, a general trend seems to be that governments are departing from some of their earlier tasks and transferring them to the market actors, while at the same time retaining their key capabilities to enforce decisions. This implies that governments want to stick to their ultimate legal powers conferred to them by the principle of sovereignty. Compared with that, the role of coercive, military power for the operation of governments may be diminishing; more and more international problems are treated as criminal acts rather than risks to traditional national security.

In most industrialised countries, one can speak of an informal alliance between governments and "their" transnational business actors. In real life, such an alliance is perceived to reduce the free political choice of citizens and distance political leaders from their concerns. This tends, in turn, to generate opposition that, especially today, comes from outside the established party system. This opposition is muted, however, by the fact the government/corporate nexus is much more informal than during the heyday of corporatism and the Cold War. Today, governments do not enlist corporations to serve the national politics of hegemony and rivalry; neither do companies necessarily need governments to back them up in politically contested regions. In reality, in many developed countries, the political and corporate elite seem to have developed a common code of understanding that does not need to be enacted or enforced by daily behaviour.

Political resistance to globalisation has been directed both against overbearing, "faceless" corporations and governments, which have supported its expansion instead of regulating it. International regimes, such as the IMF and the WTO, are perceived by the critics as the illegitimate offspring of this relationship. In other words, "the new international rules of trade are designed expressly to create markets – not to control them. Trade rules are designed to control the activities of nations and this is in the heart of agreements" (Cohen, 2000: 205).

On the other hand, relations between states, corporations and NGOs are not fixed; any two tips of the triangle may forge a coalition against the third, although an NGO-TNC (transnational corporation) coalition against the state has not been very common. Yet, it has been argued that the criticism by NGOs and the corporate response to it – for instance, the enactment of voluntary ethical codes – have created a new interdependent relationship between these two types of private actors that is realised largely outside the purview of governmental control (Gereffi, *et al.,* 2001).

Hybrid Forms of Governance

The multiplicity of actors in global governance is a new fact of international life. This observation concerns, first of all, humanitarian, and possibly some environmental issues in which NGOs have become key actors in contributing to and even implementing policy decisions. However, the multiplicity of actors can be increasingly witnessed also in economic and security policies. Thus, a predominant trend is towards *hybrid forms of governance,* in which different types of actors at different levels of the international system have to cooperate with each other to be able to govern complex and multifaceted issue areas.

There are many sectors of the world economy in which private governance is almost a rule, although possibly within broad limits decided by governments and intergovernmental organisations (IGOs). These areas include risk analysis and bond-rating agencies, online commerce, computer standards, business ethics and maritime transportation (Cutler, *et al.*, 1999). A recent example of private governance is the establishment of a common set of global accounting standards monitored by a body of technical experts. This development has been possible because of the homogenisation of business cultures, especially in the transatlantic context (Jesswein, 2001). In areas like accounting, governments play only a limited role, but when it comes, for instance, to the governance of intellectual property rights, there is no way to manage the task without involving governments and their common organisations.

In areas requiring governmental intervention, there seems to be a tendency to climb up to higher levels of governance, from the national to the regional and from the regional to the global level. Competition and antitrust laws provide good examples of this tendency. National, bilateral and even regional (in particular the EU) arrangements to promote market competition by preventing excessive concentrations of economic power have proved to be inadequate. The question is not only about a public interest in regulating transnational business activities, companies also have their own interests to avoid being paralysed by contradictory rulings of disparate national regulatory systems. (The situation is somewhat similar in the area of patents and copyrights.) Therefore, there are both political and business arguments in favour of shifting competition law to the global level. The EU, the US and other actors continue to disagree, however, on how binding global competition rules should be and where they should be negotiated.

These examples refer mostly to hybrid business/government cooperation in global governance. However, in many areas national and transnational NGOs also play a major role. Their contribution can be approached either as a normative or an empirical issue. From the prescriptive point of view, NGOs are often considered a vehicle to restore democracy to global governance as they can open up channels of action and influence from the grass roots level upwards (Falk, 1995).[3]

In a more empirical vein, one can, for instance, explore the myriad of ways in which NGOs have criticised the policies of international financial

[3] Of course, the problem of democratising global governance is a much broader and complicated issue. For comprehensive analyses of the demands on democracy in global governance and various strategies to pursue this goal, see Fox and Roth, 2000 and Camilleri, Malhotra and Tehranian, 2000. For a more sceptical historical view, see Gilbert, 1999.

institutions (IFIs) and made the (transnational) civil society a permanent factor in the lives of these institutions. In fact, much before the recent wave of anti-globalisation protests, NGOs developed working relationships with intergovernmental organisations that they have later decided to blame for various kinds of misbehaviour. The NGO input has, in particular, concerned environmental, gender, human rights and labour issues.

Roughly, one can say that the demands emanating from civil society have expanded the governance agenda, in particular of the World Bank. Such issues as transparency and accountability, corruption, military spending and human rights violations have become a part and parcel of the Bank's activities. On the other hand, the critics claim that the World Bank has embraced those initiatives that can be integrated in its own agenda and given less heed to demands that would have required deeper changes in its approach (Higgot, et al., 2000; O'Brien, et al., 2000; Nelson, 2000a; Nelson, 2000b).

The United Nations

In theory, the United Nations is the umbrella organisation for global governance; it has a universal and multisectoral mandate, some, though inadequate, administrative and material resources, and political experience for international engagements. However, according to more exacting standards, the UN role in global governance has remained limited, with the exception of some peacekeeping and peacebuilding operations, and development programmes. In Kofi Annan's words, there has been a "gap between aspiration and accomplishment" (Annan, 1998: 128).

In particular, in the governance of the global economy, the impact of the UN headquarters has been modest. Neither have the international bodies created directly by the UN, such as the United Nations Conference on Trade and Development (UNCTAD) and the United Nations Industrial Development Organization (UNIDO), been able to gain global influence of any consequence. The responsibility of economic governance has been borne by international organisations, such as the World Bank, the IMF and the WTO, which are only indirectly – or not at all – linked with the United Nations.

This has created a lasting political dilemma in which the supporters of the UN have suggested that its capabilities for dealing with the challenges of economic development and financial stability should be augmented, while many others have rejected this idea. Typically, the supporting proposals have favoured either the consolidation of its disparate development bureaucracies or the establishment of new, more powerful structures. Most UN reforms in the 1990s, including Annan's effort in 1997 to reorganise the Secretariat's work around five core areas, have aimed at consolidation. It has also been suggested, among other things, that an economic security council should be set up to give greater bite to UN actions in the development field (International Commission on Global Governance, 1995: 153–62).

The critics have countered these proposals by saying that the UN's inefficient performance is due to a legitimacy gap rather than a capability gap. Its limited legitimacy undermines any justification to allocate additional resources to the organisation. This tug of war between the two camps (one liberal, the other conservative) has produced some good by pressing the need to reform and streamline the UN structures and practices – something that has, indeed, been long overdue. However, much of the debate has been fruitless posturing and political manoeuvring and, thus, more of an obstacle than a contribution to global governance.

Under Kofi Annan's leadership, the UN has taken a new tack that seems to comprise three distinct elements; (a) a new philosophy of globalisation; (b) a search for new solutions to old global dilemmas; and (c) a new approach to TNCs and the private sector in general. The formulation of a *new thinking on globalisation* was launched in September 1998 in a speech delivered by the Secretary-General at Harvard University. Even before that, Annan (1998: 124) had acknowledged that "globalisation is perhaps the most profound source of international transformation since the Industrial Revolution". The Harvard speech struck a balance between a critical interpretation of globalisation and the search for a constructive solution.

On the one hand, Annan noted that "today, globalisation is rapidly losing its lustre in parts of the world" because it is seen "not as a term describing objective reality, but as an ideology of predatory capitalism". This perception incites nationalism, populism, and other "illiberal solutions". On the other hand, Annan stated that "globalisation is made the scapegoat of ills which more often have domestic roots of a political nature". However, to ensure that globalisation survives, its supporters must take the criticism seriously and ascertain that it becomes inclusive and distributes resources also to the poor. In Annan's words, globalisation "must deliver rights no less than riches. It must provide social justice and equity no less than economic prosperity" (Annan, 2000).

This basic message – the need to combine global market and equity – has been repeated since then by Annan on a number of occasions and has almost become a mantra in the political mainstream. In 2000, the exhortation that the success of globalisation requires social inclusion and reforms provided an agenda for two major international meetings: the Berlin summit in June and the UN Millennium Summit in September. To the Berlin meeting, Chancellor Gerhard Schröder had invited a dozen other social democratic and liberal world leaders (ranging from Bill Clinton to Thabo Mbeki and Fernando Enrique Cardoso). The summit in New York brought together the heads of state or government from practically all UN member states.

At the conference on *Modernes Regieren*, the participants recognised that globalisation is an economic fact that opens up new opportunities but which cannot be let loose; instead, it has to be "managed together". However, this management has to be based on greater individual initiative and a smaller and more efficient state than has hitherto been the case. In addition, economic growth generated by globalisation must be combined with a struggle against social exclusion and poverty. The Berlin Declaration paid particular attention to the stability of the international financial system, which should be promoted by a more effective monitoring and enforcement of the rules (*Süddeutsche Zeitung*, 15 June, 2000).[4]

In fact, these two themes – social inclusion and financial stability – have become the hallmarks of a centrist analysis of the conditions for the viability of the globalisation process. Social inclusion does not only spring from ethical concerns; it also aims at a kind of global Keynesianism. Thus, at the 2001 meeting of the World Economic Forum in Davos, Vicente Fox, the Mexican President, first admonished as inadequate "attempts to sugar coat the present form of globalisation with compensatory policies" and then called for a "new engine of growth" that would derive its power from a "vast expansion of economic citizenship in the market place" (*Financial Times*, 27– 28 January 2001). The concern with financial stability and efforts to placate anti-globalisation protestors have shaped the favourable positions of Lionel Jospin, and even Gerhard Schröder, towards the Tobin tax in the early autumn of 2001.

On 8 September 2000 in New York, the member states adopted *The United Nations Millennium Declaration* (A/55/L.2).[5] The rhetorical part of the Declaration stated, among other things, that:

> the central challenge we face today is to ensure that globalisation becomes a positive force for all the world's people. For while globalisation offers great opportunities, at present its benefits are very unevenly shared, while its costs are unevenly distributed . . . only through broad and sustained efforts to create a shared future, based upon a common humanity in all its diversity, can globalisation be made fully inclusive and equitable.

From that perspective, the Declaration, in addition to making references to peace and the environment, paid special attention to the eradication of poverty and the protection of the vulnerable.

[4] Tony Blair, Wim Kok, Göran Persson and Gerhard Schröder continued the debate in September by stressing the vital importance of knowledge-based production and education, the reform of the welfare state, and the centrality of civil society that helps to expand the circle of winners from globalisation; see their "The New Left Takes on the World", *Washington Post*, 6 September 2000.
[5] Along with the UN Millennium Summit, two other major events were organised in New York in September 2000: the Millennium World Peace Summit of Religious and Spiritual Leaders and the annual State of the World Forum. The former brought together over one thousand religious leaders, who issued a Commitment to World Peace, while Mikhail Gorbachev's Forum on Shaping Globalization: Convening the Community of Stakeholders involved political, business and NGO leaders. Both of these meetings primarily advocated the mainstream theme that economic globalisation is good, or at least acceptable, if it can be governed by social interests and moral values.

The leitmotiv of the Declaration is that poverty and other gaps in the world threaten to produce a backlash that will unravel the open world economy. To reduce this risk, the world leaders made a verbal commitment "to halve, by the year 2015, the proportion of the world's people whose income is less than one dollar a day and the proportion of people, who suffer from hunger and, by the same date, to halve the proportion of people who are unable to reach or to afford safe drinking water". The Declaration also recognised that governments cannot accomplish this aim alone, and that they need to cooperate with NGOs and the business community.

In 2001, as a follow-up to the Millennium Declaration, the Secretary-General prepared a "road map" for the attainment of its goals: *Road Map Towards the Implementation of the United Nations Millennium Declaration* (A/ 56/326, September 19, 2001). This document contains a comprehensive discussion on potential means for the promotion of human rights, good governance, disarmament, sustainable development and other laudable goals. The report is more specific as regards poverty alleviation and the protection of vulnerable sections of population. It suggests "concrete, time-bound indicators" of the Millennium Development Goals (MDGs) that can used to monitor their implementation, including the reduction of global poverty. A new feature in this process is the explicit commitment by the World Bank and the IMF to participate as "full partners" in the implementation of the MDGs. It is already clear that many a developing country is unable to meet these MDGs, but these goals may nevertheless have a positive role in establishing specific targets. This can potentially contribute to a new culture of accountability among national governments and international organisations.

In addition to political declarations, Kofi Annan has taken a number of concrete initiatives to open up UN relations with the business community. This approach has been in the making for some time, and Annan (1998: 134–35) stated early on that "one of my major priorities as secretary-general has been to establish a new partnership of development between the United Nations and the private sector". The UN's development units, especially the United Nations Development Programme (UNDP), have introduced new procedures to cooperate with transnational business, which in turn has an obvious interest in delivering goods and services for UN projects. There are also more ambitious plans in the air; for instance, the UNDP envisages the establishment of an independent Global Sustainable Development Facility that would involve the support of TNCs for various development initiatives. Corporations have already sponsored projects of the United Nations High Commission for Refugees (UNHCR) in Kosovo and elsewhere, not to speak of Ted Turner's billion-dollar gift to the UN Foundation (for an overview, see Tesner, 2000).

Perhaps the most concrete initiative by Annan has been *The Global Compact* which he originally put forward at the World Economic Forum in Davos in January 1999. The Compact aims to provide a new normative framework for transnational business activities, especially in issues dealing with human rights, labour and the environment. The Compact comprises nine general, main principles. In the area of human rights, the TNCs are asked to support international human rights and avoid complicity in their abuse. In the contested area of labour standards, Annan calls for freedom of association and the right of collective bargaining, the abolition of forced labour and child labour, and the elimination of discrimination in the workplace. Finally, in environmental issues, he requests the business community's support for a responsible and precautionary approach to ecological challenges, and the development and diffusion of environmentally friendly technologies.

In July 2000, the first High-Level Meeting of the Global Compact was held in New York. The meeting was attended by some 50 chief executive officers (CEOs). However, very few of them came from US corporations, as these seem to be concerned about the general and possibly ambiguous nature of the Compact principles. It is interesting to note that seven major British and US mining and energy corporations have struck a separate deal with nine human rights organisations (including Amnesty International and Human Rights Watch) and the twenty million member International Federation of Chemical, Energy and Mine Workers' Unions (ICEM). At the insistence of corporations, the guidelines are voluntary, but they promise to examine closely any allegations of human-rights abuses by themselves or host governments, and also demand the right to defend by physical and legal means the corporate property against incursions (*Wall Street Journal*, 21 December 2000).

The July 2000 meeting at the UN set the goal of recruiting 1,000 companies as the signatories of the Global Compact by 2003. The Secretary-General appointed Göran Lindahl, the retired chief executive of Asea Brown Boveri (ABB), to spearhead the recruitment effort. In all likelihood, the Global Compact will have at least some practical consequences. Thus, the Norwegian Statoil and ICEM have adopted a set of guiding principles based explicitly on the Global Compact. The guidelines will cover Statoil and its 16,000 workers in twenty-three countries. However, in reality, for many companies the decision to sign the Global Compact is yet another PR move with little practical consequence. The promise to post their experiences in implementing its principles once a year on the Compact website does not impose very demanding obligations on the participating corporations.

In addition to the Global Compact, Annan has also sponsored the new set of global Sullivan Principles which also aim to create a practical normative standard for transnational business operations to enhance their sustainability. By early 2001, some fifty TNCs had signed the voluntary principles of the Global Compact (e.g. BP, Daimler Chrysler, Nike, Unilever, Statoil and France Telecom).

These signatures are a sign of the rise of a new business ethics movement, which is reflected both in the proliferation of intra-firm ethics codes and the increasing subscription of corporations to various global and regional agreements on appropriate business standards (Williams, 2000; for a statistical analysis of international codes of conduct, see Kolk and van Tulder, 1999). Obviously, one has to ask whether these moves make TNCs new moral agents in the global society or whether various codes and standards are adopted mostly for utilitarian reasons. As good reputation is a key asset in many business sectors, it makes practical sense to get a UN stamp of approval.

The Secretary-General clearly aims to forge *a new type of UN-TNC partnership* with both a normative and practical element. By doing so, the UN would move from the sidelines of the global debate to its mainstream and even start giving political direction to it. This move may benefit the UN by making at least some business money available for its development and humanitarian activities, although it is unrealistic to assume that the UN's budget problems can ever be resolved by private corporate donations. Clearly, Annan's initiatives also have a political function; he wants the UN headquarters to assume a political and moral role in issues dealing with human rights, labour standards and the environment.

This move could lead to some political burden-sharing and alleviate the pressure falling on the international financial and trade institutions. This motive is reflected in Annan's statement that the debate on social and environmental matters has to be taken out of the WTO if a new round of global trade talks is to be launched: "The WTO was never designed and cannot handle being an arbiter in human rights, labour and environmental issues" (*Financial Times*, 28 July 2000). This means that there should be an appropriate division of labour between international political and technical bodies; let the former manage the political burden and the latter get on with their work with the regulation of the global market economy. Of course, this doctrine creates as many problems as it solves, and is not adequate to address the concerns of those who protest against the current mode of globalisation and its governance.

The Global Compact and other similar initiatives by Annan have also faced considerable criticism, especially by various representatives of NGOs. The main counter-argument is that international compacts are asymmetric in nature; corporations gain some legitimacy by subscribing to core principles that are non-binding and unenforceable, while the UN gets very little in return. On the contrary, the compacts with TNCs can potentially tarnish the UN's reputation, increase self-censorship and strain its relationship with important segments of civil society. The prevailing critical sentiment has been summarised by Cohen (2000: 209); "in designing new international institutions, the focus for discipline must shift from the nation to the international corporation".

In a sense, Annan and the United Nations are in a bind; now that the UN has been sidelined in the management of international conflicts, it has a political and institutional need to expand its activities and legitimacy to other areas, especially those related to globalisation. This requires the formulation of new ideas and the opening up of relations with new constituencies in a vital area of global relations. This may, however, turn out to be a contradictory and, in terms of its outcomes, an unpredictable process. It has even been argued that the goal of halving the proportion of the people living in poverty amounts to little more than a justification of the fact that development policies are losing their economic bite and political legitimacy (Nuscheler, 2001).[6]

Kofi Annan is not the only world leader who has started to stress the need for a new partnership between transnational business and international organisations. For instance, the Italian government submitted a proposal to the Genoa meeting of the group of seven (G7), held in July 2001, that it should convince the world's 1,000 largest companies to donate half a million dollars each. These funds would then be matched by G7 governments. In that way, one could create a trust fund of one billion dollars, jointly administered by the World Bank and the WHO, to improve health care, especially of children, in developing countries (*Financial Times*, 24 February 2001). However, the communiqué issued from the Genoa summit on 22 July 2001 did not make any reference to the host-country initiative.

This proposal comes on top of large grants that the Gates Foundations have given to the development and distribution of vaccines for the most common diseases afflicting people in the South. These and other similar initiatives aim to remedy the current imbalance in which "less than 10 percent of the global health research budget is aimed at the health problems afflicting 90 percent of the world's population" as Kofi Annan pointed out in Davos in January 2001. The corporate efforts are matched politically by transnational coalitions, such as the People's Health Assembly, which aim to bring together NGOs to "hear the unheard, to reinforce the principle of health as a broad cross-cutting issue [and] to formulate a People's Health Charter" (www.pha2000.org). The UN summit on AIDS/HIV, malaria, and tuberculosis in 2001, and commitments made there to fight these diseases by cooperative means – for instance, by setting up a $ 1.3 billion Global Fund – is an even stronger sign of how public health is assuming a more central place on the international agenda.

---

[6] In this context, one cannot but pay attention to the speech delivered by President George W. Bush at the World Bank in July 2001. Bush stated that the reduction of global poverty would be a priority of his foreign policy because "conquering poverty creates new resources". In particular, Bush suggested that, instead of giving loans to developing countries, they should be provided with grants. However, he did not suggest any new funds to underpin this radical initiative. According to some observers, the speech was intended to deflect attention from the then controversial issues of missile defence and global warming (*The Washington Post*, 18 July: A18).

Poverty Reduction
Globalisation, growth and poverty

Recent debates on globalisation and its governance have very visibly pushed the problem of poverty onto the international agenda. The issue is not new, of course, but for decades it has been intimately related to the general debate on the nature and aims of development. In the contrast between growth and equity as the main goals of development policy, the problem of poverty has been placed firmly in the context of equity. Martha Finnemore has documented in detail how poverty alleviation became, by the mid-1970s, a central development norm, largely as a result of the actions of McNamara's World Bank. Since the mid-1980s, the focus on poverty has been at least rhetorically undisputed. The Bank "institutionalised the poverty focus so that it became a necessary part of development efforts" (Finnemore, 1996: 89–127; see also Nelson, 2000b: 152–53).

The institutionalisation of a norm does not, of course, mean that all state, business and other actors necessarily respect the norm or make serious efforts to implement it. The emergence of the norm does suggest, however, that any dialogue on development, whether among policy makers or experts, is hardly possible today without taking into account the poverty problem. A sure sign of the spread of the norm is its frequent use in the IMF and World Bank documents.[7] Thus, the goal of poverty alleviation has become a general prescriptive norm that has to be taken into account in international development, trade and financial policies.

Finnemore and Sikkink (1998: 895–905) speak of the life cycles of norms from their emergence through a "norm cascade" to their internalisation. They also suggest that there is a tipping point between the first two phases of the cycle; i.e. when a norm has become pervasive enough it starts spreading more quickly and is adopted by both public and private actors. In the course of this process, the links between the domestic and international aspects of the norm grow stronger.

My impression is that the global norm of poverty alleviation is now in the cascading phase and is passing the tipping point, after having gathered sufficient political momentum in recent years. A typical example is a recent statement by Gunter Pleuger, State Secretary in the German Foreign Office, in which he lists the following priorities for global politics: the UN

---

[7] For example, James Wolfensohn urged in his speech in July 2001 at the Genoa summit of the G7 that "it is time that politicians and voters in rich countries realise that without a bright future for Africa's poor, the future cannot be bright for the rest of the world". He continued by saying that "it is hypocritical to give debt relief with one hand and then deny poor countries the ability to export their way out of poverty". Therefore, developed countries must open up their markets for imports from developing countries, but also increase their development aid to 0.7 per cent of GDP from its present level of 0.22 percent (The World Bank. Press release no. 2002/023/S, 16 July 2001).

Global Compact, the struggle against poverty, debt relief, tariff-free access of developing countries to the world market, the prevention of violence and the protection of the environment. This is standard newspeak today among the political elites of industrialised countries.

However, the norm of poverty alleviation has not yet been internalised in any deeper way in the international community, as this would mean that compliance with and enforcement of it should have become habit-driven. A process of internalisation may nevertheless be underway, as suggested by the emphasis given to the anti-poverty strategies by various international economic organisations, most notably the World Bank (World Development Report, 2000/2001). On the other hand, it has been suggested that the official emphasis on the importance of development assistance for poverty reduction is seldom empirically sustainable. In reality, it may be used more to justify the continuation of current aid policies and the national and international institutional interests embedded in it (Wolff, 2001).[8]

Neither is the anti-poverty norm yet constitutive for international relations. Such a constitution would require, among other things, a consensus on its causes and remedies. However, there is no agreement in the international academic or policy-making communities on whether free trade, and more generally globalisation, really foster economic growth and, if they do, whether this helps to promote equity and eradicate poverty. The final answer to the question of how economic openness, growth and inequality are related to each other seems to depend on the operationalisation of these variables, the consistency of methods of measurement and the sample of the cases chosen for the analysis and the degree of their disaggregation. Keeping these caveats in mind, there exists some evidence that, in developing countries, inequality and economic growth are inversely related to each other (Przeworski, et al., 2000; Knowles, 2001).

In numerous studies carried out by the World Bank, the IMF and the WTO, the most common finding is, not surprisingly, that trade liberalisation is good for growth, from which the poor, in turn, benefit as their incomes improve in tandem with those of the rich. Neither do the poor suffer disproportionately from economic crises as they can even benefit from the cutbacks in public spending (Dollar and Kray, 2000). However, economic growth can contribute most effectively to poverty reduction if it is combined with improved income equality. Without growth, there is little prospect for the reduction of poverty (Bisten and Lewin, 2001). On the other hand, growth alone is not enough to reduce inequality, but its effects must

[8] The declaration of the World Summit for Social Development and Beyond, held in Geneva in June 2000 – as a special session of the UN General Assembly and as a follow-up to the UN Social Summit in Copenhagen in 1995 – provides several examples on how the expansion of development aid and the poverty reduction are politically linked to each other.

be, at a minimum, neutral with respect to income distribution. The assumption of a trickle-down process from the rich to the poor is an illusion; only a strong policy emphasis on socio-economic equity can help to overcome the dismal levels of poverty in Africa and South Asia.

The conventional wisdom about economic openness leading to growth has been challenged, however, both by the supporters of the "new growth theory" and scholars such as Dani Rodrik. The former argue that growth follows primarily from investments in human capital, i.e., education and technology, which provide the basis for a sustainable economic expansion. In a somewhat similar vein, Rodrik's empirical study suggests that external openness does not have any direct impact on economic growth; the benefits are mostly due to imports rather than exports of goods and capital, and contingent on several other factors. More decisive than trade for economic growth is the level of domestic investment, which may benefit from an inflow of foreign resources, but may also succeed without it (Rodrik, 1999).

To my mind, it is important to make a distinction between the general phenomenon of globalisation and the neoliberal economic regime. The effects of globalisation can vary considerably from one economic structural and policy context to another. The liberalisation of trade as such does not necessarily engender increased income inequality and has, in any case, diverging effects (Blanchflower and Slaughter, 1999). The effects of neoliberalism seem, on the other hand, to converge to a greater extent and to lead to deflationary policies. Most importantly, neoliberalism gives rise to "coercive competition" which homogenises the economic policies of states and makes the promotion of socio-economic equity an uphill struggle. This is, in particular, the case if the country has to compete from an underprivileged position (Crotty, et al., 1998).

In general, economic globalisation tends to mobilise people. As a consequence, they tend to move from rural to urban areas where income levels are higher and opportunities more plentiful. The process of economic mobilisation probably expands the overall economic pie, but may, at the same time, stagnate rural economies, thus increasing relative rural poverty which accounts for two-thirds of poverty world-wide, especially in South Asia and Africa. The combination of urban economic growth, although often very lopsided, and the economic stagnation of the countryside increases urban-rural income differences (Khan, 2001). However, this distributive effect of globalisation is more limited than it is in the case of clear-cut neoliberalist policies, as their stated purpose is to skew income distribution to the benefit of the well off. Globalisation is an economic process, while neoliberalism is a political strategy.

Political response

Academic and policy controversies about its causes notwithstanding, poverty has recently taken a central place in policy debates. Most major political speeches remember to mention that 1.2 billion people survive on less than a dollar a day and a further 1.6 billion have to make do with one to two dollars a day.[9] It seems that the emphasis on poverty is one indication of the development away from the old Washington consensus and the disciplinary philosophy of structural adjustment strategies. Instead, the fight against poverty is painted both as a moral imperative and a socio-political precondition for the continuation of the globalisation process. The polarising tendencies of globalisation have to be counteracted by national and international public policies to provide the poor with resources for and access to a better life, and ultimately to empower them.

The shift from (neo)liberal market reforms, as emphasised in structural adjustment policies, through the relativisation of economic growth as a source of political stability and equal development, to the emphasis on joint ownership of the development effort has been a long one (for this trajectory in the World Bank, see Pender, 2001). My impression is that the understanding of the profound and potentially destabilising effects of globalisation has provided an important impetus for the redefinition of national and international policies on economic management; instead of dictation, sharing and ownership are needed.

The Asian financial crisis in 1997 was an important turning point in this regard. It taught political leaders that, if left to its own devices, globalisation is a vulnerable and crises-ridden process whose contagious effects can grind the entire world economy to a halt, or even worse. An authoritative study of four major financial crises has concluded that "there can be little doubt that the process of globalisation aggravated the crises that hit Latin America, Mexico, East Asia, and Russia" (Lamfalussy, 2000: 166–67, 172–73). The primary political response to this observation has been to stress the importance of institutional reforms to assure financial stability. This can be accomplished, for instance, by restructuring IFIs and strengthening national banking supervision. This response is not, of course, entirely new, and its origins can be traced back to the debt crises of the early 1980s (Wiener, 1999: 41–81).

However, the Asian and the subsequent Russian crisis also reminded us that such breakdowns can have highly destabilising social and political consequences; in Indonesia, 60–80 percent of the population are said to live

[9] A typical example is the statement issued by the G7 leaders from their Okinawa summit in July 2000: "We must tackle the root causes of conflict and poverty. We must bravely seize the opportunities created by new technologies in such areas as information technology and life sciences. We must acknowledge the concerns associated with globalization, while continuing to be innovative in order to maximize the benefits of globalization for all".

below the poverty line and in Russia the situation, especially in the countryside, is not much different. In particular in Asia, these problems have won regional and global attention; Assocation of South East Asia Nations (ASEAN), the IMF, the International Conference of Free Trade Unions and many other organisations have arranged regional meetings to consult the local social actors and draw up plans to alleviate the poverty problem.

Any serious effort to convert the rhetoric of poverty alleviation into a concrete programme of action requires both a mandate and tools. The World Bank and the IMF have clearly recognised that the international community has given them a *mandate* to work for the mitigation of poverty in the world. However, the fulfilment of this mandate requires a new approach and new policy instruments. While the World Bank, in particular, has been trying to develop such approaches, the WTO seems to be equivocating on the matter. Its leadership seems to think that the opening up of international trade is adequate as such to take care of the poor and their social problems. This may reflect the fact that the relationship of the WTO mandate and its tools to national sovereignty and democracy is particularly vexed. Many countries, among them developing ones, want to keep it away from domestic politics, which is, however, often a step towards successful socio-economic transformation (Wolfe, 2001).

The differences between these global organisations were also made visible in the comments made on the anti-globalisation protests by James Wolfensohn and Mike Moore, the heads of the World Bank and the WTO, respectively. Wolfensohn made quite sympathetic, though possibly tactical, comments on the nature of the protests (despite having been "caked" in Helsinki, Finland, in February 2001). He said about protests that "I do not resent that at all, I'm glad that they are interested . . . it's positive if its a questioning of the direction and involvement". Moore was much more critical in his statements and has gone as far as saying in Canberra on 5 February 2000 that "the people that stand outside and say they work in the interests of the poorest people . . . they make me want to vomit".

A political mandate is not, however, easy to convert into *instruments* that have real and positive effects in developing countries. To begin with, individual international organisations have different preconditions in this regard. The WTO creates rules and standards for world trade, but it does not have material resources of its own and even its enforcement powers are limited. In essence, the WTO provides the international trade regime with a political framework, which combines two main tenets of the liberal theory: (a) individuals have the right to free economic transactions; and (b) such a freedom contributes to the collective good of the community (Qureshi,1996: 10–14).

The advocates of the liberal view prefer to keep environmental and trade standards weak, because this secures access to the market and thus assures the efficiency of economic operations. In addition, the exclusion of domestic standards from the WTO agenda is consistent with requirements of national sovereignty. This way of thinking has a conservative bias; countries violate WTO rules just by introducing stricter environmental and labour standards (Bagwell and Steiger, 1999).

On the other hand, rules established or neglected by the WTO create material externalities for national and corporate economies and cannot, therefore, be reduced to individual preferences. These economic realities intersect in multiple ways with the ecological realities. This means that efforts to separate trade from environment are artificial. On this basis it has been argued that international trade policy can be viable and economically efficient over the long term only if environmental criteria and reviews are integrated in the WTO's decision-making which, in general, should be made more transparent (Esty, 2000).

It is well known that a key issue in launching the new round of global trade negotiations is the efforts to find a consensus both among the developed countries and with the leading developing countries on the agenda and goals of these talks. At the time of writing, October 2001, there is a complex negotiation process underway to adjust different, and sometimes almost contradictory national preferences to each other. This is only possible if the anticipated material compromises between the major groups of countries can somehow be fortuitously incorporated into the final agenda. The emerging agenda is very complex and ranges from agriculture and services to intellectual property rights.

It is interesting to note that the hectic diplomacy to facilitate the launch of a new round of trade talks has changed in tone after the protests in Seattle and other places. The technical jargon has been replaced by political speeches which note, as Romano Prodi did in his speech to the UN Millennium Summit on 8 September 2000, that the WTO can only succeed if it addresses the problem of poverty in a serious way and listens to civil society.[10] In keeping with the latter argument, the EU sent an official letter to the WTO stressing that NGOs must be given reasonable access to its ministerial meeting in Doha (Qatar) in November 2001.

The best instrument, according to the EU, for reducing poverty is to open the markets of developed countries, in particular, to the products of the least developed countries. For this reason, the Union decided in February 2001 to eliminate all quotas and duties on all products from these countries by adopting the so-called "Everything but Arms" trade initiative.

---

[10] More specifically, Prodi stated that "at this time of great expectation, the emergence of a genuine world economy, underpinned by colossal technological forces, calls for a vastly improved system of global governance, that is a common core of values, rules and practices . . . [I]n the international arena there is no alternative to strong multilateral institutions based on impeccable democratic legitimacy. Decisions and procedures must be as transparent as possible. Civil society must be involved more directly. Only improved multilateralism will ensure that globalisation appears not so much as a threat as an opportunity not to be missed" (http://europa.eu.int/comm(trade/whats_new/prodiun).

The activist Foreign Trade Commissioner, Pascal Lamy, noted that this decision is "a worldwide first . . . we are serious about getting the most disadvantaged to share in the fruits of trade liberalisation"(http://europa.eu.int/comm/trade/miti/devel/eba3, 27 February 2001).[11] The principles behind the initiative cannot but be lauded, but, as usual, the devil is in the detail – and in the schedule of its implementation. The plan seems to be limited, and slow to rectify the imbalances that various rounds of tariff-reduction have created in trade relations between the developed and developing countries.

Outside the WTO, there are three tools available for the international community to reduce poverty: multilateral loans by IFIs, development assistance, and international private flows of goods and capital. These different instruments are often at cross-purposes with each other. The general level of official development assistance (ODA) has been declining; for instance in Sub-Saharan Africa its per capita value has fallen from $ 32 in 1990 to $ 19 in 1998. The percentage of ODA by the developed countries of their GDP fell from 0.33 per cent in 1985 to 0.24 per cent in 1998. In foreign direct investments, there has been a strong secular growth in the 1990s, but the capital seldom goes to most impoverished regions plagued by poor infrastructure and political instability. Even in more promising areas, some three-fourths of the capital needed in investment are raised from local sources.

If these two trends are combined, an inevitable conclusion follows; the inflows of private investment and public concessionary money cannot solve the problem of poverty. There is simply not enough money and, even if there is, it does not go to those most in need. As a result, the scarcity of alternative forms of funding leads to burgeoning levels of external debt. The accumulation of debt is due to both the real needs of the borrowers and defensive lending by international institutions. The increasing debt burden cannot, in turn, but have detrimental social consequences that erode any efforts at poverty eradication.

Debt Relief

Active management of sovereign debt has at least a twenty-year history. By the early 1990s, it had progressed from a containment strategy through the emphasis on growth in the Baker Plan to market-oriented solutions in the

---

[11] It is interesting to note that Kofi Annan assumed an active role in promoting the trade initiative *within* the EU against the opposition of France and Spain, which wanted to water down some of its key provisions. In his letter to the EU Presidency, Sweden, Annan, following his general line of globalisation policy, urged the Union to send "a clear signal that the world's richest countries are genuinely prepared to put into practice their oft-stated intention to accord priority attention to the plight of the world's poorest" (Guy Jonquieres, "Annan Steps into EU Imports Dispute", *Financial Times*, 23 February 2001).

Brady Plan (Corbridge, 1993: 41–86). However, none of these policies has solved the basic problems of highly-indebted developing countries. Depending on the country, they have suffered from volatile fuel and commodity prices, natural catastrophes, geographical isolation, counterproductive economic policies, corruption and other forms of bad governance, political instability and capital flight. In various combinations, these factors have led to spiralling debt burdens.

In the 1990s, the debt problem has increasingly concentrated on the least developed countries that have borrowed most of their money from multilateral institutions (in contrast to countries like Brazil, Mexico and Poland, which borrowed mostly from the open market). The debt problem has also escalated. In 1970, the total external debt of the developing countries amounted to $ 90 billion, or 15 percent of their GDP, but in 1998 it had risen to $ 2,000 billion or 37 percent of their GDP. Over time, it has become increasingly clear that the economic and social development of heavily-indebted countries cannot take off unless their debt burden is reduced by concerted international action (for additional information and analyses, see World Economic Outlook, 2000: 136–42, 262–70; Kampffmeyer, 2000; Roodman, 2001).

It seems that the problem in debt relief has not depended so much on the availability of funds as on perceived risks of moral hazard and bad precedents. It has been widely felt in the developed world that some kind of conditionality is needed if concessionary debt relief is to be launched in a serious manner. This insistence can be contrasted with the fact that the political success of conditionalities, at least in development cooperation, has been limited at best (Crawford, 2001: 183–200). The answer to the dilemma of debt relief has been the Heavily Indebted Poor Countries (HIPC) initiative which was launched by the G7 at its meeting in Lyon in 1997, and expanded at the Cologne meeting in 1999. The decision was, in part, a response to public pressure by a new NGO coalition called Jubilee 2000, which had both organised rather large demonstrations and extensively lobbied political leaders.

The HIPC initiative is a critical move in several respects. Its success is not only important for the heavily indebted countries, but also for the future role and influence of the IMF and the World Bank. From the debtors' point of view, the initiative has been criticised because it "demands too much from debtors in terms of policy reform and offers too little in terms of debt reduction" (Roodman, 2001: 149; see also Kampffmeyer, 2000). A rather common view is that the redistributive effects of HIPC are modest and that it cannot, with a few exceptions, be expected to be a key instrument of poverty alleviation. Its main function is rather to permit the return of highly-indebted countries to the global private capital market. The HIPC initiative is a long step in the right direction, but its structural consequences still remain too modest to alter the situation on the ground. For this, much larger external transfers of resources are needed (Dagdeviren and Weeks, 2001; Abrego and Ross, 2001).

The HIPC initiative does not mean safe sailing for the IMF either. In effect, the strongest pressure to restructure the Fund does not come from the streets, but from its own key member states and various leaders of public opinion. Thus, the International Financial Advisory Commission, set up by the US Congress and chaired by Allan Meltzer, demanded a major re-structuring of the Fund. Such political demands have been amplified by academic critics (see e.g. Sachs, 2000; Stiglitz, 2000), who have largely focused on the manner in which the IMF managed, or failed to manage, the Asian financial crisis. Some other well-known economists, such as Steve Hanke and Robert Barro, have either demanded the liquidation of the IMF or a reduction of its size. In Barro's view, the tasks of the Fund should be limited to the provision of short-term liquidity to solvent economies threatened by a potential crisis (*Business Week*, 10 April 2000).

The dominant idea in proposals, including those by the US government, to reform the IMF is that the Fund should return to its core functions of short-term emergency lending. This would mean that it should withdraw from a number of enhanced long-term commitments, now absorbing some forty percent of its lending, that were made in 1994–99 in the management of financial and economic crises, especially in Africa and Eastern Europe. However, the decision to go back to basics would not only be hard to implement, it may also have inadvertent consequences. Paul Mosley (2001) has argued in detail that the Fund cannot pursue any short-term focused strategy without being committed to crises-ridden countries also over a long term. For instance, the financial extent of the HIPC initiative is so modest that it is unable to replace the long-term commitments made by the Fund. In 2000, the share of funds allocated to HIPC of the total debt stock of $ 250 billion was less than one percent (Mosley, 2001: 623).[12]

Under various (cross)pressures, the IMF is changing, but more in operational than in structural ways (for various observations and suggestions, see Woods, 2001). The Fund has started to demand greater transparency in the financial sector of the member states to be better able to perform its role in surveillance, early-warning, and crisis prevention. At the same time,

---

[12] This is, however, inconsistent with more recent figures which suggest that in 2001 total debt relief, at net present value (NPV), amounted to $ 20.7 billion and, thus, to some eight percent of the total debt stock (Dagdeviren and Weeks 2001: 23). Yet another estimate indicates that the total value of the HIPC initiative, now applying to 41 countries, is $ 50 billion which would be a debt reduction of some 20 percent. As of 2001, 22 countries of the total 41 have reached the so-called decision point and seven the completion point, leaving 12 countries at the very start of the debt relief process. The Poverty Reduction and Growth Facility (PRGF), run by the Bank and the Fund, estimate that the external indebtedness of the countries that have reached the decision point will be reduced by two-thirds, or from $ 53 billion to $ 20 billion (IMF and the World Bank, 2001c).

it has had to make its own operations more transparent and accountable. The Fund has also started a process to reduce the number of conditions it imposes on borrowing countries and thus streamline its activities. Yet, it is too early to say whether the rather orthodox economic philosophy that has guided IMF actions in the past has been re-evaluated in any fundamental manner.

The critical aspect in the HIPC initiative is the explicit link established between debt relief and poverty reduction after heavy criticism of the original plans which, by and large, overlooked the poverty problem. This link is set out in Poverty Reduction Strategy Papers (PRSPs), in which the partners specify the ways in which debt relief is used to alleviate poverty. The exercise has just started, but it is expected to evolve and deepen in the near future (IMF and the World Bank, 2001a). The PRSPs are a novel, international instrument to fight poverty, but, at the same time, they are also partial and controversial. There will always be voices, and perhaps rightly so, criticising the Bank and the Fund for dictating the conditions from the outside rather than building on local needs. In addition, the capability and willingness of individual debtor countries to implement their provisions has varied greatly.

The hardest cases are obviously those countries which have not yet even reached the decision point. They include, among others, Burundi, the Democratic Republic of Congo, Ethiopia, Myanmar, Sierra Leone, Somalia and Sudan, all of which are involved in major domestic or international conflicts. Without peace and some elemental stability, it is difficult to imagine that they could meet the criteria of debt relief or that this relief would even make much of a difference. Against this stark backdrop, the exhortation of the G7 from its Genoa summit in July 2001 sounds rather lame: "we call upon those countries involved in military conflicts to lay down their arms, and implement necessary reforms. We confirm our willingness to help them take measures needed to come forward to debt relief".

In general, one has to recognise that debt relief, although an important step forward, does not alone offer a solution to the dilemma of development financing. Even its indirect positive effects, such as better access to private capital markets, will not do much to change the prevailing situation. Even the Bank and the Fund have to acknowledge that the maintenance of long-term debt sustainability requires many more measures that would address, for instance, the export vulnerability and the lack of investment capital in developing countries (IMF and the World Bank, 2001b). The UN has made a useful contribution by producing in January 2001 an extensive report for the conference on development financing in March 2002 (DEV 2275PI/1323).

The report specifies a total of eighty-seven remedies to finance development. Many of them concern the promotion of trade and private investment, but others deal with the closing of global tax loopholes and debt relief. The report sees debt relief as just one of the available instruments, but admits that in some desperate cases – and Zambia is often mentioned as an example – "debt burdens represent insurmountable obstacles and need to be addressed urgently", without debt relief other measures would be ineffective.

Conclusion

The international political climate has changed in a major way over the last few years. The process and consequences of economic globalisation are perhaps assessed more carefully and critically than ever before. This concern grows partly out of a fear that, if left to its own devices, globalisation, carried on by transnational business and often in an unregulated manner, will self-destruct and threaten the present mode of political stability as well as the distribution of wealth and power in the world.

For this reason, various institutions and instruments of global governance are promoted by the self-interests of the developed countries and their elites. However, these elites are not necessarily united; there is no global ruling class in any meaningful sense. Rather we can discern various elite factions that have come to understand the importance of creating a political framework for the globalisation process. As the US-European disagreement on the implementation of the Kyoto Protocol shows, these elite factions may disagree on the solution of contextual problems.

This particular disagreement boils down to the difference between market liberalism and reformist models. If the issue at hand does not have a direct connection with the market and concerns tangible negative externalities, problems of collective action between developed countries may be easier to solve. The common fight against transnational terrorism is an obvious example of how political differences can be quickly overcome if the risk is perceived to be high enough and to emanate from outside the developed countries. In other words, market liberalism and reformism are united by several common traits, while the critical perspective easily becomes sidelined in issues such as terrorism.

The critical perspective has had more to say on issues such as the environment and globalisation. Its adverse effects have elicited a strong counterreaction from civil society which is not united either. Part of this reaction stems from material self-interests. Thus, the strong support by the US and Canadian trade unions to North American anti-globalisation protests has been primarily informed by their fear of losing jobs and members. On the other hand, much of the protest has been motivated by non-material concerns with the environment, poverty, health and labour conditions. Demands for biodiversity, poverty reduction, the availability of inexpensive drugs to fight AIDS or malaria in developing countries, and decent working conditions for sweatshop workers, cannot be explained by material self-interests, but by the spread of a more ethical *Weltanschauung*.

In practice, this new global ethic is manifested in concrete aims, such as the promotion of fair labour standards and debt relief, around which demonstrations and (transnational) networking activities can be organised. In this regard, there seem to be differences between various sectors; most transnational networks focus on specific environmental and health issues, while they are less influential in such broader areas as poverty reduction and global climate change, where expert communities seem to dominate (Reinicke and Deng, 2000).

The articulation of new demands to redirect and regulate the globalisation process has fostered new forms of global governance. On the one hand, traditional mechanisms of governance – especially the WTO, the IMF and the World Bank – have gained new powers to regulate governmental policies and, to a lesser degree, corporate behaviour. However, this development has provoked strong criticism and demands for change. These demands do not only come from the protest movements; a number of governments, including some in the developed world, have risen to claim back some of the regulatory powers they had handed over to international institutions.

This demand to restructure old institutions of global governance has been accompanied by a rise of new institutions and instruments of governance. Many of these transnational institutions are private or hybrid in nature. In the latter case, they combine governments, business actors and even NGOs in a joint effort to regulate a particular area of international action. In sum, we are witnessing several pertinent trends: (a) reformism is being strengthened at the expense of market liberalism, partly because it provides more relevant responses to the critical challenges; (b) old institutions of global governance have to restructure and reposition themselves, albeit only in a gradualist manner; and (c) new forms of governance are emerging outside the traditional state- and business-centric frameworks.

An interesting phenomenon has been the repositioning of the United Nations in debates and policies pertaining to global governance. This is largely the result of initiatives taken by Kofi Annan who has, in a number of ways, breathed new air into rather stale UN approaches of the past. Annan has, of course, been criticised for his efforts to integrate transnational business in UN operations. Yet, his efforts come closest to creating a political philosophy and framework which can make the "great transformation" brought about by globalisation a sustainable and reasonably equitable process.

Obviously, the UN effort does not only manifest a new political spirit, it is also institutionally anchored; like the EU, the UN also has to find new ideas and policies to defend its relevance in a world that is quickly refashioning itself. The emerging constellation of actors and issues does not easily fit into the traditional images and institutions of politics. Moreover, many global problems have become contextual in nature and cannot be tackled in the same "rational", actor-centric manner as externalities and collective-action problems.

The fight against global inequality, the source of poverty and marginalisation, is a key example of issues to which entirely new approaches are
needed. Lasting solutions appear, as Pogge (2001) argues, to be possible
only if the rich countries are prepared to make binding global commitments
to redistribute resources on a major scale – and stick to these commitments
over a long period of time.

References

Abrego, L. and D. Ross, 2001, *Debt Relief under HIPC Initiative: Context and Outlook for Debt Sustainability and Resource Flows*, Washington, D.C.: International Monetary Fund, August.

Annan, K., 1998, "The Quiet Revolution", *Global Governance*, vol. 4, no. 2, pp. 139–56.

Annan, K., 2000, "The Politics of Globalization", in O' Meara, P. , Mehlinger, H. and M. Krain (eds.), *Globalization and the Challenge of A New Century*. Bloomington, IN: Indiana University Press.

Arrighi, G., 1994, *The Long Twentieth Century. Money, Power, and the Origins of Our Times*. London: Verso.

Axelrod, R. and R.O. Keohane, 1986, "Achieving Cooperation under Anarchy: Strategies and Institutions", in Oye, K. (ed.), *Cooperation under Anarchy*, Princeton, N.J.: Princeton University Press.

Bagwell, K. and R.W. Staiger, 1999, *Domestic Policies, National Sovereignty and International Economic Institutions*, Cambridge, MA: National Bureau of Economic Research, Working Paper 7293.

Barnett, M. N. and M. Finnemore, 1999, "Power and Pathologies of International Organizations", *International Organization*, vol. 53, no. 4, pp. 699–732.

Beitz, C. R., 1999, "Social and Cosmopolitan Liberalism", *International Affairs*, vol. 75, no. 3 (1999), pp. 515–29.

Bigsten, A. and J. Levin, 2001, *Growth, Income Distribution and Poverty: A Review*, Paper prepared for the WIDER conference on Growth and Poverty, Helsinki, 25–26 May.

Blanchflower, D. and M. Slaughter, 1999, "The Causes and Consequences of Changing Income Inequality", in Fishlow, A. and K. Parker (eds.), *Growing Apart. The Causes and Consequences of Global Wage Inequality*, New York: Council on Foreign Relations Press.

Bleiker, R., 2000, *Popular Dissent, Human Agency and Global Politics*, Cambridge: Cambridge University Press.

Botcheva, L. and L. Martin, 2001, "Institutional Effects on State Behavior: Convergence and Divergence", *International Studies Quarterly*, vol. 45, no. 1, pp. 1–26.

Cable, V., 1999, *Globalization and Global Governance*, London: The Royal Institute of International Relations.

Camilleri, J., Malhotra K. and M. Tehranian, 2000, *Reimagining the Future. Towards Democratic Governance*, Melbourne: LaTrobe University.

Cerny, P., 1993, "Plurilateralism: Structural Differentiation and Functional Conflict in the Post-Cold War World Order", *Millennium*, vol. 22, no. 1, pp. 27–51.

Chin, C. and J. Mittelman, 1997, "Conceptualizing Resistance to Globalisation", *New Political Economy*, vol. 2, no. 1, pp. 25–37.

Clapham, C., 1996, *Africa and the International System. Politics of State Survival*, Cambridge: Cambridge University Press.

Coglianese, C., 2000, "Globalization and the Design of International Institutions", in Nye, J.S. Jr and J.D. Donahue (eds.), *Governance in a Globalizing World*. Washington, D.C.: The Brookings Institution Press, pp. 297–318.

Cohen, M.G., 2000, "Rethinking Global Strategies", in McBride, S. and J. Wiseman (eds.), *Globalization and Its Discontents*, London: Macmillan, pp. 200–213.

Corbridge, S., 1993, *Debt and Development*, Oxford: Blackwell.

Crawford, G., 2001, *Foreign Aid and Political Reform. A Comparative Analysis of Democracy Assistance and Political Conditionality*, London: Palgrave.

Crotty, J., Epstein, G. and P. Kelly, 1998, "Multinational Corporations in the Neo-liberal Regime", in Baker, D., Epstein G., and R. Pollin (eds.), *Globalization and the Progressive Economic Policy*, Cambridge: Cambridge University Press, pp. 117–43.

Cutler, C., Haufler, V. and T. Porter (eds.), 1999, *Private Authority and International Affairs*, Albany, NY: State University of New York Press.

Dagdeviren, H. and J. Weeks, 2001, "How Much Poverty Could HIPC Reduce?", Paper prepared for the WIDER Conference on Debt Relief. Helsinki: WIDER, 17 August.

Della Porta, D. and M. Diani, 1999, *Social Movements. An Introduction*. Oxford: Blackwell.

Dollar, D. and A. Kray, 2000, "Growth is Good for the Poor", www.worldbank.org/resea/growth/absddolakray.htm.

Doyle, M., 2000, "Global Economic Inequalities: Growing Moral Gap", in Wapner, P. and L.E. Ruiz, (eds.), *Principled World Politics. The Challenge of Normative International Relations*, Lanham, MD: Rowman and Littlefield.

Emmott, B., 1997, "Managing the International System over the Next Ten Years", in Emmott, B., Watanabe, K. and P. Wolfowitz, *Managing the International System over the Next Ten Years. Three Essays*, New York: The Trilateral Commission.

Esty, D.C., 2000, "Environment and the Trading System: Picking Up the Post-Seattle Pieces", in Schott, J.J. (ed.), *The WTO after Seattle*, Washington, D.C.: Institute for International Economics.

Falk, R., 1995, *On Humane Governance. Toward a New Global Politics*, University Park, PA: The Pennsylvania State University Press.

Finnemore, M., 1996, *National Interests in International Society*, Ithaca, NY: Cornell University Press.

Finnemore, M. and K. Sikkink, 1998, "International Norm Dynamics and Political Change", *International Organization*, vol. 52, no. 4, pp. 887–917.

Firebaugh, G., 1999, "Empirics of World Income Inequality", *American Journal of Sociology*, vol. 104, no. 6, pp. 1597–1630.

Fox, G. and B. Roth (eds.), 2000, *Democratic Governance and International Law*, Cambridge: Cambridge University Press.

Garrett, G., 1998, *Partisan Politics in the Global Economy*, Cambridge: Cambridge University Press.

Gereffi, G., Garcia-Johnson, R. and E. Sasser, 2001, "The NGO-Industrial Complex", *Foreign Policy*, July–August, pp. 56–65.

Gilbert, A., 1999, *Must Global Politics Constrain Democracy? Great-Power Realism, Democratic Peace, and Democratic Internationalism*. Princeton, NJ: Princeton University Press.

Gilpin, Robert, 2000, *The Challenge to Global Capitalism. The World Economy in the 21st Century*, Princeton: Princeton University Press.

Gourevitch, P. A., 1999, "The Governance Problem in International Relations", in Lake, D.A. and R. Powell (eds.), *Strategic Choice and International Relations*, Princeton, NJ: Princeton University Press.

Halliday, F., 2001, *The World at 2000*, London: Palgrave.

Higgott, R., Underhill, G. and A. Bieler (eds.), 2000, *Non-State Actors and Authority in the Global System*, London: Routledge.

Hurrell, A., "Global Inequality and International Institutions", *Metaphilosophy*, vol. 32, nos. 1–2, 2001, pp. 34–57.

IMF and the World Bank, 2001a, *Poverty Reduction Strategy Papers – Progress and Implementation*, Washington, D.C., 20 April 2001.

IMF and the World Bank, 2001b, *The Challenge of Maintaining Long-Term External Debt Sustainability*, Washington, D.C., 20 April 2001.

IMF and the World Bank, 2001c, *Heavily Indebted Poor Countries (HIPC) Initiative: Status of Implementation*, Washington, D.C., 20 April 2001.

International Commission of Global Governance, 1995, *Our Global Neighbourhood*, Oxford: Oxford University Press.

Jackson, R., 1990, *Quasi-States. Sovereignty, International Relations and the Third World*. Cambridge: Cambridge University Press.

Jesswein, K., 2001, "Global Accounting Harmonization: A Comparison of US and Germany", in Fatemi, K. (ed.), *International Public Policy and Regionalism at the Turn of the Century*, Amsterdam: Pergamon.

Jones, C., 1997, "On the Evolution of the World Income Distribution", *Journal of Economic Perspectives*, vol. 11, no. 3, pp. 19–36.

Kampffmeyer, T., 2000, "Lösungsansätze für die Verschuldungsprobleme der ärmsten Entwicklungsländer", *Das Parlament. Aus Politik und Zeitgesichte*, no. 9.

Kaplinski, R., 2001, "Is Globalization All It Is Cracked Up To Be?", *Review of International Political Economy*, vol. 8, no. 1, pp. 45–65.

Keck, M.E. and K. Sikkink, 1998, *Activists Beyond Borders. Advocacy Networks in International Politics*, Ithaca, NY: Cornell University Press.

Khan, M.H., 2001, Rural Poverty in Developing Countries. Washington, D.C.: IMF Economic Issues, No. 26.

Knowles, S., 2001, *Inequality and Economic Growth: The Empirical Relationship Reconsidered in the Light of Comparative Data*, Paper prepared for the WIDER conference on Growth and Poverty, Helsinki, 25–26 May.

Kolk, A. and van Tulder, R., 1999, "International Codes of Conduct and Corporate Social Responsibility: Can Transational Corporations Regulate Themselves", *Transnational Corporations*, vol. 8, no. 1, pp. 143–80.

Krasner, S.D., 1999, *Sovereignty. Organized Hypocricy*, Princeton, NJ: Princeton University Press.

Lamfalussy, A., 2000, *Financial Crises in Emerging Markets. An Essay on the Financial Globalisation and Fragility*, New Haven, CT: Yale University Press.

Landes, D., 1998, *The Wealth and Poverty of Nations*, New York: W.W. Norton.

Lentner, H., 2000, "Globalization and Power", in Auklah, P. and M. Schecter (eds.), *Rethinking Globalization(s)*, London: Macmillan.

Mandle, J., 2000, "Globalization and Justice", *The Annals of the American Academy of Political and Social Science*, vol. 570, pp. 126–39.

Margalit, A., 2000, "Rogini's Law", *The New Republic*, 11 September, pp. 30–33.

McGinnis, M., 1999, "Rent-seeking, Redistribution, and Reform in the Governance of Global Markets", in Prakash, A. and J. Hart (eds.), *Globalization and Governance*, London: Routledge.

Mearsheimer, J., 1995, "The False Promise of International Institutions", *International Security*, vol. 19, no. 1, pp. 5–49.

Miller, D., 1999, "Justice and Global Inequality", in Hurrell, A. and N. Woods (eds.), *Inequality, Globalization, and World Politics*, Oxford: Oxford University Press.

Mosley, P., 2001, "The IMF after the Asian Crisis: Merits and Limits of the 'Long-Term Development Partner' Role", *The World Economy*, vol. 24, no. 5, pp. 597–629.

Nelson, P., 2000a, "Whose Civil Society? Whose Governance? Decisionmaking and Practice in the New Agenda at the Inter-American Development Bank and the World Bank", *Global Governance*, vol. 6, no. 4, pp. 405–31.

Nelson, P., 2000b, "Internationalising Economic and Environmental Policy: Transnational NGO Networks and the World Bank's Expanding Influence", in Vandersluis Owen, S. and P. Yeros (eds.), *Poverty in World Politics. Whose Global Era?*, London: Macmillan.

Nuscheler, F., 2001, "Halbierung der absoluten Armut. Die Entwicklungspolitische Nagelprobe", *Das Parlament. Aus Politik und Zeitgeschichte*, no. 18–19, pp. 6–12.

O'Brien, R., Goetz, A.M., Scholte, J.A. and M. Williams (eds.), 2000, *Contesting Global Governance. Multilateral Economic Institutions and Global Social Movements*, Cambridge: Cambridge University Press.

Pender, J., 2001, "From 'Structural Adjustment' to 'Comprehensive Development Framework'. Conditionality Transformed?", *Third World Quarterly*, vol. 22, no. 3, pp. 397–411.

Pogge, T., 2001, "Priorities of Global Justice", *Metaphilosophy*, vol. 32, nos. 1–2, pp. 6–24.

Qureshi, A.H., 1996, *The World Trade Organization. Implementing International Trade Norms*, Manchester: Manchester University Press.

Regeringskansliet, 2001, *En rättvisare globalisering*, Interim report, Stockholm.

Reinicke, W., F. Deng, *et al.*, 2000, *Critical Choices. The United Nations, Networks, and the Future of Global Governance*, Ottawa: International Development Research Centre.

Rodrik, D., 1999, *The New Global Economy and Developing Countries: Making Openness Work*, Washington, D.C.: Overseas Development Council. Policy Essay No. 24.

Roodman, D. M., 2001, "Ending the Debt Crisis", in L. Brown, *et al.*, *State of the World 2001*, New York: W.W. Norton/ The Worldwatch Institute, pp. 143–165.

Ruggie, J.G., 1998, *Constructing the World Polity, Essays on International Institutionalization*, New York: Routledge.

Sachs, J., 2000, "A New Map of the World", *The Economist*, 24 June, pp. 81–83.

Sandler, T., 1997, *Global Challenges. An Approach to Environmental, Political and Economic Problems*, Cambridge: Cambridge University Press.

Sarkar, P., 2000, "North-South Uneven Development: What the Data Show", *Review*, vol. 23, no. 4, pp. 439–58.

Schechter, M., 2000, "Globalization and Civil Society", in Schechter, M. (ed.), *The Revival of Civil Society. Global and Comparative Perspectives*, London: Macmillan, pp. 61–101.

Schultze, G. and H. Ursprung, 1999, "Globalisation of the Economy and the Nation State", *The World Economy*, vol. 22, no. 3, pp. 295–352.

Schwartz, H.M., 2000, *States versus Markets. The Emergence of a Global Economy*, New York: St. Martin's Press (second ed.).

Sen, A., 1999, "Global Justice. Beyond International Equity", in Kaul, I., Grunberg, I. and M. Stern (eds.), *Global Public Goods. International Cooperation in the 21st Century*, New York: UNDP/Oxford University Press.

Sen, A., 2000, *Development as Freedom*, New York: Anchor Books.

Stiglitz , J., 2000, "The Insider. What I Learned at the World Economic Crisis", *The New Republic*, 17 April, pp. 56–60.

Tan, Kok-Chor, 2000, *Toleration, Diversity, and Global Justice*, University Park: The State University of Pennsylvania Press.

Tesner, S., 2000, *The United Nations and Business. A Partnership Recovered*, New York: St. Martin's Press.

Väyrynen, R., 1997, "International Stability and Risky States: Enforcement of International Norms", in Schneider, G. and P.A. Weitsman (eds.), *Enforcing Cooperation. Risky States and Intergovernmental Management of Cooperation*, London: Macmillan, pp. 37–59.

Väyrynen, R., 2001, "Sovereignty, Globalization, and Transnational Social Movements", *International Relations of the Asia-Pacific*, vol. 1, no. 2, pp. 26–47.

Wade, R., 2001, "Global Inequality: Winners and Losers", *The Economist*, 28 April, pp. 72–74.

Wiener, J., 1999, *Globalization and the Harmonization of Law*, London: Pinter.

Williams, O. (ed.), 2000, *Global Codes of Conduct. An Idea Whose Time Has Come*, Notre Dame, IN: University of Notre Dame Press.

Wolf, C., 1979, "A Theory of Nonmarket Failure: Framework for Implementation Analysis", *The Journal of Law and Economics*, vol. 22, no. 1, pp. 107–39.

Wolfe, R., 2001, *See You in Geneva? Democracy, the Rule of Law and the WTO*, Paper presented to the 41st Annual Convention of the International Studies Association, Chicago, 21–24 February.

Wolff, J., 2000, "Armutsbekämpfung durch Entwicklungshilfe", *Das Parlament. Aus Politik und Zeitgeschichte*, No. 9.

Woods, N., 2001, "Making the IMF and the World Bank More Accountable", *International Affairs*, vol. 77, no. 1, pp. 83–100.

146

World Economic Outlook, May 2000, Washington, D.C.: International Monetary Fund 2000.
World Development Report 2000/2001, *Attacking Poverty*, Washington, D.C.: The World
   Bank 2000.
Young, O., 2000, *Governance in World Affairs*, Ithaca, NY: Cornell University Press.

5. The Post-Westphalia Enigma

Richard Falk

Introducing a Post-Westphalia Perspective
The Westphalia benchmark

To comprehend the significance of a post-Westphalia framework for global politics, it is helpful to clarify the Westphalia reality to the extent possible. In brief, the Westphalia rubric is ambiguous as it serves both as shorthand to designate a state-centric, sovereignty-oriented, territorially bounded global order, and to identify a hierarchically structured world order shaped and managed by dominant or hegemonic political actors. In effect, the term "Westphalia" contains an inevitable degree of incoherence by combining the territorial/juridical logic of equality with the geopolitical/hegemonic logic of inequality.

Such a statist/hegemonic structure of world order had been preceded in thought and practice by a medieval conception that emphasised with greater consistency the interaction between Christian universalism – establishing a normative community among Christians – and territorial localism associated with various heterogeneous forms of political control arising from feudal land tenure and employment relations. This foundation for world order, besides being implicitly and operationally Eurocentric, also generated a sharp contrast in identity between the civilised "we" and the barbaric "them", which became formalised much later in the colonial era. The initial breakdown of this pre-Westphalia framework was partly a consequence of cleavages within Christianity, especially the Protestant break with Rome, and partly a consequence of the military and economic benefits of more centralised political actors with greater capabilities to mobilise resources and establish order within large, yet manageable, territorial units.[1]

This Westphalia system originated in Europe, formalised by treaties at the end of The Thirty Years War in 1648, but enlarged by stages to encompass the world, combining at each stage its statism (the logic of equality) with hegemonic actualities (the logic of inequality). The decades after World War II represented the climax of the Westphalia conception of world order, that is, the extension of the states system to Asia and Africa via the dynamics of de-colonisation, the continued control over global economic policy by states, a preoccupation by governments with security in relation to war and

---

[1] On the emergence of the sovereign state and states system as the dominant form of political organization, see Spruyt, 1994. For an assessment of its prospects under conditions of intensifying interdependence and declining capacity, see Camilleri and Falk, 1992.

peace, and a geopolitical focus on "bipolarity" that reflected the centrality of the encounter between two superpowers and their respective blocs of subordinate allies.

This Westphalia world was juridically structured through the agency of such foundational norms of international law as the equality of states, sovereign immunity, and the doctrine of non-intervention. This juridical conception of international society *as statist* has also controlled membership and participation in all of the most significant international institutions. Only fully sovereign states are treated as possessing the qualifications for full membership and participation, although moves toward regional representation, especially for EU countries, have complicated the realities of global diplomacy. Matters of human rights, civil discord, and the choice of governing ideology are treated by the United Nations Charter exclusively as matters of "domestic jurisdiction" in deference to the Westphalia frame of reference. Such deference can also be explained as recognition of the limited capabilities of the UN as the institutional expression of the organised international community. When these limits are not respected, as has been arguably the case with respect to humanitarian diplomacy in the 1990s, the UN is ineffective, and its activities generate embittered criticism.[2]

This Westphalia model also effortlessly accommodated the realities of radical inequality among states in size, wealth, power, and international role. This inequality generated its own distinctive form of global governance, relying on the performance of special managerial roles by leading state actors, known as "the Great Powers", and more recently discussed as "hegemonic geopolitics" (Bull, 1995; Gilpin, 1981).[3] Such a model was historically conditioned by the evolutionary dynamics of a Eurocentric world that included imperial forms of multi-state governance, and was gradually challenged in the 20th century by the rise of the United States and Russia. These states emerged as the first "superpowers" in the era of the Cold War, dominating tight alliances designed to deter expansion by their rivals while avoiding the onset of World War III, and possessing weaponry of mass destruction that could be delivered to any part of the planet in devastating quantities. Since 1945, even the strongest states have been inherently vulnerable to catastrophic destruction as a result of the development of nuclear weaponry, and the means for its delivery in minutes from great distances. As of 2001, every state is vulnerable to attacks with weaponry of mass destruction, and many actors possess such a capability to some degree.

---

[2] For a severe critiques of the role of the United Nations in the Balkans and Rwanda during the height of peacekeeping diplomacy in the 1990s, see Rieff, 1995; Malvern, 2000. As Malvern makes particularly clear, the UN must be understood as an agent of the main Western states, especially the United States.

[3] For influential formulations, a more recent distinguished addition to this literature of statist endorsement is Jackson, 2000.

With the end of the Cold War, a further restructuring has led Westphalia realists to view the hegemonic position of the United States as establishing "a unipolar moment" in the history of the states system, which is currently being sustained by a combination of economic, technological, diplomatic, cultural, and military instruments of influence. It is also being challenged in various ways by counter-movements and patterns of resistance. Such phenomena as the zero-casualty NATO war in 1999 over Kosovo, and the American quest for nuclear ballistic defence and space-based weaponry, manifest the practice and mentality of unipolarity. It also reflects a geopolitical shift from a traditional Westphalia search for balance and countervailing power and, at most, military superiority, to a more controlling effort to establish and maintain dominance (Lodal, 2001).

It is important to note two further Westphalia features of world order. Against the background of Machiavelli, Hobbes, and Clausewitz, the prevailing view of international society has been one in which the role of law and morality has been kept marginal in relation to statecraft and the shifting calculus of relative power. This marginality has been interpreted in the contemporary period by such thinkers as Morgenthau, Kennan, and Kissinger on the basis of a sceptical view of human nature that is conditioned by ambition, fear, and selfishness. It has led to a political orientation that regards security as virtually synonymous with power, and an outlook towards conflict associated with differing forms and degrees of "realism".

Such thinkers as E.H. Carr, Raymond Aron, Hedley Bull and Robert Cox have modified the outlook of pure realism.[4] These influential thinkers, although sharing a concern about the power of states, have many differences in emphasis and outlook. For instance, Aron and Bull conceive of international virtue modestly as consisting of "prudence" in statecraft, as well as inferring from statism the existence of an "anarchical society". The latter is seen as a minimal form of societal reality that depend upon a generalised recognition of the benefits of elementary forms of international cooperation, arising in turn from good faith compliance with international treaties, from customary respect for diplomatic immunities, and from a general willingness to abide by norms of non-intervention.

Carr and Cox are more inclined to consider seriously alternative forms of future world order, based either on the relevance of "dreams", or on leverage that might be exerted over time by transnational social forces. The character of international society reflects the historical circumstances, including struggles between opposed worldviews, and evolves as these circumstances alter. Such an international society possesses limits of sociability, which if exceeded, lead to disillusionment. More specifically, realist patterns of thought conceive it to be futile and disillusioning to seek to prohibit re-

---

[4] For an analysis along these lines see Falk, 1997a.

course to force in international life, or to attempt to punish leaders of sovereign states for their transgressions against international law.[5]

The Westphalia ethos has also generated variants of structural realism that relate behavioural features of international relations ahistorically to the way in which power is distributed among leading states. Such trust in the explanatory power of rational analysis is partly an effort to give the study of international relations a scientific basis. Realist critics imbued with classical approaches, resting on the historical and conceptual interpretation of world politics, regard this effort to achieve scientific rigor as essentially misconceived, because the subject-matter of international life is not susceptible to the abstraction needed to carry out experiments and deduce laws. This whole enterprise of scientific explanation amounts in the end to little more than one more instance of a confusion of science with "scientism".[6]

To summarise, the Westphalia framework continues to contain dual reference points that encompass the equality of states under international law, and the hierarchy of states in the actual operation of international relations. It is only by combining these contradictory ordering logics that the complex character of Westphalia is comprehended. The shared outlook of these two ideas relates to their focus on power, either as the territorial sovereignty of the state, or the geopolitical control of relations among states by way of hegemonic mechanisms (for instance, Great Power diplomacy or superpower arrangements). To the extent that "failed states" exist within recognised territorial boundaries and to the degree that no state or states exercise leadership roles, the quality of Westphalia order tends to diminish. This quality can also be diminished by the emergence of militarist and dissatisfied states and by the suppression of human rights at home and aggression abroad.

The Westphalia approach to world order tends toward the fulfilment of its *normative* potential when governance at the state level is internally moderate, democratic, and observant of human rights (including economic, social, and cultural rights) and when leading states are externally dedicated to the promotion of global public goods as well as to the preservation of their specific strategic interests. As a matter of historical experience, this normative potential has never been achieved, or even clearly and fully advocated, although the extent of failure has varied over time.[7] Genocidal politics and

[5] Perhaps most clearly articulated by Bull in "The Grotian Conception of International Society", in Butterfield and Wight, 1966. See also Aron, 1966; Cox with Sinclair, 1996.

[6] See Kenneth Waltz for the most rigorous argument to this effect in Waltz, 1979.

[7] Prominent partial and non-utopian advocates of a global peace system include Czar Alexander, Woodrow Wilson, Franklin Roosevelt, and more recently Olof Palme, Mikhail Gorbachev, and Nelson Mandela. Wilson can be regarded as utopian in the important sense of proposing a mechanism that lacked the capability to achieve the proclaimed goal; i.e., the League of Nations as constituted did not have the authority or the capacity to supplant a balance of power approach by institutionalising collective security.

major international and civil wars are indicators of extreme failure, as assessed by common Westphalia standards of performance.

The degree to which legal obligation deserves respect in international political life remains a matter of controversy. According to the Hobbesian variant of Westphalia realism, law can function *within* the state because an agency of enforcement exists, but *outside* the state there is no enforcing mechanism. It is a war zone that can be kept non-violent only by means of deterrence. Bull, in particular, challenged this view, suggesting that a distinctive form of sociability among states is an imperative of international life, but that the maintenance of security depends on leading states retaining discretion to use force in times and places of their choosing, so as to maintain balance and stability among sovereign states.[8] Throughout the Westphalia period there existed counter-traditions that emphasised morality and law to a far greater extent, and envisioned the emergence of a normatively accountable global polity by stages. Such perspectives are often grounded in and inspired by Kant's seminal essay, *Perpetual Peace* (1795), which served as the starting point for such persisting perspectives as international liberalism and the related espousal of "democratic peace", i.e. the view that democratically organised states do not wage war against one another.[9]

The United States between World War I and the end of the Cold War was the main champion of this counter-tradition, often called "idealism" in contrast with "realism". It is associated with the formative ideas and outlook of Woodrow Wilson, but draws on deeper and abiding ideas of American exceptionalism ("a Lockean nation in a Hobbesian world").[10] Whether this Wilsonianism persisted in the United States during the Cold War era is a matter of ongoing debate, but its weight was (and is) felt in liberal patterns of support for the United Nations, foreign economic assistance, humanitarian diplomacy, and human rights.[11]

These strands of liberal/idealist thought often derive from and are associ-

[8] For Bull's views on Hobbes see his essay, "Hobbes and the International Anarchy", reprinted in Alderson and Hurrell (eds.), 2000.

[9] In the Clinton presidency this idea was formalised as the doctrine of "enlargement", seeking to expand the domain of constitutional democracy as a strategy for extending peace to the peoples of the world. In the Clinton formulations, "constitutional democracy" was understood as implying the existence of a market economy.

[10] Of course, there is also the America of Jesse Helms, and George W. Bush, that prides itself on anti-internationalism, isolationism, and an affirmation of strong sovereign rights, while still insisting upon its moral exceptionalism in world politics. Increasingly, others regard these claims with suspicion in the period since the end of the Cold War, viewing the United States as a typical arrogant, domineering, and self-seeking state whose unilateralism undermines respect for international law and the United Nations.

[11] For an influential interpretation that argues against the alleged Wilsonian legacy of moralism see Kissinger, 1994, pp. 218–45 and 762–835. On Wilson's views on world peace and related diplomacy after World War I, see Knock, 1992.

ated with *inclusive* forms of religious belief.[12] Inclusive orientations, whether religious or secular humanist, emphasise human solidarity as desirable and possible, thereby challenging either directly or indirectly Westphalia complacency about radical inequality and war as intrinsic to international reality, as well as to the existential limits of community. The liberal/idealist outlook is more hopeful about human nature, species identity and world order prospects than are realists. Secular versions of such idealism rest their underlying optimism upon the emancipatory impacts of human reason over time and, especially, on the degree to which technological innovation improves material wellbeing and contributes to better communication and understanding among the peoples of the world.

Of course, these simplistic distinctions miss some crucial aspects of hybridity of thought-realists who exhibit an optimism about the persistence of a Westphalia world despite global warming and the spread of weaponry of mass destruction; liberal/idealists who are convinced that such persistence will trigger a catastrophic breakdown of order, together with a major regression in human circumstances. The latter tend to believe that rational human action can prevent catastrophic future developments, whereas most realists mainly rely on little other than their capacity to inflict destruction on adversaries and are sceptical about internationalism of all kinds, especially institution-building, other than defensive alliances. Of course, there are many varieties of realism distributed throughout a spectrum of views on such matters, some of which incorporate liberal convictions about human rights and international institutions and some of which are hostile to such goals.

Despite such normative counter-traditions, the postulates of realism have shaped the behaviour of states during the modern era, with the possible exception of the behaviour of the liberal democracies – especially the United States – in the period between the end of World War I and the onset of World War II. It would be a mistake to regard the establishment of the League of Nations or the United Nations as an indication that the Westphalia statist/geopolitical framework was being superseded by either design or practice.[13] The realist predominance is manifested by the continuing tolerance of genocide, massive poverty, acute civil discord in those realms of international society where a geopolitics of indifference prevails, and contrasts with the emergence of patterns of robust intervention in circumstances where important strategic interests of the intervenors are at stake. It is a question of some significance for the assessment of post-Westphalia prospects to gauge

---

[12] The contrast here is with *exclusive* forms that emphasise special access to truth and salvation, and regard those without such access as evil or as infidels. This distinction, and its relation to contemporary patterns of world order is the main theme of Falk, 2001a.

[13] For mainly sceptical assessments of supra-nationalising claims, see Lyons and Mastanduno (eds.), 1995.

the extent to which realism is intrinsic to a statist framework of world order, or is more of an expression of values prevailing in the political culture, or of the ethics associated with the market. A related question is whether realism is capable of conceiving of national and strategic interests as long-term, which would enable a realist to be deeply concerned about the impacts a generation or a century hence of environmental deterioration either by way of global warming or ocean pollution.

One way to concretise such an inquiry would be with respect to the viability of an approach to security at the state level that proposes reliance on "human security", a terminology recently introduced into the language of diplomacy to express a less militarist and more normative conception of security. Would a statist system genuinely operating on the basis of and organised in relation to human security, continue to be usefully labelled as "Westphalia"? Or, would not the adoption of human security by leading governments have a transformative impact on world politics, validating some sort of post-Westphalia designation? To the extent that such questions are rhetorical they suggest that the Westphalia state-centric and geopolitical managed world presupposes a pluralist orientation toward the definition of wellbeing, development, and destiny. Such pluralism would be consistent with extensive cooperation to address global-scale challenges to ecological sustainability. It would not, however, be arguably consistent with the elimination of self-help features of a decentralised world order constituted by sovereign territorial states.

The relation of state and nation is also a crucial aspect of Westphalia. The invention of militant nationalism in the 18th century served to consolidate state power, enhancing its mobilising capacity, as well as accentuating the contrasts between "inside" and "outside", between "citizen" and "alien", and even between "civilised" and "barbaric". The idea of the nation-state served partly as a mobilising fiction and project to ensure loyalty to the state and partly as a legalistic designation of nationality, as conferred by the state without regard to specific ethnic identity. Such nationalism weakened bonds with outsiders, but served over time to construct meaningful political communities, as well as to erode many hierarchies and patterns of discrimination based on class, race, and ethnic identity within territorial boundaries. And yet, as of the early 21st century, an array of anti-state and ethnic nationalisms poses a crucial challenge to political stability in many states. This challenge is directed not at statism as such, but at the failure of existing states to be nation-states in psycho-political respects. It is also directed toward overcoming the plight of "captive nations" and embittered micro-nationalisms trapped within the boundaries of existing states. The modern system of states was premised on secular assumptions of multi-ethnicity and juridical nationhood, and so any major trend in the direction of invalidating such states would tend toward the nullification of mature Westphalia forms of world order.

For this reason, the practice and theorising on the right of self-determination since the end of colonialism and the Cold War has placed in jeopardy the persistence of the modernist ethos a Westphalia world, which favoured in principle ethnic diversity and religious pluralism.[14] To the extent that 3,000–8,000 distinct ethnicities exist as "nations", the legitimation of their claims to independence, or even autonomy (sometimes identified as "internal self-determination"), would alter the world order in fundamental respects. In effect, the legitimacy of states that are ethnically diverse and, in this sense, multi-national to the extent that minorities conceive of themselves as nations, is an indispensable feature of the Westphalia world.

It is obvious that the states system is at the core of the Westphalia experience, but in itself both a guiding and incoherent myth that does not now – and never did – correspond with patterns of behaviour in international politics that were shaped by war and inequalities of power/wealth. What is more, the character of the state is fundamentally ambiguous on this central matter of nation-state, and the operating modes of statecraft certainly evolve over time, especially reflecting the impact of changes in technology, values, geopolitical goals, and guiding ideology. As such, it is misleading to essentialise the Westphalia reality as if it was not embedded in a changing historical matrix of ideas, technologies, ideologies, structures, and practices.

What endures to give world order its Westphalia shape over the centuries is the primacy of the territorial state as political actor on a global level, the centrality of international warfare, the autonomy of the sovereign state to govern affairs within recognised international boundaries, the generalised tolerance of "human wrongs" committed within the scope of sovereign authority, the special leadership role in geopolitics claimed by and assigned to leading state(s), and the absence of strong institutions of regional and global governance. The veto power conferred on the five Permanent Members of the Security Council is a formal recognition of inequality as part and parcel of the Westphalia reality as of the early 21st century. As such, it is an explicit acknowledgement that the equality of states is a diplomatic concept but not one that is politically descriptive of the workings of world order.[15]

The decision to abandon or alter the Westphalia label for world order is a matter of both assessing empirical trends and advancing prescriptive goals. To embrace a post-Westphalia perspective involves an endorsement of cer-

---

[14] The controversy about the proper limits of the right of self-determination in the post-colonial era is far from resolved. It has flared up in concrete circumstances of bloody encounter in such diverse settings as Kosovo, Chechnya, Kashmir, and Palestine. For views expressive of the range of claims see Kly and Kly (eds.), 2000. For a more cautious set of views about the scope of the right of self-determination see Danspreckgruber with Watts (eds.), 1997.

[15] Ken Booth has vividly conceptualized this critique of the Westphalia impact on human wellbeing in Booth, 1995. For a series of essays exploring the relevance of this critique by Booth, see Dunne and Wheeler (eds.), 1999.

tain forms of transformative agency currently active in the world, as well as a process of re-labelling due to subversive trends that have been unleashed in recent decades. There are two sets of actors that are moving consciousness and perception beyond Westphalia categories: global corporations and banks that conceive of the world as a marketplace for production, consumption, and investment, and the civil society transnational actors that conceive of the world as a human community in which the human needs and basic rights of all persons are upheld. Both of these transformative agents seek alignment with governments, and both have had a measure of success. Corporate globalisers have enjoyed the general support of the leading states in promoting their objectives, whereas the civic globalisers have had to cobble together coalitions with shifting clusters of states seeking to uphold global public goods in relation to such international goals as arms control, human rights, and environmental protection.

A post-Wesphalia world is *not yet*, although the dynamics of behavioural and linguistic subversion are eroding Westphalia foundations. Reliance on the descriptive terminology of "globalisation" in some way expresses the insufficiency of early discussions of international relations that kept their entire focus on the states system. Also, the interest in civilisational perspectives, whether to depict new conflict formations or to encourage dialogic relations, is another recognition that our interpretative categories need to be revised to capture the most significant aspects of contemporary reality. In some genuine sense, the Westphalia world no longer exists,[16] but neither has a post-Westphalia world been brought into being.[17] Westphalia frames for international reality no longer generate confidence, but globalisation, as another framing is too vague and uncrystalised to be a serious candidate for replacement.

A final feature of the Westphalia outlook was the horizoning of reality in relation to the state, whether on maps or in the political and cultural imagination, although there were notable exceptions who earlier conceived of collective human experience in civilisational terms.[18] Such horizoning could

---

[16] Unconditional territorial sovereignty never did except as an "ideal type". See Krasner, 1999. See also Hashmi (ed.), 1997.

[17] It is for this reason that I have elsewhere referred to this period of hybridity and transition as "a Grotian moment" in which the old order persists, yet is increasingly challenged by an emergent new order. It was a truly great achievement of Grotius to provide a synthesis that created conceptual and political space for the new without requiring a repudiation of the old. For my assessment, see Falk, 1999.

[18] Although statist views predominated in international relations, there has been a macro-historical tradition that regarded civilisational units as the basic constitutive force in world affairs. Leading examples of this tradition include Spengler, 1926–28; Toynbee, 1934–61 (12 vols.), Braudel, 1980; McNeill, 1963. A recent example of this genre is the fine study of Barzun, 2000, *From Dawn to Decadence: 1500 to the Present*. Important as a corrective to the Western preoccupations of this macro-historical work is Edward Said's *Culture and Imperialism*, 1993. A perceptive overview of the civilisational approach as it relates to international relations is O'Hagen, 2000.

be reconciled with feeble forms of regionalism and globalism, but without much relevance for the lifeworld of human existence or political behaviour, which was dominated by states. For this reason, conjectures of the imagination that depicted such horizons as constitutive were generally derided as "cultural" or "utopian", more suitable for the realms of literature and religion. Utopia has, of course, the revealing and humbling etymology of meaning "no where". It is this shift in horizoning that may be the most decisive indication that we are currently experiencing a post-Westphalia dawn. It is no longer possible to ignore *politically* the following non-statist horizons: that of "humanity", of "globality", and of "regionality".[19] Such shifts in language signal deeper behavioural and perceptual adjustments. They parallel the radical behavioural implications of the global religious resurgence and the rise of civilisational thinking.

The post-Westphalia framing of political reality must accordingly be mindful of this set of tendencies, identified most prominently in relation to an impending "clash of civilisations". Here, the Westphalia war system is given a renewed relevance by being resituated in a civilisational rather than statist structure of conflict.[20] The religious resurgence adds weight to this outlook, although migration patterns of intermingled civilisations make spatial mapping of inter-civilisational relations impossible. The emphasis on a "dialogue of civilisations" is mainly a normative effort to appreciate the relevance of the civilisational interpretation of the historical situation, at the same time seeking to avoid reproducing the Westphalia war system in the emergent inter-civilisational context. It also seeks to avoid confusing geographical categories of delimited regions with civilisational contours that overlap one another to significant degrees.

The Post-Westphalia Perspective

The prescriptive imperative

Modernity has given rise to two sorts of escapist projections: a nostalgic return to small local communities premised on high degrees of integration, perhaps epitomised by pre-modern images of self-determination affirmed by many representatives of indigenous peoples; and an evolution toward encompassing communities that were premised on low degrees of integration, but looked toward the emergence of a planetary polity in some form.

---

[19] These awkward words are used here to get away from such heavily freighted alternatives as globalisation and regionalism.

[20] This provocative interpretation of international relations is set forth fully in Huntington, 1996. Huntington's geopolitical approach distracted commentators from the innovative side of his assessment of the future of international relations centering upon a shift in the main axes of significance from statism to civilisationalism. In this respect, Huntington's outlook can be understood as one type of post-Westphalia scenario.

During the whole course of the Westphalia reality there were those on the sidelines of political life who dreamed of a unified world order that maintained peace and security, and spread a set of preferred values, almost always their own.[21] Already in the 14th century Dante gave expression to such a self-serving hope in his *De Monarchia*, conceiving of Rome as the foundation for achieving a much desired global political unity. It was a visionary solution to the problems of political fragmentation that was set forth long before the formation of the European state system. Subsequently, there were a stream of peace plans and visions of a stateless world that were viewed as part of a utopian tradition of reflection and aspiration, but also tended to express in concealed forms, grandiose expansions of the power structures associated with the various authors.

Ever since Dante, such projects for world unification tended to emanate from the existing centre of global dominance, and institutionalise that reality in a morally attractive form that was presented as beneficial to the whole of humanity. Such visionary thinking seems generally to represent a good faith effort to promote human wellbeing, but it is greeted with suspicion because such thinking so invariably emanates from existing power centres. It is assessed sceptically because such individuals are writing on their own, without any political base that might make more believable a transition from here to there.

At least since the end of the 19th century, on the occasion of the Hague Peace Conferences of 1899 and 1907, there was a constituency for the thesis that war was at once integral to the Westphalia world of interacting sovereign states, and increasingly intolerable as a recurrent international practice. After World War I, the World Federalists put forward proposals for world government that attracted considerable grassroots support in Europe and North America. After World War II, these proposals were revived, especially as a result of the shock effects associated with the initial uses of the atomic bomb, which gave rise to a mood of "utopia, or else". This outlook remained rather influential in the months following Hiroshima and Nagasaki. For the next decade or so, this kind of thinking was given some attention, possibly most influentially in the plan for a strengthened United Nations that would be converted into a type of limited world government. It was published in a sequence of three editions by Grenville Clark and Louis B. Sohn under the title *World Peace Through World Law* (1966, third ed.).[22] But the Cold War managed to stifle such thinking about alternative world orders based on the centralisation of authority. The absence of any use of nuclear weaponry during the Cold War, and the refusal of nuclear weapons states to part with their capabilities even in the absence of strategic rivalry,

[21] For overview, see Hemleben, 1943. For more recent visionary thinking, see Wooley, 1968.
[22] For a recent proposal along similar lines see Yunker, 1993.

has effectively removed such proposals from serious consideration even among anti-Westphalias. The Soviet Union was also widely interpreted as a failed utopian project that suggested the bloody dangers and fundamental misconceptions about human nature that pertained to all efforts to transform the utopian genre, from an occasionally inspiring literary pursuit to guidance for lifeworld politics.

In a more modest, less Western format, the World Order Models Project (WOMP), working with a transnational group of scholars since 1967, produced a series of volumes under the title "preferred worlds for the 1990s" that were published in the period of 1975–1980.[23] These volumes were designed to formulate "relevant utopias" that could achieve attainable improvements in the human condition, but were accompanied by a strategy that could credibly interpret "the political space" between what exists and what is preferred. Such projections were certainly less anchored in Westphalia assumptions than was mainstream thinking, especially with respect to the relevance of ethical considerations on the formation of global policy. Unlike the pessimism of realists, the WOMP conjectures, while generally accepting the persistence of the state as dominant actor, were far more optimistic about reformist potentialities, ranging from substantial demilitarisation and denuclearisation through to the development of a more egalitarian world order, to the build-up of regional and global institutions.

A later extension of this line of prescriptive thinking looked hopefully at the emergence of transnational social movements as creating the political basis for a global civil society that could over time generate a structure of humane global governance. In a sense, this post-Westphalia outlook regarded the ecological stability of the planet and its increasing interdependence as establishing a functional foundation for moving beyond the operational codes of an anarchical society. Such transnational activism was also viewed as a positive expression of resistance to the reach and impact of global corporations and banks.

It is also true that economistic versions of this kind of post-Westphalia world began to surface toward the end of the 20th century. The image of a borderless world dominated by markets, global corporations and banks attracted a certain following. More recently, these images were reinforced by the rise of cyber-consciousness with its affinities for "self-organising systems" and libertarian critiques of government. In these economistic/cyber visions of the future, the Westphalia system is displaced from within and below, rather than superseded by a layer of supranational institutions.

A final important prescriptive conception is associated with the degree to which "human wrongs" (Ken Booth) are given "a safe haven" by the Westphalia

---

[23] Mendlovitz (ed.), 1975, provides a summary of the diverse models of preferred futures for the 1990s.

charter of sovereignty. The failure of the world to react to the Nazi policies of persecution, or more recently to the genocide occurring in Cambodia or Rwanda, has inspired critics to postulate capabilities for overriding deference to territorial supremacy.[24] Proposals to establish genocide-prevention forces under UN authority is one direction of assault upon hard core Westphalia ideas of sovereignty. The support for humanitarian intervention is another direction, although a contested one, especially in the aftermath of the Kosovo War of 1999. The experience of the *ad hoc* tribunals to prosecute those indicted for crimes in relation to the break-up of the former Yugoslavia and in Rwanda, as well as the Pinochet litigation, are still other directions. They indicate the existence of procedures for imposing accountability on leaders of sovereign states that commit crimes against their own peoples.[25]

As already mentioned, two other prescriptive trends implicitly posit a post-Westphalia world: the transition from national security to human security as the basis for governmental engagement in world politics; and the insistence that states to be legitimate must be nation-states in an ethnically homogeneous rather than a juridical sense, or at least constitute an existentially coherent community. Note that the advocates of "democratic peace" do not challenge the essential character of the Westphalia framework, including its structure of radical inequality. Such a project of re-formed statism seeks to reformulate the qualifications for international legitimacy at the level of the state, so as to reconcile the protection of basic political and civil rights at the level of the individual with the exercise of territorial sovereignty. This reconciliation is believed to enhance prospects for a generally stable, cooperative, and, above all, peaceful interaction among existing states.

From a prescriptive outlook, such views are post-Westphalia in partial and questionable respects: the obsolescence of international warfare and some mechanisms for external accountability to ensure compliance with international human rights standards. These reforms would qualify as basic and beneficial modifications of the Westphalia reality, *if systemically implemented*, but would not seem sufficiently transformational so as to merit unfurling the "post-Westphalia" banner. Perhaps, instead, the label of "neo-Westphalia" would seem to offer an appropriate degree of acknowledgement that the framework had changed in important respects, but that its statist character remains. Naming is an interpretative act with significant effects. The naming of world order, particularly its re-naming, generates both ex-

---

[24] Take note of cynicism in the face of genocide: Khmer Rouge exempted for geopolitical reasons associated with the "China card", while Rhodesia was "overlooked" because the country was seen as without strategic concern. See Cooper, 2001; see also Malvern, 2000.

[25] For fine books on these themes, see Bass, 2000; Minow, 1998; Barkan, 2000.

pectations and controversy. It highlights disagreements about global trends, and it signals the wish to affirm or avoid restructuring of authority patterns that give shape and direction to world order.

As will be discussed in subsequent sections, the emergence of certain forms of regionalism and of global democracy will be treated in this essay as transformational, and thus cannot be conceptually accommodated within the Westphalia framework. Such an insistence does not imply "the end of the state", although it does mean that world order can no longer be usefully depicted by an exclusive focus on the role and interactions of states. At the same time, the state and statecraft are sufficiently robust and resilient to remain essential features of any non-utopian form of post-Westphalia world order that can be set forth. All in all, if these democratising and regionalising developments come to pass, a new organising concept will be needed. Until it can be agreed upon, the new reality is suggested by employing the post-Westphalia label. The added advantage of this non-committal label is also to avoid either accepting or rejecting the terminology of globalisation.

Some empirical observations

Reliance on the terminology of globalisation is an attempt to highlight a major shift in global trends that have become especially pronounced in the period since the end of the Cold War. It also represents an attempt to find a terminology that is less statist, and yet not suggestive of moral progress or drastic innovation. Globalisation can be understood either modestly as identifying a dominant trend in an economistic era of late Westphalia geopolitics, or more dramatically, as signalling the birth of a planetary structure that is dominated by market forces. The slippery and ambiguous nature of the term globalisation is partly a result of this uncertainty about how, at this stage, to specify these emergent structures of world order that seem to be shaping current history in new directions. At issue, also, is the role and future of the territorial state, and that of the states system. Of concern is whether it is more accurate and helpful to conceive of globalisation as the latest phase of the Westphalia Era, or being the constitutive process of radical restructuring associated with the claim that some variant of post-Westphalia reality is upon us. Of course, the debate is an interpretative one that cannot be resolved.

The minimum content of globalisation involves the compression of time and space on a planetary scale. Other aspects include the intensification of cross-border interactivity, the transnational penetration of territorial space, the effects of information technology (IT) on global business operations, the dissemination of a consensual view of political legitimacy based on market liberalism and elective constitutionalism, and the pervasive impingement of global market forces on governmental processes. Such a presentation of globalisation emphasises its linear character as a sequel to a more state-centric, war-oriented phase of international history. The state is re-instrumentalised by market forces to promote, to a far greater extent than previously, the priorities of business and finance as these relate to trade, investment, and consumption *around the world*. Not all states are re-instrumentalised to the same degree, which contributes to an overall impression of an uneven relationship between globalisation and the policymaking discretion of states, i.e. some governments maintain much greater freedom of manoeuvre with respect to their foreign economic policy than do others.

This prevailing account of globalisation misses some critical aspects of the new reality, especially the challenge being mounted by transnational social forces to alleged adverse impacts of globalisation: rapidly increasing inequality at the level of society, of the state, of the region; the tendency toward the social disempowerment of the state; the decline in support for public goods at all levels of social interaction. The Seattle demonstrations against the WTO at the end of 1999, the Genoa riots sparked by the G8 meeting in mid-2001, and others that have occurred with growing militancy at sites where globalisation elites convene, are expressions of a vibrant global movement that currently lacks clear goals and a consensus as to tactics. Anti-globalisation forces do possess a shared and deepening resolve to resist the social, economic, and cultural deformations attributed to corporate globalisation. It seems useful to consider this resistance as manifesting mainly a commitment to "another globalisation" that is animated by strong commitments to the enhancement of human wellbeing, and as such is people-oriented rather than market-driven.

There is also a nationalistic component of this anti-globalisation movement that tends toward protectionism, and is centred upon a struggle to preserve a territorial conception of world order based on the primacy of the nation-state and its citizenry. Parts of organised labour and non-competitive sectors of national economies are hostile to globalisation, mainly for materialist reasons, and in the spirit of statist populism. There is a subsidiary component of the anti-globalisation movement that harbours strong suspicions about the effects of integrative technology, and seeks to encourage de-industrialisation. It favours an austere economic approach that rejects growth as a societal goal, opting for small-scale environmentally benign technologies associated with sustainable political communities.[26]

I have elsewhere referred to corporate globalisation as "globalisation-from-above", and the civic globalisation as "globalisation-from-below" (e.g. Falk, 1993). This dichotomising terminology is far from satisfactory, as it overlooks and homogenises the distinct strands of belief that are bound together in these encompassing orientations. It also neglects the sort of patterns associated with collaboration between transnational social forces and

---

[26] A coherent presentation along these lines can be found in Daly and Cobb Jr., 1989.

governments that are seeking to sustain their identity as socially responsible political actors with primary allegiance to the wellbeing of their citizenry. Familiar examples of such collaboration include the overall political process that produced the Anti-Personnel Landmines Treaty, and the Rome Treaty establishing an International Criminal Court (ICC). These collaborative patterns, although exploratory and situational, do raise up the possibility of a new internationalism that is neither statist, nor populist, yet combines the capacities of states with the energies of people, and breaks down the state/society dividing line.

Putting the cosmodrama of globalisation into the context of an inquiry into post-Westphalia prospects suggests that globalisation is a decidedly unfinished narrative that could go forward in different directions. This rather cautious line of interpretation suggests that the real impact of globalisation will depend significantly on the outcome of the ongoing struggle for "the soul of the state" (see Falk, 1997b). At issue is whether the state continues to be predominantly *instrumentalised* by and responsive to market forces, or manages to be *socially reempowered* through the agency of transnational activism as reinforced by social democratic elites, and by an accommodation with what is called "humane regionalism" in a later section.

In the case that globalisation-from-above wins out by instrumentalising the state, completing the process of social disempowerment and political demobilisation, it would be appropriate to consider globalisation as having produced one possible post-Westphalia scenario. However, for reasons only alluded to, such an outcome should be treated as a dysutopia. If the state is socially re-empowered, there would exist a renewed regulatory relationship of governance structures and processes to the market, and a shift away from adherence to the policy postulates of neo-liberalism. If this eventuality fails to come to pass, then the locus of power would remain configured in such a manner as to reaffirm the persistence and legitimacy (although in a somewhat contested and diluted condition) of the Westphalia framework.

Of course, there are many intermediate positions relating to the role of the state that could reflect compromise. Different states might respond in quite disparate ways to the mobilisation of, and pressures exerted by, reformist orientations with respect to the role of the state in relation to globalisation. The responses range from accommodation to rejection, and both possibilities could occur under circumstances of varying balances of internal power. Differences in political culture and the presence or absence of effective leadership on one side or the other could also push the process of encounter in one direction or the other.

The rise of transnationalism, the growth of human rights and associated ideas of criminal accountability of political leaders, and the role of international institutions might, if these tendencies persist, justify adoption of an ambivalent label such as a "Neo-Westphalia" scenario even without taking globalisation into consideration (Risse-Kappen, 1995). A Neo-Westphalia world order would continue to be understood primarily through the prism of statist geopolitics, although accompanied by a conceptual acknowledgement that normative concerns are integral (relevance of international law and morality) and that transnationalism (localism, regionalism, and cosmopolitanism) are significantly more relevant than in the Westphalia era. The search for forms of global governance and the protection of vulnerable and disadvantaged peoples, would also represent Neo-Westphalia concerns that were not given prominence during the Westphalia period.

As already suggested, there is a subjective element present. The terminology chosen reflects the will and perceptions of the observer as well as the objective circumstances that arguably call for a re-labelling of reality. The counter-intuitive irony present in this analysis of globalisation is that the more hopeful interpretation of its evolution now relies on the reinvigoration of the state.[27] More pessimistic lines of thinking anticipate the decisive weakening of the state, as assessed from either a humanistic perspective of global public goods or from a more Westphalia perspective of the wellbeing of the territorial citizenry. It should be understood that this endorsement of a renewal of "the strong state" as the basis of regulating global market operations should not be confused with an endorsement of the military and coercive dimensions of state power. As the current approach of the United States government suggests, high-intensity militarisation is quite consistent with an ardent embrace of neo-liberal ideology with regard to state/society relations. This deadly combination of militarism and globalisation can be expressed more concretely: a huge investment by the US government in Ballistic Missile Defence is not seen as a departure from the gospel of free trade as preached at Quebec in 2001 by President George W. Bush at the Summit of the Americas.

What seems evident is that "globalisation" conveniently encodes the confluence of empirical trends that dominate the political imagination at the moment. Whether these trends are better interpreted as establishing a new structure of interaction, or involve merely a modification of the old structure, is a matter of persisting, and essentially unsolvable, controversy. As the next section argues, from a normative perspective of human values and from an empirical perspective of likely prospects, some of the more familiar projections of post-Westphalia outcomes are best treated as dead ends. Their advocacy is regressive in relation to the ripening goal of envisioning and realising humane global governance as a practical and indispensable political project. The most profound challenge to the political and moral imagination at the present time is to depict a Post-Westphalia scenario that

---

[27] This is counter-intuitive because previous thinking on global reform had consistently regarded states and sovereignty as obstacles to the establishment of a more humane world.

is sufficiently rooted in emergent trends to engender widespread hope and mobilise social forces on behalf of such a commitment.

Of course, as should be evident, not all post-Westphalia forms of world order are being pursued by those seeking peace, sustainability, human rights, and global community, i.e. the main elements of what is here being identified as "humane global governance". A post-Westphalia world organised around short-term market forces, with ever-widening gaps, deepening pockets of poverty, numerous "black holes" of collapsed governance structures, and control mechanisms dominated by increasingly sophisticated technology at the disposal of elites who serve the interests of business and finance. Other post-Westphalia dysutopias that need to be taken seriously involve intensifying trends toward religious and ethnic exclusivism as the claimed basis for fulfilling a right of self-determination, and an array of chauvinistic backlashes that seek to hijack government to carry out an anti-immigrant agenda.

Three Post-Westphalia Dead Ends

It is important to exclude certain commonly discussed post-Westphalia scenarios as essentially unattainable or undesirable, or both. Such scenarios distract attention from what is happening and, more significantly, from the *normative potential* implicit in the present phase of global politics. A systematic exploration of normative potential is partly a prescriptive, partly an empirical assessment of the prospect for realising a specific series of world order goals or values, such as development, human rights, peace, and ecological sustainability. The World Order Models Project launched such an inquiry as a prelude to hope for political action, implicitly subscribing to the slogan, "thought without action equals zero".[28]

Although these post-Westphalia scenarios are presented as "dead ends" because of their lack of feasibility and their challenge to widely shared world order values, it should be appreciated that each contains a measure of plausibility with respect to global trends and aspirations. Each also provides some insight into the originality of the present historical moment. But each also turns a blind eye to difficulties of realisation, as well as to pitfalls implicit in their preferred future.

The global marketplace

One theme in post-Westphalia literature is associated with the global ascendancy of market-driven forms of political and ideational structure giving rise to the first genuine global civilisation. Such conceptions envision the

---

[28] For elaboration see Mendlovitz (ed.), 1975.

radical subordination of territorial states, the anachronism of specific civilisational and religious identities, and the disappearance of such modalities of statecraft as diplomacy and warfare. At best, states would survive as subordinate facilitators of market relations and existing civilisations would become secondary sources of identity, providing some administrative backup and cultural specificity for an otherwise homogenised "global civilisation" premised on Western consumerist priorities and a stream of technological innovations (Mozaffari, 1999).[29]

Such a conception of the future overlooks the dialectical character of globalisation, which strengthens rather than overcomes civilisational, religious and ethnic identities. It also underestimates the resilience of the state, and the role of force in a world of persisting inequality of material standards. The only way that such a mega civilisation could become a political project, would be in relation to the hegemonic ambitions of an existing centre of power to exert global dominance. Then it would be either inherently oppressive or result in intense resistance. The darkest reading of the American global strategy is to conceive of it as animated by such an imperial vision of the future, but such a reading probably exaggerates US ambition and underestimates the friction that would result if such an attempt were to be seriously undertaken. Already, the awakening of civilisational identity throughout the non-western world, and even the forward momentum of European regionalism can be seen partially as a defensive hedge against attempts at the Americanisation of the world.

World government

There has been a naïve view in the West that a peaceful and just world depends on the establishment of a centralised core of political institutions operating in accordance with a constitutional framework. Such a projection has been a frequent utopian refrain in the face of debilitating warfare for the last century or so, and was given a strong impetus by the carnage of the two world wars of the 20th century and by the advent of nuclear weaponry. World government was often posited by long-range thinkers and reformers as the only serious alternative to apocalyptic catastrophe. More idealistically, world government was envisaged as the natural sequel to the era of sovereign states, a culmination of an evolutionary march of reason toward the institutionalisation of unity on an ever-grander scale (see Schell, 1982).[30]

As with other conceptions of unification, the idea of world government engenders scepticism and disbelief. The implicit transfer of peacekeeping

---

[29] For a critique see Korten, 1995; Barnet and Cavanagh, 1994.
[30] See also references cited in note 23.

authority, especially with respect to security seems so remote, considering the continuing vitality of nationalist sentiments, as to be hyper-utopian. The inequality of material standards and emergent resource scarcities also make the acceptance of a common democratic framework appear threatening both to the rich and the poor. The former fear a levelling down in the name of global equity, while the latter fear the impact of coercive authority for the sake of law and order in the face of social activism and likely unrest. World government seems to lack any current mobilising appeal, both because it seems unattainable and because its establishment is generally seen to be either the triumph of global tyranny or leading to menacing forms of large-scale civil warfare. Nationalism and civilisational identities remain too robust to risk their absorption in the name of forming a global constitutional polity, and besides the Westphalia structure ensures protection for diversity and experimentation.

Global village

The influential media guru, Marshall McLuhan, insisted that the impact of TV would create such a sense of shared awareness and inter-connectivity as to justify the label "global village". These undoubted insights into the impact of media and technological innovation have been extended in recent years to account for the impact of the Internet, information technology, and a generalised conviction that citizenship is being superseded by netizenship and cyberpolitics.[31] Such perspectives tend to embrace a libertarian ethos that reinforces market distrust of regulation and public sector solutions for human suffering and societal deficiencies. As such, it reinforces the neo-liberal downward pressure on the allocation of resources relating to the production of public goods, with the notable and revealing exception of defence. This cyber-consciousness is disposed toward a faith-based reliance on self-organising systems and the flow of technological innovations to sustain societal and ecological balances, and generate a hopeful posture toward the future.

The deficiencies of this post-Westphalia scenario are associated with a kind of reductionism, syndocheism, which substitutes a part for the whole. Undoubtedly, the impact of IT is significant, even crucial, but there is little prospect that it will overwhelm the structures and attitudes of modernity in the foreseeable future, rather than be mainly accommodated by them. Also, IT generates a dialectical response rather than merely a linear one, which leads to a variety of defensive strategies designed to maintain identity and

[31] For the most comprehensive account see Manuel Castels three volumes *The Rise of the Network Society*. See also Dery, 1996; Hall and Hughes, 1998; Paul and Cox, 1996; Robertson, 1998.

autonomy in the face of admitted global village tendencies that are regarded by most of the non-western world as hegemonic in intention and effect. Thus, regionalism, traditionalism, self-determination, collective rights, as well as international terrorism and transnational criminalisation, are among the reactions that inhibit the emergence of global village consciousness and arrangements.

There is in this scenario the possibility of a mutually reinforcing collaboration with the social forces associated with globalisation-from-above, but even so the resistance of an activated civil society, globalisation-from-below, seems capable of preventing the global village metaphor from becoming the defining reality of world order.[32]

The Post-Westphalia Prospect in the Early 21st Century
Noting the historical moment of lost opportunity

As the Cold War ended, the Soviet Union disintegrated, the world economy flourished, constitutional democracy was robust, there existed a historical moment of unprecedented opportunity to salvage the Westphalia legacy. Salvaging would have involved a mixture of initiatives designed to promote humane global governance: especially, demilitarisation, the build-up of UN peacekeeping capabilities, and a Marshall Plan for Africa. To seize the occasion, depended on American leadership, which was timid and ambivalent, retreating from any claim to promote what had earlier been called "liberal internationalism". Unlike the endings of the two world wars of the 20th century, the ending of the Cold War did not give rise to grassroots demands for global reform. Instead, the prevailing mood was complacent and foolishly optimistic about the future, triumphalist in response to the outcome of the East/West struggle, and economistic in its sense of what needed to be done to secure human wellbeing.

There was some recognition of the opportunities and challenges of the 1990s. George Bush in 1990–91 aroused interest and built support during the lead up to the Gulf War by constantly referring to the possibility of establishing "a new world order", by which he meant a functioning collective security process under UN auspices. Humanitarian diplomacy was also taken seriously in this period, both in relation to the protection of the Kurdish minority in Iraq, the response to the humanitarian catastrophe in

---

[32] The more normatively, less technocratically, grounded image of "global neighbourhood" seems similarly out of touch with the predatory elements of the main currents of globalisation in lethal interaction with neo-liberal ideas and hegemonic geopolitics. See the Commission on Global Governance, 1995; Falk, 1999a. I have preferred the terminology of "humane global governance" as goal and ideal, as well as potentiality, but without the implication that such a phrase is descriptive of current world order or the most probable future.

Somalia, and the effort to avoid ethnic cleansing in Bosnia. But for reasons too complicated to discuss here, disillusionment ensued, and the more promising implications of such initiatives never materialised. Among the more hopeful initiatives was the effort of Lloyd Axworthy, while Foreign Minister of Canada, to champion a shift from "national security" to "human security" as the basis for the role of the sovereign state, a conceptualisation earlier given currency in an annual volume of the Human Development Report. Instead, the United States led a return to Westphalia geopolitics in its narrower state-centric ethos, a backlash against the United Nations, and a primary reliance on the world economy to address problems of human suffering (including, poverty and the AIDS epidemic) and ecological sustainability.

The opportunity to initiate comprehensive negotiations to abolish nuclear weapons was not even seriously considered during this period, nor were proposals to establish a UN volunteer peacekeeping force that could respond to humanitarian catastrophes rapidly, without passing through the realist and nationalist filters of leading states. Such states were reluctant to bear the financial or human costs of a diplomacy that could not be validated by traditional criteria associated with national security and strategic overseas interests. (For example, to put the matter most starkly, oil is worth dying for, but the prevention of genocide is not, especially in a Third World setting.) As a result, the main deficiencies of Westphalia were preserved: the war system of global security and the vulnerability of the peoples of the world to various forms of oppressive governance.

Yet, the case for drastic global reform was being made in various arenas, and if not attainable within the Westphalia framework, then possibly its realisation could be achieved through the agency of transnational social forces and the emergence of post-Westphalia structures of governance. What was this case? What were these social forces? Essentially the plausibility of post-Westphalia perspectives involved the rise to high visibility of a multidimensional normative agenda: implementation of human rights, accountability for past crimes of state, abridgements of sovereignty, and the rise of humanitarian peacekeeping.

Beyond the agenda, there were steps taken to achieve institutionalisation: an increasingly willingness of national judicial bodies to apply international legal standards as relevant; greater reliance on multilateral approaches to global security, especially under the auspices of the United Nations; the impressive growth of regional governance, especially in Europe, with mandates to promote human rights, to sustain a social contract between citizens and market forces, and to facilitate trade and investment. Such goals by their nature could not be realised without compromising the internal autonomy of sovereign states, and this would not happen without the agency of political actors other than the state. In effect, drastic global reform, if it is to occur, will eventuate in a post-Westphalia scenario of transformed state structures and strengthened transnational, regional, and global formal and informal institutional procedures.[33]

Of these developments, the most currently promising is the campaign to promote cosmopolitan (or global) democracy and the various movements to build comprehensive regional frameworks for democracy, human rights, and political identity. If cumulatively effective, the impact will be to view the outcome as post-Westphalia: states become subject to external and internal standards of accountability, the Rule of Law, and the discipline of democratic practices. Regional institutions become vital actors that adhere to frameworks that ensure constitutionalism and collective wellbeing. World order is thus no longer state-centric, although the role of states remains crucial, even if reconfigured in light of legal and ethical norms.

The dusk of Westphalia can be best understood in relation to the setting sun of sovereignty and the rising sun of regional and global policy, rather than by supposing that the state itself will disappear, or will be marginalised.

The campaign for cosmopolitan democracy

Until recently, "pro-democracy" advocacy was understood to refer to ensuring that state/society relations provided electoral mechanisms to obtain the consent of the governed by way of periodic, free elections, and sufficient constitutionalism to protect citizens from governmental abuse. Democracy and democratic theory were essentially *internal* frameworks for domestic governance. The operation of international institutions and global arenas of decision, were from this perspective not treated as particularly relevant to the existence and establishment of democracy on a global scale. The annual assessments of "freedom" made by Freedom House presupposed that the state was the only significant unit of democratisation, and that human rights were only of the civil and political variety. The Kantian tradition of speculating about the global effects of the adoption of democracy at the level of the state is a purely Westphalia approach that does not regard regional and global arenas of authority as constitutionally or structurally relevant.

Cosmopolitan democracy theorises in a much more extensive manner. It regards democratic values as pertaining to all domains of life, although adjusted to reflect the particular setting. On the one side of everyday existence, democratic accountability and transparency extends its reach to the domain of gender and workplace relations, but also to the undertakings of governments themselves. No one is either above or below the law, which

---

[33] There are some complexities present, as strong states are needed to resist the predatory aspects of globalisation, and the transformation of the state would involve its greater responsiveness to normative demands, including the effort to commit a higher proportion of the national budget to the financing of global public goods. See generally Kaul, Grunberg, and Stern (eds.), 1999.

poses a mission impossible if directed at contemporary realities, given the radical inequalities that exist in relation to all dimensions of concern within the current system of world order, however labelled. On the other side, democratic participation, accountability, and transparency are to be extended to such international (regional and global) institutional settings as the United Nations, the IMF, the World Bank, the WTO, and the European Union. Such extensions of democracy blur the inside/outside red line of sovereignty associated with international boundaries as well as the public/private sector blue line of domestic governance, and as such challenge the equality/ inequality structure that has so far prevented equals from being treated equally in the implementation of international standards.

From Seattle to Pinochet, there is a multi-dimensional ferment that seeks democratic procedures of accountability, participation, and the Rule of Law in *all* arenas of decision that affect human wellbeing. In effect, the campaign for cosmopolitan democracy is closely associated with the establishment of a regime of representative governance associated with human security, but with the role of ultimate guardian of rights and responsibilities entrusted to the peoples of the world. The overall character of cosmopolitan democracy is a work-in-progress. We will not even be able to discern its contours for some decades to come, but it is an emergent reality, and it has become the unifying thread in the spectrum of undertakings associated with globalisation-from-below. Some illustrative initiatives can be briefly mentioned to convey the spirit of this campaign (see Archibugi and Held, 1995; Archibugi *et al.*, 1998)

But first, some cautionary words. Globalisation-from-below can be understood in at least two distinct ways: as the normative strivings associated with the various elements of the movement resisting globalisation-from-above, or as the general populist orientations of the political culture that is operative within the world at this point in history, and is segmented in terms of state, religion, ethnicity, and class. As the anti-globalisation demonstrations have confirmed, among the participants are violently disposed anarchists (the so-called "black blocs") and anti-technologists (often identified as Luddites or Neo-Luddites). Such orientations cannot contribute positively to the realisation of humane global governance even if they join the ranks of those most militantly opposed to the regressive implications of globalisation-from-above.

If one thinks more broadly about political culture in general, then there are grounds for growing concern, as both consumerism and militarism seem to enjoy strong majoritarian support in the richest and most influential countries. It is quite possible that if globalisation-from-below is identified with democratic preferences of society as a whole, then there exists little or no tension between governing elites and the citizenry, and that globalisation-from-above is entitled to claim legitimation according to standard criteria of the consent of the people. But such an acceptance by majoritarian consent is not enough to ensure legitimacy, given the militancy of opposition, even if this opposition is acknowledged to be a minority.

In this chapter, globalisation-from-below is used in the narrower, normative sense of dissenting from the neo-liberal ideology and practices associated with corporate globalisation, but not necessarily from the application of technology to productive processes so as to achieve economic growth and a variety of social gains in such areas as health and education. The anti-globalisation movement that is challenging the legitimacy of globalisation-from-above in its current form, puts its main stress on failures to distribute the gains of economic growth among the peoples of the world on an equitable basis and in greater accordance with human needs. The movement also is directed at the failure to provide democratic oversight with respect to the operation of global market forces, as well as its tendency to bypass global public goods such as environmental protection and the operations of international institutions.

The following projects promoted by the anti-globalisation movement are illustrative of a commitment to humane global governance, but are selective in the sense of both rejecting violence as a means and accepting the contributions of technological innovations to the making of a better world.

(1)International Criminal Court. The Rome Treaty of 1998 calls for the establishment of an international criminal court once sixty countries have deposited instruments of ratification with the United Nations. Both the process and the outcome are essential building blocks for a global democratic framework premised on the Rule of Law, extending even to those who exercise pre-eminent political and military authority on behalf of sovereign states. The process by which this treaty is becoming law was decisively facilitated by a coalition of civil society actors that pushed governments and collaborated with those governments seeking to reach a similar goal. In other words, the very act of establishment embodied "a new internationalism" that can be viewed as a Westphalia hybrid, combining transnational civil society activism with traditional state actors to reach a very non-Westphalia result. The outcome represents a great victory for the ethos of accountability, making those who use governmental power abusively to face the possibility of being held criminally accountable for their misdeeds, as measured by accepted *international* standards relating to human rights, crimes against humanity, and international humanitarian law. The detention of Pinochet, the indictment of Milosevic by the International Criminal Tribunal for the former Yugoslavia, the recent discussion of the indictability of Henry Kissinger, Ariel Sharon, and Saddam Hussein, as well as the recent litigation associated with World War II slave labour and comfort women are suggestive of a broader trend toward accountability (Bass, 2000; Minow, 1998; Barkan, 2000).

Of course, the accountability breakthrough, also discussed in relation to a backlash against "the culture of impunity" should not be exaggerated. The

Rome Treaty contains many important concessions to Westphalia conceptions, including deference to the primacy of national criminal authority and a major role for the UN Security Council in authorising or prohibiting prosecution, which gives several of the leading geopolitical actors an extensive veto. Such states are likely to remain outside the ICC legal regime for the foreseeable future. But the existence of a permanent international criminal court is a reminder to the representatives of state power that their officials are not above international law, even in the manner with which they treat their own citizens. The refusal to implement its authority in a consistent manner will also provide civil society, especially in liberal democracies, with a powerful instrument by which to challenge the legitimacy of government and of specific official conduct. Also, complementary mechanisms of accountability are likely to be emboldened. Especially domestic courts will be more encouraged than ever to conceive of themselves as agents of the international legal order with respect to crimes of state. Post-Pinochet discussion of these issues is already indicative of a trend toward international accountability, although there are also sceptical responses to these developments.[34]

In critical discussions mention is being made of the stark unevenness of implementation due to the power realities of world politics that is certain to damage the overall credibility of these law-based efforts to impose accountability on political leaders for their official acts. A second line of criticism stresses the degree to which the pursuit of leaders currently holding office can disrupt diplomacy if impartially applied to those charged with violating basic international legal standards, and the related importance of retaining the idea of sovereign immunity for heads of state. And yet, shielding leaders charged with flagrant Crimes Against Humanity seems to relegate the whole effort to impose individual accountability to the marginal role of rectifying past abuses only. As such, the project of establishing an ICC can be understood as a modest and symbolic step toward imposing the rule of law on heads of state, but leaving much work to be done if the process is to achieve the goal of treating equals equally

(2) A Global Peoples Assembly. The articulation of the agenda of global civil society as the foundation for cosmopolitan democracy has encountered great difficulties given the degree to which *representation* of interests and values takes place within a Westphalia structure that, with increasingly apparent artificiality, confers membership only on states. Transnational social forces and civil society actors have been trying to find spaces within this

---

[34] Guidelines for national courts to proceed with the indictment and prosecution of individuals accused of crimes against humanity, genocide, and other serious crimes of state are contained in *The Princeton Principles on Universal Jurisdiction*, brochure published by Program in Law and Public Affairs, Princeton University, 2001. The Princeton Principles are the product of discussion and analysis by a group of international law specialists and practitioners.

structure that allow some expression of views that are not statist in character. Among the most effective of these improvisations was the establishing of a strong presence at major conferences held under United Nations auspices on global policy issues such as environment, women, population, and social wellbeing. The media increasingly acknowledged such people-oriented perspectives. Their agitation was welcomed by some governments seeking to increase their own impact on the plan of action and declaratory documents that come at the end of such proceedings.

This process of participation reached a climax in a series of such conferences in the early 1990s, and suggested the vitality of these exploratory moves in the direction of accommodating the demands of cosmopolitan democrats. Such a dynamic was so successful from this democratising perspective that it generated a statist backlash designed to close off such avenues of populist participation. Leading states defended their turf with such lame arguments as the waste of money associated with UN conferences that were derided as "talkfests" and "spectacles". Earlier, these same governments welcomed civil society participation, mainly because of their expected co-opting effect on grassroots criticism, hopefully making these actors part of the process as a way of muting their opposition. But this governmental effort was frustrated by the militancy and effectiveness of these transnational civic presences that were clear about their goals. As a result, this avenue of societal participation has been closed off, at least for the present.

An alternative line of participation that has emerged late in the 1990s has been more militant, taking the form of protest demonstrations in the streets of cities that are the scene of high-visibility inter-governmental meetings concerned with the functioning of the world economy. These demonstrations have been particularly directed at the institutional manifestations of corporate globalisation, and have occurred in relation to meetings of the WTO, the IMF, and the World Bank, as well as such occasions fashioned by market forces, as the meetings of the G8 and Davos annual sessions of the World Economic Forum. Such expressions of resistance have been effective in stimulating a debate about the shortcomings of globalisation, including its regressive distributive patterns and the anti-democratic operating modalities of its institutional support structure. The result has been calls for more participation and transparency, as well as a demand that social and equity concerns of a distributive character be given weight, alongside the priority accorded trade expansion and capital efficiency.

Yet, the *ad hoc* character of demonstrations and activism as methods of achieving participation and influence are not satisfactory in any sustained way. The calls for reform are often misunderstood by most of the public and misrepresented in the media, and are easily deflected because of their episodic expression, the focus on encounters with the police, and the inevitable incoherence of objectives among the demonstrators with diverse, even antagonistic, agendas.

Instead of concentrating on the substantive issues at stake, the media, especially TV, treat these events as actual or potential spectacles of violence, despite the fact that over ninety percent of the demonstrators themselves reject violence as a tactic and seek to express their militancy by symbolic and persuasive means alone. Focusing on the violence also allows the governmental and business/finance elites to deflect criticism, and to concentrate on arranging their future meetings in a manner that poses obstacles for those organising popular demonstrations. One idea being considered by G8 leaders, after the explosive 2001 Genoa G8 and Gothenburg European Union meetings, is to hold future meetings in remote rural settings that can be more easily sealed off from demonstrators and media.

What these populist efforts to penetrate the Westphalia edifice in its globalisation phase disclose, is the need for some more durable and institutionalised form of participatory opportunity for the voices of civil society. It would seem beneficial to establish a parliamentary organ representative of the peoples of the world as a constructive step at this stage, preferably taken within the formal UN System, but not necessarily so. There are many complexities and obstacles associated with the establishment, operations, and funding of such a parliament or assembly.[35] These can be overcome in practice. The experience over time of the European Parliament (EP) is inspirational in this regard. As with the proposal for a Global Peoples Assembly (GPA), the EP too was dismissed for decades as frivolous. Only recently has the EP taken its place as a vital element in the overall structure of the European Union, and assumed the role of being the indispensable guarantor of its democratic commitment to the peoples of Europe. The legitimacy of the EU evolution is certainly helped by having a functioning parliamentary organ of governance.

A more substantive confirmation of the value of this recommended initiative has been demonstrated by the experience of the Assembly of the Peoples of the United Nations organised on a grassroots basis and held every second year in Perugia during the last decade. Delegates come from many countries, financed by Italian urban communities, and engage in discussion of salient global and local issues for several days, then make a dramatic march of solidarity to the nearby spiritually renowned town of Assisi. While the selection of delegates is presently unsystematic and there is a certain chaotic quality pertaining to the mode of discussion and recommendations, there is an exciting and compelling quality about the establishment and conduct of such a forum. A significantly different discourse emerges from that associated with meetings of inter-governmental and economistic elites, with a strikingly distinct hierarchy of priorities and expectations.

---

[35] The case for a Global Peoples Assembly is elaborated by Falk and Strauss, 2000; Falk and Strauss, 2001.

In this sense a GPA would, at the very least, help fashion a creative tension between the perspectives associated with corporate globalisation and those emanating from the various elements composing globalisation-from-below, including those of reactionary character. As with any expression of democratic sentiment, there can be no guaranty that the forms taken by the process will be substantively beneficial. There are risks and uncertainties, but the whole movement of progressive politics since the French Revolution has been to endow the people as citizens with increasing authority in shaping the dynamics of governance. An experiment with some type of GPA should be thought about in this spirit.

(3) *The International Rule of Law.* A positive post-Westphalia world order would upgrade the role of law in structuring relations among participants in international life, thereby diminishing the influence of unequal power, wealth, and capabilities. It would also provide for far greater reliance on third-party procedures for dispute settlement and conflict resolution. The spread of international tribunals in such specialised areas as trade, oceans, and human rights is already suggestive of a trend in this direction that partly reflects growing normativity. So far these innovations are, however, best understood as mere functional adjustments to growing complexity and interactivity. Such tendencies toward legalisation should not be overstated, but at the same time impressive and unanticipated outcomes can arise from humble beginnings.[36] The relevance of geopolitics and militarism is almost certain to remain central to the structuring of security policy as pursued by leading states for the next decade or so. Although even here the resonance of the global security discourse is suggestive of discomfort with the old paradigmatic enclosures based on national security.

Achieving Humane Regionalism[37]

In important respects, the Westphalia world order was a European regional system for most of its operative period, gradually developing a global outreach that attained its climax in the colonial era. Indeed, the regionality of world order began its decline after World War I, with the rise of the United States and Russia to positions of prominence and influence that eclipsed Europe after World War II. This type of Eurocentric regionality lost almost all of its relevance as a description of the overall Westphalia reality with the collapse of colonialism, the emergence of Japan as an Asian financial super-power, and the more recent pronounced rise of China as a world power.

---

[36] See symposium on these themes under the rubric of "Legalization and World Politics", edited by Judith Goldstein, Miles Kahler, Robert O. Keohane, and Ann-Marie Slaughter in *International Organization*, vol. 54, no. 3, esp. introduction by editors, 385–389.

[37] My thinking here is influenced by Björn Hettne, especially Hettne, 1999.

The universality of statist participation in the United Nations, as well as constitutive rules that make membership an exclusive prerogative of states, embodies the formal idea of a Westphalia world.

The erosion of this world has been increasingly acknowledged by the current Secretary General, Kofi Annan, who has associated his leadership of the UN with the central idea of enlisting in the Organisation the meaningful participation of corporate and civil society actors, and arguing that only by weakening its statist character can the UN hope to retain its relevance to a globalising world order. Significantly, by appealing to global civil society and to global market forces, Annan has understated the relevance of regional actors to the sort of neo-Westphalia United Nations that he seems to be intent upon crafting during his period of tenure. Perhaps, this is less an oversight than a recognition that regionalism is such an uneven force in human affairs at this time if region to region realities are taken into account. But is such regional unevenness greater than the disparities that exist among states, or in relation to the leverage of civil society or business/finance actors?

Without question, the boldest, most successful international institution-building process has taken place over the last five decades, within the European setting, eclipsing in important respects both the growth of the United Nations System and that of Global Economic Governance (the combined operations of the IMF, the World Bank, and the WTO, as co-ordinated with treasury officials of leading economies).[38] Such a process has the intriguing feature of arising from the relation among the states that generated and dominated most of the Westphalia era, inventing and structuring Eurocentric patterns of ideological, political, economic, and cultural control. Indeed, their loss of dominance due to the results of two world wars, the weakening and collapse of overseas empires, the overshadowing power of the United States and Russia, and the self-destructive bloodshed of intra-European cycles of warfare, were among the factors that led several notable European visionaries to embrace the regional idea in its more modest and literal form as integrative for Europe and as a hedge against war-making.

The initial benefits of European regionalism were perceived in mainly intra-regional terms as post-war reconstruction and as a mean to weaken inter-state rivalries that had led to the recurrence of large-scale destructive wars. More recently, this European embrace has also been advocated as a way of both competing with and resisting the adverse impacts of economic and cultural globalisation. It has proceeded so far as to give rise to various analogies to state-building precursors and to anticipations of an emergent European polity operating within a constitutional framework, engendering loyalty and political identity.

[38] For elaboration of this point see Falk, 2001b.

The outcome in Europe and its wider relationships to other regionalisms remains uncertain, and is likely to remain so for several more decades. Nevertheless, to the extent that European regionalism is perceived elsewhere as a success, it is likely to be replicated, although with dramatic adjustments taking account of the particularities of culture, geography, stage of development, styles of governance, and policy priorities. Regionalism presupposes the will and capacity of states to engage cooperatively, thus involving some minimum degree of mutual respect and perception of equal benefits and burdens. With the spread of human rights and democratic forms of governance, these preconditions are being met. Also, with globalisation being perceived as posing a threat to cultural identity and as a vehicle for Westernisation (and even Americanisation), regionalism presents itself as a line of defence.

It aggregates the capabilities of distinct states engaged in bilateral relations, and in collective efforts to insulate such civilisational groupings from unwanted extra-regional encroachments. The assertive side of regionalism posits "Asian values" or Islam as transnational bonding that validates and intensifies regional claims of identity, and underpins calls for a dialogue of civilisations. From a hegemonic perspective such regionalism is seen as antagonistic, leading to a "clash of civilisations" and an era of "culture wars". Beyond these differing lines of interpretation, regionalist understandings move beyond Westphalia categories by positing the significance and potentialities of non-statist criteria as essential to the construction of our image of world order. Their prominence is itself evidence of a post-Westphalia emergence.

However, as Hettne helpfully suggests, drawing on Polanyi, part of the regionalist impulse needs to be seen in the historical shadow being cast by globalisation. Especially its weakening of the territorial autonomy of the state, and diminished social expectations relating to the capacity of the state to promote the wellbeing of its own citizenry. This internationalisation of the state, converting it primarily into a non-territorial instrument facilitating the expansion of the world market, gives rise to an effort to recover a territorial base for autonomous action that can better relate governance to people. Regionalism in Europe, and even in Asia and Latin America, is achieving and may in the future achieve more impressive results. And in more extreme settings of Africa and the Caribbean, even without the juggernaut of globalisation, regionalism offers some aggregation of influence to mitigate the extreme weakness of the states constituting "the region".

Yet regionalism is not unconditionally beneficial. It could be the prelude to the establishment of enclaves of reaction in the world that reject the universalising influence of the human rights discourse. Such possibilities definitely seem to cast a shadow over Asian regionalism, which in other respects seems promising. But the insulation of China from criticism, the "constructive engagement" of Burma, and the opposition to UN efforts to mount justifiable humanitarian interventions as in the Balkans, suggests that regionalism can operate in a reactionary manner with respect to the pursuit of normative goals.

Regionalism may produce new dangerous forms of conflict, and withdraw energies and resources from the United Nations system. It may also excuse the richer countries from duties toward poorer regions that are experiencing a variety of humanitarian catastrophes, particularly Africa. As such, regionalism works against the sort of human solidarity needed to take on such global challenges as global warming, ocean pollution, and the militarisation of space.

It should be appreciated that the linear growth of regionalism, even in Europe, cannot be assumed. A reversible of trends is quite possible, particularly if the world economy performs poorly, if regionalisation does not seem to benefit a particular country, and if nationalistic sentiments grow stronger as a backlash to immigration and other unwanted developments attributable to regionalism and globalisation. In this regard, it may be too soon to dismiss the possibility of a return to a more decidedly Westphalia framework, even within the wider context of globalisation which, unlike regionalism, does not seem reversible. There are presently indications that in Europe, regionalism is far more popular among elites than with the citizenry of the respective countries. European regionalism will be tested in the years ahead by the ambitious monetary innovations, especially the replacement of national currencies by the Euro. If this succeeds, it is likely to provide the foundation for strengthening other dimensions of European regionalism, and of influencing non-European regionalisms to move ahead. However, if it fails, the dampening effect in Europe and elsewhere could be quite dramatic.

Europe currently offers the best arena within which to assess the historical and normative relevance of regionalism as a post-Westphalia enhancement of world order. The protection of human rights, the provision of safety nets to address issues of poverty and unemployment, the sense of ethnic autonomy for minorities that displaces their secessionist demands, the mobility of labour as more comparable to the mobility of capital, the formation of a citizenry that is multi-ethnic, multi-national while retaining its statist and nationalist bonds of primary affiliation, and a prosperous peace system – are among the yardsticks by which to assess whether Europe lives up to its promise, or even exceeds what it now seems to be.

A Concluding Note

A definite post-Westphalia scenario is not likely to take shape within the next decade or so. Hence, the contours of a new emergent world order are not likely to change dramatically as the structure and dynamics of globalisation evolve in the years ahead. The global setting is very unstable due to the impact of dramatic technological shifts and the volatility of market forces in an under-regulated world economy. In this regard, the immediate situation calls upon us to acknowledge the double reality of a neo-Westphalia world order of the sort described above, and of a more distant emergent post-Westphalia world order that could move in either positive or negative directions (as appraised from the perspective of humane global governance). What seems least likely is for the classical framing of international relations in Westphalia terms to be regarded as satisfactory in either policymaking or academic circles.

The pace and direction of transition to a post-Westphalia world will depend upon many factors: the degree to which elites can legitimise globalisation-from-above, the extent to which the anti-globalisation movement can collaborate with governmental forces that are dissatisfied with the manner in which the world economy is functioning, the creativity of reformist and transformative politics within regional and global arenas, and the extent to which the state can demonstrate its problem-solving competence in response to a variety of global challenges (global warming, transnational crime, genocide, illegal immigration and refugees).

The agents of positive change are in the process of formation. There are in the background the well-established transnational NGOs that have been active and effective with respect to human rights (especially on civil liberties, racial discrimination, and gender issues) and the environment. In the foreground are more amorphous civil society actors that have been on the front lines of the struggle against various manifestations of corporate globalisation – whether in local efforts to oppose large dams or with respect to global policymaking arenas, such as the gathering points for the G8 or the World Economic Forum. The potency and impact of this activism cannot now be discerned in any very clear way. The success of these efforts will largely depend on the ability to form collaborative and durable relationships with those governments that share a commitment to the establishment of humane global governance. It will also depend on the capacity to shape a consensus in global civil society that is dedicated to democratisation and the repudiation of tactical violence.

What seems likely to persist in various formats is the struggle to deepen and extend democratic practices and procedures. This struggle is likely to consist of a series of rather divergent regional and global initiatives, and experiments involving the specific interplay of state, market, region, and world. These divergencies will reflect varying cultural circumstances that are freighted with a range of historical memories, and increasingly agitated by a revival of religious influence in different guises that are often closely linked to nationalist and civilisational revivalism. Also of importance are the perceived impacts of environmental tendencies and technological breakthroughs, especially with respect to the adequacy of prevailing regulatory frameworks to protect short and intermediate term human health and wellbeing, and with respect to identifying the limiting conditions of humanity (cloning, robots).

The conclusion reached here is that Westphalia modes of regulatory authority are already insufficient and will turn out to be more so in the future, but that Westphalia resistance to adjustments by the leading centres of state power will remain formidable, blocking creative innovations. In the face of this reality, the movement for humane global governance (the preferred post-Westphalia scenario) is likely to grow stronger. It may, however, be inclined to aim for and accept neo-Westphalia modifications of statism that realise the normative (ethical and legal) potential of a statist world. This reformist prospect will in turn be strengthened and guided by the existence of a lively and plausible, if visionary, understanding of a post-Westphalia architecture constructed by reference to the premises of humane global governance. Indeed, such world order inconclusiveness is an insignia of this era!

References

Alderson, K. and A. Hurrell (eds.), 2000, *Hedley Bull on International Society*, New York: St. Martin's Press.

Archibugi, D. and D. Held (eds.), 1995, *Cosmopolitan Democracy: An Agenda for a New World Order*, Cambridge, UK: Polity.

Archibugi, D., Held, D. and M. Köhler (eds.), 1998, *Re-imagining Political Community: Studies in Cosmopolitan Democracy*, Cambridge, UK: Polity.

Aron, R., 1966, *Peace and War: A Theory of International Relations*, London, UK: Weidenfeld & Nicolson.

Barkan, E., 2000, *The Guilt of Nations: Restitution and Negotiating Historical Injustices*, New York: Norton.

Barnet, R.J. and J. Cavanagh, 1994, *Global Dreams: Imperial Corporations and the New World Order*, New York: Simon & Schuster.

Barzun, J., 2000, *From Dawn to Decadence: 1500 to the Present*, New York: HarperCollins.

Bass, G., 2000, *To Stay the Hand of Vengeance*, Princeton, NJ: Princeton University Press.

Booth, K., "Human Wrongs and International Relations", *Journal of International Affairs*, vol. 71, 1995, pp. 103–26.

Braudel, F., 1980, *On History*, Chicago: University of Chicago Press.

Bull, H., 1966, "The Grotian Conception of International Society", in Butterfield, H. and M. Wight (eds.), *Diplomatic Investigations*, London: Butterworths.

Bull, H., 1995, *The Anarchical Society: A Study of Order in World Politics*, London, UK: Macmillan.

Bull, H., "Hobbes and the International Anarchy", reprinted in Alderson, K. and A. Hurrell (eds.), 2000, *Hedley Bull on International Society*, New York: St. Martin's Press.

Camilleri, J.A. and J. Falk, 1992, *The End of Sovereignty? The Politics of a Shrinking and Fragmenting World*, Hants, UK: Edward Elgar.

Castels, M., 1996–98, 3 vols., *The Rise of the Network Society*, Oxford, UK: Blackwell.

Clark, G. and L.B. Sohn, 1966, *World Peace Through World Law*, third ed., Cambridge, MA: Harvard University Press.

Commission on Global Governance, 1995, *Our Global Neighborhood*, New York: Oxford University Press.

Cox, R.W. with T. J. Sinclair, 1996, *Approaches to World Order*, Cambridge, UK: Cambridge University Press.

Cooper, G., 2001, "U.S. Memos Reveal Delay on Rwanda", *Washington Post*, August 8, A20.

Daly, H.E. and J.B. Cobb Jr., 1989, *For the Common Good: Redirecting the Economy Toward Community, the Environment, and a Sustainable Future*, Boston: Beacon.

Dery, M., 1996, *Escape Velocity: Cyberculture at the End of the Century*, London, UK: Hodder & Stoughton.

Danspreckgruber W. with A. Watts (eds.), 1997, *Self-Dermination and Self-Administration: A Sourcebook*, Boulder, CO: Lynne Rienner.

Dunne, T. and N.J. Wheeler (eds.), 1999, *Human Rights in Global Politics*, Cambridge, UK: Cambridge University Press.

Falk, R., 1993, "The Making of Global Citizenship", in Brecher, J., Childs, J.B. and J. Cutler (eds.), *Global Visions: Beyond the New World Order*, Boston: South End Press.

Falk, R., 1997a, "The critical realist tradition and the demystification of interstate power", in Gill, S. and J. H. Mittelman (eds.), *Innovation and Transformation in International Studies*, Cambridge, UK: Cambridge University Press.

Falk, R., 1997b, "State of Seige: will globalization win out?", *International Affairs*, vol. 73, no. 1, pp. 123–36.

Falk, R, 1999a, *Predatory Globalization: A Critique*, Cambridge, UK: Polity.

Falk, R., 1999b, *Law in an Emerging Global Village*, Ardsley, NY: Transnational, NY.

Falk R. and A. Strauss, 2000, "On the Creation of a Global Peoples Assembly: Legitimacy and the Power of Popular Sovereignty", *Stanford Journal of International Law*, vol. 36, no. 2, pp. 191–219.

Falk, R. and A. Strauss, 2001, "Toward Global Parliament", *Foreign Affairs*, vol. 80, no. 1, pp. 212–20.

Falk, R., 2001a, *Religion and Humane Global Governace*, New York: Palgrave.

Falk, R., 2001b, "Meeting the Challenge of Multilateralism", in Henriksen, T.H. (ed.), *Foreign Policy for America in the Twenty-first Century: Alternative Perspectives*, Stanford, CA: Hoover Institution Press.

Gilpin, R., 1981, *War and Change in World Politics*, Cambridge, UK: Cambridge University Press.

Goldstein, J., Kahler, M., Keohane, R.O. and A. Slaughter, 2000, "Legalization and World Politics", *International Organization*, vol. 54, no. 3, pp. 385–389.

Hall, K.A. and J.E. Hughes, 1998, *Cyberpolitics: Citizen Activism in the Age of the Internet*, Lanham, MD: Rowman & Littlefield.

Hashmi, S.H. (ed.), 1997, *State Sovereignty: Change and Persistence in International Relations*, University Park, PA: Penn State University Press.

Hemleben, S.J., 1943, *Plans for Peace Through Six Centuries*, Chicago: University of Chicago.

Hettne, B., 1999, "Globalisation and the New Regionalism: The Second Great Transformation", in Hettne, B., Inotai, A. and O. Sunkel (eds.), *Globalism and the New Regionalism*, New York: St. Martin's.

Huntington, S.P., 1996, *The Clash of Civilizations and the Remaking of World Order*, New York: Simon & Schuster.

Jackson, R., 2000, *The Global Covenant: Human Conduct in a World of States*, Oxford, UK: Oxford University Press.

Kaul, I., Grunberg, I. and M.A. Stern (eds.), 1999, *Global Public Goods: International Cooperation in the 21st Century*, New York: Oxford University Press.

Kissinger, H., 1994, *Diplomacy*, New York: Simon & Schuster.

Kly, Y.N. and D. Kly (eds.), 2000, *The Right to Self-Determination*, Collected Papers & Proceedings of the First International Conference on the Right to Self-Determination & the United Nations, Geneva, Atlanta, GA: Clarity Press.

Knock, T.J., 1992, *To End All Wars: Woodrow Wilson and the Quest for a New World Order*, New York: Oxford University Press.

Korten, D., 1995, *When Corporations Rule the World*, London: Earthscan

Krasner, S.D., 1999, *Sovereignty: Organized Hypocrisy*, Princeton, NJ: Princeton University Press.

Lodal, J., 2001, *The Price of Dominance*, New York: The Council on Foreign Relations.

Lyons, G. and M. Mastanduno (eds.), 1995, *Beyond Westphalia? State Sovereignty and International Intervention*, Baltimore, MD: Johns Hopkins University Press.

Malvern, L.R., 2000, *A People Betrayed: The Role of the West in Rwanda's Genocide*, London, UK: Zed.

McNeill, W.H., 1963, *The Rise of the West: A History of the Human Community*, Chicago: University of Chicago Press.

Mendlovitz, S.H. (ed.), 1975, *On the Creation of a Just World Order*, New York: Free Press.

Minow, M., 1998, *Between Vengeance and Forgiveness*, Boston: Beacon.

Mozaffari, M., 1999, *Mega Civilization: Global Capital and New Standard of Civilization*, Aarhus, Denmark: Aarhus University.

O'Hagen, J., 2000, "Conflict, Convergence or Co-existence? The Relevance of Culture in Reframing World Order", *Transnational Law & Contemporary Problems*, vol. 9, no. 2, pp. 537–67.

Paul, G.S. and E.D. Cox, 1996, *Beyond Humanity: CyberEvolution and Future Minds*, Rockland, MA: Charles River Media.

Rieff, D., 1995, *Slaughterhouse*, New York: Simon & Schuster.

Risse-Kappen, T. (ed.), 1995, *Bringing Transnational Relations Back In: Non-State Actors, Domestic Structures, and International Institutions*, Cambridge, UK: Cambridge University Press.

Robertson, D.S., 1998, *The New Renaissance: Computers and the Next Level of Civilization*, Oxford, UK: Oxford University Press.

Said, E., 1993, *Culture and Imperialism*, New York: Knopf.

Schell, J., 1982, *The Fate of the Earth*, New York: Knopf.

Spengler, O., 1926–28, *Decline of the West*, New York: Knopf.

Spruyt, H., 1994, *The Sovereign State and Its Competitors*, Princeton, NJ: Princeton University Press.

The Princeton Principles on Universal Jurisdiction, brochure published by the Program in Law and Public Affairs, Princeton University, 2001.

Toynbee, A., 1934–61, 12 vols., *A Study of History*, Oxford, UK: Oxford University Press.

Waltz, K., 1979, *Theory of International Politics*, New York: McGraw-Hill.

Yunker, J.A., 1993, *World Union on the Horizon*, Lanham, MD: University Press of America.

Wooley, W.T., 1968, *Alternatives to Anarchy: American Supranationalism Since World War II*, Bloomington, IN: Indiana University Press.

6. Alternative Forms of International Governance and Development Cooperation

Bertil Odén

What are the implications for development cooperation of the various forms of governance that are formulated in the four paradigmatic chapters? As can be expected, the conflict-development nexus differs strongly, depending on the features of the globalisation process that are focused upon. This was also the intention when commissioning the studies. Slightly surprising is that some common features can also be identified when comparing them, despite their differing points of departure.

The Future of Westphalia

Some more extreme scenarios on the effects of globalisation tend to focus on the eradication of the state as a major actor, either due to the total triumph of market forces, (e.g. Ohmae, 1995) or due to the effects of uncontrolled conflicts (e.g. Kaplan, 1994). They can be considered as the extremes of the category of *hyper-globalists* (McGrew, 1998). According to McGrew, for this category

> economic globalization is associated with the de-nationalization of economies as a consequence of the transnationalization of networks of production, trade and finance. In this 'borderless' global economy national governments are relegated to little more than transmission belts for global capitalism or alternatively catalysts for nurturing mechanisms of governance at the local, regional and global levels more compatible with the logic of global marketplace (pp. 9–10).

The four forms of governance in this book distance themselves from such predictions. Even Richard Falk, who provides the main discussion on the post-Westphalia perspective, opposes the idea of the end of the state, insisting that the state and statecraft are sufficiently robust and resilient to remain essential features of any non-utopian form of post-Westphalia world order. Instead he argues that "Westphalia frames for international reality no longer generate confidence, but globalisation as another framing is too vague and uncrystalized to be a serious candidate for replacement." Therefore a post-Westphalia world is not yet a reality.

The multilateral world order, with its hybrid forms of governance is based on active states, even though they have to share the influence of governance with other actors. These states have significant power to reform international institutions and provide governance at regional or global level, even when they have a compact with the private sector or invite civil society organisations into the process.

In the Liberal Globalist Case, explored by Indra de Soysa and Nils Petter Gleditsch, one main focus is the global economy's creation of stronger interdependence between states through trade and investment. De Soysa and Gleditsch argue that it is a mistake to talk in terms of states versus markets. Instead the question is one of the degree to which the state is involved in governing the economic life of its citizens. International institutional frameworks have to be created by states and a national economic environment conducive to trade and investment can only be provided by states. States are therefore crucial actors for the creation of a more integrated world economy. This increased interdependence in turn reduces the risk for armed conflicts.

The multilateral and plurilateral perspective, provided by Raimo Väyrynen, is by definition strongly based on states as crucial actors. In this model there is a strong belief in the power of legislation, agreements and other regulatory approaches which define the limits of what is permitted. Once the rules have been established, the state has the primary responsibility to monitor that they are followed and enforced in the case of non-compliance.

Mark Duffield argues that if the notion of durable disorder can be reprised, "ideas of state enfeeblement and paralysis do not take us very far". Globalisation processes do not erode "metropolitan" states. Durable disorder arises not out of paralysis of these states, but from their will to govern, now with aid as the main instrument. However, Duffield points out that this is difficult, as the translation of central calculations into actions in the borderlands is problematic, due to the multiplicity of private actors that intervene in the process.

The authors of the four chapters thus agree that the state will not vanish or disintegrate. They also agree that the role of the state will change and the scope for governance at nation state level will change substantially, as other actors become increasingly involved in governance at various levels, from the local to the global. However, they differ in their discussions on whether the forces of change will be strong enough to transform the world order into something that best could be labelled *post-Westphalia* or *neo-Westphalia*. In this chapter we will focus on the implications for the role, scope and mode of relations between the North and the South that may follow from the different perspectives in the previous four chapters, with particular emphasis on development cooperation.

The Meanings of Globalisation

The concept of globalisation cannot be very rigorously defined, when the contributors have as different perspectives as those in this volume. Therefore the editors did not attempt to provide a common definition to be used by all authors. Some further comments on the issue, related to the discussions in the previous chapters, should however be added. As Hettne points out in the introduction, globalisation can in many respects be seen as a long-term historical process, but at the same time it is qualitatively new, due to new information and communication technologies and a new organisational logic. Globalisation in economic terms and in its current form can be conceived as a further deepening and expansion of the market system, a continuation of the Great Transformation, i.e. the 19th century market expansion, disrupting traditional society and provoking various kinds of political interventionism. This time the process of market expansion, including its social repercussions, takes place on a truly global scale.

This stress on the relative novelty of the present forms of globalisation can be related to a recent article by James Rosenau, in which he listed various types of transformative dynamics:

> Among the most powerful of these dynamics are the microelectronic revolution that has facilitated the rapid flow of ideas, information, pictures and money across continents, the transportation revolution that has hastened the boundary-spanning flow of elites, tourists, immigrants (legal and illegal), migrants and whole populations, the organisational revolution that has shifted the flow of authority, influence and power beyond traditional boundaries, and the economic revolution that has redirected the flow of goods, services, capital and ownership among countries (Rosenau, 1998: 37).

The balance between these factors differs according to the authors, depending on their perspective

Arguing the liberal globalist case, de Soysa and Gleditsch have as their point of departure that globalisation is generally understood as a process of economic, political and social integration of states and societies, both horizontally and vertically, in tighter webs of interdependence. Globalisation is a process and not a qualitatively different end state, where the state has receded and the market has taken over. Integration of nation states in the global economy is currently taking place via at least two major visible and measurable processes – the rapid spread of foreign capital and trade, and the spread of the ideas of political democracy and market economy to an extent never before witnessed in modern history.

To Duffield the open market as the archetypal self-regulating process is at the heart of the liberal interpretation of globalisation, which dominates the international discussion. To him the paradox of globalisation is not that deregulated markets produce poverty and disorder for some at the same time as creating wealth and stability for others; because this is the propensity, which has made it possible for capitalism to reform itself for two hundred years. The paradox of liberal globalisation is that instead of more effective and self-adjusting powers of regulation, the reforms and institutions necessary for its existence appear to be creating the conditions for widening systems of autonomy and resistance. This process does not however result from state enfeeblement. Instead it is the result of the collateral effects of innovative response and engagement of metropolitan states in the face of non-conventional security threats. This also requires an expansion in the field of diplomacy and negotiations.

Väyrynen emphasises that historically the rise of the nation state and capitalism has taken place in tandem. When the expansion of global capitalism took place later, this economic globalisation emerged under the auspices of the leading power of the system. This is not sufficient, however. The stability of a globalised economy requires the extension of political institutions and norms to the transnational level. There is, however, significant concentration on state-centric strategies of global governance.

The problem of "stateness" is complicated already in the industrialised countries and further so in developing countries, of which only a few have an adequate record of political stability and sustained economic development. Global governance in this context is a new mode of problem-solving cooperation between private economic interests and public politics to cope with new challenges. This new mode of national, but increasingly private-public relationship is constantly challenged by social non-state actors, who tend to consider it detrimental to democracy, equity, and other social values.

Falk suggests that the minimum content of globalisation involves the compression of time and space on a planetary scale. Other aspects include the intensification of cross-border interactivity, the transnational penetration of territorial space, the effects of IT on global business operations, the dissemination of a consensual view of political legitimacy based on market liberalism and elective constitutionalism, and the rise of global market forces. Such a presentation of globalisation emphasises its linear character as a sequel to a more state-centric war-oriented phase of international history.

According to Falk, this prevailing account of globalisation misses some critical aspects of the new reality, especially the challenge being mounted by transnational social forces to the alleged adverse impacts of globalisation: rapidly increasing inequalities at the level of society, state and region; the social disempowerment of the state; and the decline in support for public goods at all levels of social interaction.

Implications for Governance at Various Levels

It seems as if the authors of this volume share one opinion regarding the impact on governance of the various forces of globalisation. This is the reduced impact of homogeneous and territorial authorities and the increased impact of de-territorialised, heterogeneous collectivities, based on a multiplicity of rule systems in a world that in some areas becomes more multi-centric. This can be seen as a challenge to democracy, but not necessarily. It is certainly a challenge to some democratic institutions at the nation state level, as e.g. Rosenau points out in a rather sinister way:

> the world's territorial politicians may increasingly (and unknowingly) relinquish their decision making authority to a diverse array of unaccountable leaders – from corporation executives to drug lords, from issue experts to foundation officials, from crime bosses to populist demagogues – whose domains of power and influence are shaped by both globalizing dynamics and their localizing counterparts (Rosenau, 1998: 47).

The events of 11 September 2001 remind us that terror groups or networks should be added to Rosenau's list.

The distinction between challenges to democracy and challenges to existing democratic institutions at the national level is important. In a sense, challenges to the power of national governments in states with democratically elected governments and reasonably democratic institutions may be perceived as a challenge to a democratic system. In Falk's perspective, stronger rule-based international institutions as well as non-governmental organisations (NGOs) may strengthen democratic processes at the global level, while sometimes challenging national democratic institutions. The previous chapters also give evidence that erosion of national democratically-based state institutions may pave the way for new forms of democratic governance institutions at other levels

The room for manoeuvre for national governments has changed in, *inter alia*, the following domains.

1. The scope for repression and violation of human rights has been reduced with the increasing focus on individual or human security. In case of serious such violations, a national government risks "humanitarian" intervention from the international community or from a group of countries such as the EU or NATO. The probability of external intervention is higher in the case of countries that are considered less important economically and/or politically than in countries playing an important role for the world order, such as China.

2. The "securitisation of aid", in accordance with Duffield's analysis, is related to this. It has played an important role in encouraging the emergence of public-private networks, linking all levels and categories of actors and has legitimised a growing involvement of non-state actors.

3. The scope for welfare policy at the nation state level is reduced, in the developed countries as an effect of liberalised capital markets, making some national tax bases more mobile and thus eroding the funding of existing national welfare systems. The same development is observed in the poor-

est countries due to low economic growth and institutional capacity and the strong budgetary discipline, which is a prerequisite for support from the IMF, the World Bank and major bilateral donors. Many of these countries are heavily dependent on aid inflows to improve social services.

4. The scope for governments to implement a national economic policy, which is inconsistent with the global market economy norm, is almost nil. For smaller countries such attempts are totally impossible, as they will imply an exclusion from the world market and no or only limited private or public capital inflows.

5. The influence on national governance of private sector and civil society has increased. In many of the third world countries this trend is enhanced by the *Poverty Reduction Strategy* process, which is strongly pushed by the IMF, the World Bank, and most other donor agencies, as part of the Heavily Indebted Poor Countries (HIPC) Debt Relief system. Also in many OECD countries there are stronger links between governments, the private sector and civil society. This trend is also visible at the international level, with the involvement of a large number of transnational non-governmental organisations and networks in major international conferences and with the UN compact with the private sector as some examples.

6. Organised international crime and terrorism contribute to the erosion of the power of national governments in a number of ways. This is most visible in poor African countries, but also in some of the transition economies. The links between the various levels, from the global to the local, of the unofficial economy – on which organised crime and terrorism are based – may also fuel durable disorder. On the other hand, they may give states and politicians leading them arguments for strengthening the power and capacity of the state.

7. Globalisation processes result in an increasing need for institutions providing public goods at the global and regional levels.

The other side of this coin, implying a reduced scope for national governments and public sector actions, is an expansion in scope at other levels and in new forms of cooperation.

Implications of the Common Features for Development Cooperation

According to many international policy statements the basic objective for development cooperation is poverty reduction.[1] To which extent can the

---

[1] A recent example is the adoption of the International Development Targets, with the main objective of reducing the share of the global population living under abject poverty by half by 2015. However, it should be noted that after the end of the Cold War, a number of other objectives have also influenced the allocation and forms of aid.

world order models of this book contribute to that objective? There are some common features among them, which could be strengthened by international development cooperation, including:

- Increasing impact of the human security concept, which in turn has increased the legitimacy of external humanitarian interventions and the introduction of "human rights conditionality".
- The spread of common norms regarding democracy and human rights to an increasing number of countries in the world, and the emergence of new institutions based on those norms.
- Stronger focus on conflict prevention, peace keeping and post-conflict reconstruction, as a consequence of increased numbers of new types of conflicts.
- Greater influence of non-state actors in international governance.

All these trends are visible and have already had important implications for international development cooperation during the past decade. Together their influence on development thinking and practice is significant. Should the trends listed above be further enhanced, which follows the logic of the governance frameworks in this volume, further changes of institutions for global and international governance will be needed. This can also be expected to influence the international development agenda and relations between rich and poor countries and people.

The contemporary thinking of the major aid agencies on security motivated development cooperation can be found in *DAC Guidelines on Conflict, Peace and Development at the Threshold of the 21 Century* (1997) and its supplement *Helping Prevent Violent Conflict: Orientations for External Partners* (2001). In these documents aid has a clear role to play in a broader foreign policy context. Reducing violent conflicts in the borderlands (which is not the term DAC uses) is a measure to reduce the risk of various transnational threats, such as drug trafficking, organised crime and terrorism and irregular arms trade.

> 'Moving upstream' to help prevent violent conflict at its source is a shared goal of the development co-operation community. Donors are learning to apply a conflict prevention 'lens' to policies in many departments to make them coherent and comprehensive. The 'lens' is a metaphor for looking at how conflict prevention can be incorporated into all arenas of policy e.g. from development to trade, investment and foreign policy (DAC, 2001: 6).

International and regional humanitarian intervention and conflict-resolution efforts have had a mixed record. To what extent this is related to the way "durable disorder" is perceived should be further looked into. The literature on this and related issues is voluminous. For Africa, see, for instance, de Waal (1997). For an empirical overview of the conflict – poverty links in Africa, see Luckham, *et al.* (2001). For the "Greed and grievance" discussion, see Collier and Hoefler (2000). For the discussion on Livelihood conflicts – poverty and environment as causes of conflict, see Ohlsson (2000).

During the past decade we have also experienced an increasing influence on government policy and implementation from non-state actors, both private companies and civil society organisations. This is what Väyrynen calls hybrid governance. The increased influence of transnational companies and NGO networks may reduce the power of states in international governance, but may also improve the legitimacy of institutional reforms and changed norm systems. It may also strengthen the democratic legitimacy of companies, organisations and other civil society participants. Thus, it is not a zero-sum game. It raises the democratic legitimacy not only of some states but also of companies, organisations and other civil society participants. On the other hand, if the influence of private sector and other actors emerges as part of decision-making processes which are perceived as being less transparent, it may dilute the democratic legitimacy of these states.

Duffield emphasises another aspect of hybrid governance, namely that influence is not mainly channeled through such actions as lobbying and other peaceful means, but through the mechanisms of network wars and the effects of threats or violent actions that actually occur against the dominating states. Here, of course, 11 September 2001 comes to mind.

As Hettne points out in the introduction, the recent change of focus from state security to human security in the development discourse has already had implications on both the rhetoric and implementation of development cooperation. As Falk suggests in his rhetorical question: would not the acceptance of human security by leading governments have a transformative impact on world politics, validating some sort of post-Westphalia designation? And if so, what "post-Westphalia" development cooperation would emerge out of such a development. We have seen how the legitimacy factor with respect to intervention into what was previously called domestic affairs has grown stronger in the last decade. The number of interventions motivated as support to democracy and human rights has also increased. This trend is part of the narrative in all four cases, albeit in different contexts and with different interpretations. Assistance provided as a support for democracy in the form of e.g. support to opposition parties or mass media, can also be interpreted as a challenge to the sovereignty of the ruling government, particularly if this government is formed as a result of internationally accepted democratic elections.

The trends discussed above have so far not influenced total development cooperation. The main body continues along the same lines as before, based on agreements between international organisations and bilateral aid agencies on one hand and the governments of receiving countries on the other.

These are firmly based at the national level and imply agreements between governments of individual states or international organisations, and implementation of the agreements by state institutions. Another trend regarding the modalities of development cooperation is a greater share of budget support and general sector programme support. Both these modalities have a potential to provide increased influence for the national government.

Thus, while some of the issues put forward in the chapters of this volume imply the possibility of significant changes in role and mode for development cooperation, there are other processes going on in parallel, which tend to strengthen national institutions and also national governments using them. A prerequisite is that governments are prepared to follow the existing and gradually changing Washington consensus regarding macroeconomic policy and governance.

Implications of Various Forms of Governance

What immediate implications for development cooperation would be the results of the four different governance frameworks? This is, of course, a highly speculative question. Hoping that we may provide some food for further discussion we present some tentative suggestions for each of them. It should be noted that we do not discuss the plausibility of the respective framework or our own reactions to them. Instead we consider them as given and look into their possible implications for development cooperation.

We start with the two scenarios in which the forces of globalisation are considered to be strong enough, either to create such a strong interdependence that the risk of armed conflicts is almost eliminated (de Soysa and Gleditsch) or to create a more or less permanent disorder in some parts of the world, in which wars should be taken as a given and not as an abnormal situation (Duffield). The multilateralist/pluralist model (Väyrynen) is the most typical neo-Westphalia. Finally, the post-Westphalia enigma (Falk) is discussed, in which stronger norms and new actors, particularly transnational civil society networks are increasing their impact on the global governance process.

The liberal globalist case

De Soysa and Gleditsch mainly discuss the implications of economic globalisation on governance and conflicts. Their perspective oscillates between the neo-liberal and social market economy.

On poverty reduction in the poor countries, the main argument of de Soysa and Gleditsch is the need for integration of the poorest countries into the international economy and the role of foreign investment and trade in this context. The main problem for governments in poor countries is to improve the economic environment in order to attract foreign direct investments (FDI), which are in most cases the same factors that strengthen domestic economic development – peace, political stability, good governance and macroeconomic policy and social and physical infrastructure.

One basic perspective is thus the need for the poorest countries to be further integrated into the world economy and polity. Problem areas in terms of poverty and peace are, in this perspective, the areas that have by and large been bypassed by global economic forces. Conflict and bad governance, which seem to be closely allied, are not related to global processes but to conditions that favour predation over production within poor states. These conditions are not produced because of market forces, but because of the capture of states by politicians with other agendas than liberal development, and state-instituted macropolicies that provide the wrong incentives.

De Soysa and Gleditsch argue that interdependence reduces the risk of conflict and increases the scope for democracy. If this thesis is accepted, the linking of the poorest countries to the world economy and to various international organisations and institutions should be pursued as strongly and as quickly as possible. This scenario is an argument for further enhancing the liberalisation agenda and the one which would probably imply the smallest changes in present international development cooperation policy. The premise of this scenario is that it is the most growth-creating. The correlation between globalisation and growth is not questioned. However, some of the present globalisation critics argue that the growth rates of the late 1990s are lower than during the 1960s and early 1970s, when international trade and capital flows were much more regulated than today.

In the field of trade liberalisation the international financial institutions (IFIs) have a strong influence on poor countries' policies, but much less so on the policies of their major shareholders. The WTO regulatory framework has not so far been effective in opening the markets of the OECD countries for producers in development countries. Another well-known target for criticism within this framework is the protectionist trade policy of the European Union against imports from the third world. The "Everything but arms" decision in 2001, according to which the EU member countries will open their markets for products from the least developed countries, albeit with an eight-year transition period for the most important ones, can be considered a small step towards more liberalisation. However, radical reforms of the EU Common Agriculture Policy (CAP) are also needed in order to avoid heavily subsidised EU agriculture exports continuing to derail the domestic production of the same products in poor countries.

An obvious role for development cooperation in the liberal globalist case is to strengthen the capacity of the poor countries to participate in international negotiations and to support all efforts to open the markets of rich countries for exports from producers in the poor countries. Existing pressure from international NGOs in this field should therefore be further strengthened. Furthermore, the liberalisation and integration of those countries in the world economy should continue. The logic of this scenario leads to the conclusion that all efforts to support such a development should be high on the development cooperation agenda.

Integration in the world economy becomes a main instrument for poverty reduction via trade and investments, creating growth. This perspective is close to the on-going reform-based macroeconomic financing system, led by the Bretton Woods institutions and supported by most bilateral development agencies and governments. It would therefore not imply significant changes in present international development cooperation. It is also consistent with the trend towards increased macro level assistance to countries that combine a large number of poor inhabitants with sufficiently good macroeconomic policy, governance, financial management, and implementation capacity. The logic of this scenario also reduces the relative importance of special poverty-reduction programmes, as creating the right environment for trade and investments is considered more important.

Thus, while there is little need for major reforms in present development cooperation, it is clear that the import regimes of most OECD countries have to be significantly liberalised in order to fit into the discourse, argued by de Soysa and Gleditsch.

Although not explicitly discussed by de Soysa and Gleditsch, the issue of regional cooperation/integration between a group of neighbouring countries is important in this context. Regional integration can be seen as a stepping stone towards a more liberalised and integrated global economic system, although some of the strong trade liberalists, such as Bhagwati, are highly sceptical. They see regional integration as a stumbling block, rather than as a stepping stone towards global trade liberalisation. (A number of contributions on this issue can be found in e.g. De Melo and Panagaryia, 1993, and Teunissen, 1998.) There is significant scope for external support to strengthen regional institutions and instruments to share experiences from other regional projects.

Durable disorder

In his chapter Duffield is highly critical of the interpretation of the new wars as a failure of modernity. He argues that they are reflexive forms of resistance and adjustment to the process of globalisation. To look at them as failure of modernity conceals the actual predicament, but it also wrongly interprets political resistance as forms of social regression, which can be solved technically. "Rather than seeking political solutions, the securitisation of aid holds out the illusory promise that, through aid based control technologies, organised violence can be mollified and massaged away." Duffield points out that the technologies of risk, performance and auditing, through which the securitisation of aid is operationalised require machine-like prediction for their success. There is a serious gap between this technological approach and the reality of the new wars, as their main feature is their unpredictability.

Duffield suggests as a way out of this impasse, that a political vision is needed to replace the social claims of aid discourse. "aid should be 'de-securitised' and, in conflict zones, returned to its more modest but no less important role of impartial humanitarian assistance." At the same time, the field of diplomacy and negotiation should expand. Political actors need to address the multileveled and transborder nature of network war.

Accepting Duffield's perspective, aid agencies and politicians will need to negotiate and cooperate with different regimes at various levels and with various levels of legitimacy, confined to a specific territory. The alternative is to take full responsibility for aid provided to the territories they control. The latter option has an in-built restriction, as the regime controlling the territory can block access. This is a familiar situation to NGOs and governmental aid agencies, implementing humanitarian aid activities in conflict areas. One special aspect, which has been discussed for many years, is the role of emergency aid as provider of food for warring forces, rebels or government troops, depending on the situation (Andersson, 1996). This is not explicitly elaborated on by Duffield, while it is a concern to various NGOs and aid agencies.

It is interesting to compare Duffield's view on aid as an instrument for control of the borderlands by the centre, with the role aid can be assumed to have in the liberal globalist case. In the latter, aid is an instrument to integrate also what Duffield calls the borderlands in the world economy by creating an economic and political environment, which supports integration in the world economy. This is another strategy and a different analysis, but the objective to pacify the geographical territories that may develop into a threat against the centre, is implicitly similar.

Duffield's perspective contains the strongest challenge for those sectors of development cooperation that deal with conflict areas. In the wake of 11 September 2001, the major trend may move in the contrary direction to Duffield's vision of "de-securitised aid" – in the form of increased support to those regimes that are prepared to support the USA in its war against terrorism, irrespective of their record of human rights and democracy.

Finally, it should be noted that only about five percent of total official development assistance (ODA) funds, mainly in the form of emergency assistance, is allocated to territories labelled borderlands by Duffield. An interesting topic for further research is whether this share can be expected to increase or decrease.

Multi- and plurilateral approaches

Raimo Väyrynen presents one neo-Westphalia perspective, supporting governmental intervention in the market, especially to promote equality and stability, but without leading to its total political control. He discusses some contextual aspects, the issue of inequality and governance and the main actors involved in global governance, particularly the IMF, the World Bank, the WTO, the UN system and private and civil society actors. In the context of development cooperation, a main feature is the reforms of the UN that have been initiated during the period of Kofi Annan as Secretary General. A crucial concept used by Väyrynen is that of hybrid governance, meaning a new mode of problem-solving cooperation between private economic interests and public politics to cope with international challenges. He also discusses how this new mode of national, but increasingly private-public relationship, is challenged by social non-state actors, who tend to consider it detrimental to democracy, equity and other social values.

An important factor in this context that affects global governance are the new global ethics and global norms that are emerging, and which have already influenced the substance of development cooperation and its institutions and put pressure for organisational reforms of international institutions. Here, Väyrynen's perspective links to that of Richard Falk, although he is more interested in the potential of a reformed UN system, while Falk focuses more on the potential for the creation of new institutions based on a bottom-up perspective.

Besides the potential of hybrid governance in order to deal with collective and contextual aspects of global governance, Väyrynen penetrates global inequality issues, siding with those in the ongoing international debate on poverty and inequality who emphasise the inequality aspect. His main points for the discussion on possible implications for development cooperation in a global governance perspective, are to be found in the interface between the potentials of hybrid governance to take on the task of reducing ongoing inequality processes at both global and national levels.

Väyrynen discusses the possible role of some of the major international institutions, particularly the IMF, the World Bank, the WTO and the UN system. He points out that the articulation of new demands to redirect and regulate the globalisation process has fostered new forms of global governance. Traditional mechanisms such as the WTO, the IMF and the World Bank have gained new powers to regulate governmental policies. This has been accompanied by the rise of new institutions that are private or hybrid in nature. A strong criticism has emerged from mainly civil society actors against this development, focusing on some of the most powerful international institutions, particularly the IMF, the World Bank and the WTO.

Väyrynen particularly emphasises the repositioning of the UN in debates and policies pertaining to global governance. Under Kofi Annan's term of office as Secretary-General the organisation has also pioneered some hybrid mechanisms, including the Global Compact as a mechanism to cooperate with and mobilise resources from large international companies. Väyrynen also points out the risk that many companies perceive membership of the

Global Compact as a low-cost public relations activity. These are also part of attempts to reform the UN system, improve its efficiency and move the UN from the sidelines of the global debate to its mainstream.

With the strong scepticism from the US administration and even more so from the US Congress, this is a project that probably falls on the shoulders of the European Commission and the European Union member states. In the case of Sweden, support for such reforms has been strong and Sweden has been positive towards the report *Our Global Neighbourhood* by the International Commission of Global Governance (1995). This report proposes a number of institutional reforms of the UN system, including a strengthened Economic and Social Council (ECOSOC), to be responsible for global development issues. It also implies that the influence of countries other than the major industrial nations increases, at least marginally

A large number of initiatives have already been taken in this field, particularly on the instruments for conflict resolution, peace keeping and conflict prevention both within the UN system and the OECD. If successful, political stability may be improved at both national and regional levels and better conditions created for long-term development.

Väyrynen's perspective gives great scope for institutional development and reforms. It fits in well both with ongoing capacity and institution building at the national level of the "good performers" among the Heavily Indebted Poor Countries (HIPC) and arguments for increased support to the supply of global public goods (Kaul, *et al.*, 1999). In this context, the concern should be noted, expressed by political leaders from the poorest countries, that too strong a focus on global public goods will erode the direct flow of resources to the poorest countries. These countries have experienced a significant reduction in aid during the past decade due to a combination of reduced overall volume and flows to transition economies.

A globalisation of human rights-based norm systems and harmonised global ethics will provide increased pressure for reforms of existing international institutions and perhaps also demands for new such institutions. Out of this may also emerge new compacts and internationally agreed development targets and benchmarks, against which progress could be measured. While such targets and benchmarks have failed many times, there is still hope that they could contribute to mobilisation of additional resources.

One aspect of the hybrid approach, as discussed by Väyrynen, is its potential for mobilising resources outside government financed aid budgets, as well as conditions as regards the use of such resources and the influence of the new sources. For the international community involved in development and a reduction in inequality these issues are certainly not uncontroversial. One challenge is to keep instruments to be used alongside hybrid governance firmly within a poverty reduction perspective, and avoid some of the distortions that may be the result of restrictions as to sectors, countries or procurement, etc. Emerging hybrid governance in UN and other international institutions and networks, has potentially significant implications for the organisation of development cooperation, particularly for bilateral aid agencies.

Compared to the Liberal Globalist Case, the Multilateral Approach, as presented by Väyrynen, puts stronger emphasis on the institutional side and on the seriously negative effects of great and increasing inequality both at the national and the global level. On the latter issue, the Multilateral Approach includes a certain scepticism regarding the positive effects of trade and capital liberalisation without a sufficient normative regulatory framework and looks for possible room for manoeuvre for activities directly focusing on reducing poverty.

Humane global governance

In his chapter on The Post-Westphalia Enigma, Richard Falk suggests that "a positive post-Westphalia scenario will not take shape in all likelihood in the next decade or so". Still some of the trends regarding the post-Westphalia prospect will have and in some cases already have had implications in the field of development cooperation. One important point is that a post-Westphalia world would not imply that the state will disappear or even be marginalised, but that the sovereignty concept is changing and that this process will continue. A different sovereignty concept has strong implications for the power of the state.

Falk argues that a positive post-Westphalia world order would upgrade the rule of law in structuring relations among participants in international life. It would also provide reliance on third-party procedures for dispute settlement and conflict resolution, as well as new international courts using not national legislation but international norms and agreed principles.

This is also one reason for the sceptical attitude from many countries, particularly those with repressive governments. This sceptical attitude is shared by some of the largest and most powerful states, such as the USA, China and Russia. To them international rule of law would threaten their states' sovereignty, as their citizens, and even those in governing positions would be liable to legal action for actions taken in their official position.

The implications of rights-based development have not yet been fully analysed and if this concept is taken seriously, it will have a significant effect on the forms and objectives of development cooperation that are currently in use. Should governments of poor countries, in which the right to health, education, etc., for all citizens is not provided for, always be held responsible for this and if so, what type of external interventions should then be undertaken? What is the responsibility of governments and other actors in the richest countries? Such questions are old, but still unsolved, and they come to the surface in this context.

This issue is also discussed in the chapter by Väyrynen on multilateralism

– although from another perspective, but it comes out more clearly in Falk's text. It is probably one of the most important "new" items on the development cooperation agenda. It links to such issues as the sovereignty of states in many aid-receiving countries, who the specific private sector and NGO actors represent when involved in governance issues, and the mandate of these actors and their democratic legitimacy. It is also related to the old issues of aid dependency and the erosion of government authority that takes place if conditions for macroeconomic policy are decided outside the country by actors who do not have national political responsibility.

A more recent issue in this context is to what extent aid agencies should allow themselves to support various opposition groups and civil society activities in countries in which democratic elections have been held, but where governments are violating human rights and eroding democratic institutions. Are there limits for aid motivated as human rights and/or democracy support in formally democratic partner countries?

Three aspects of the ongoing discussion on global public goods can be linked to the perspective of Falk's chapter. One is the need for institutions to provide human rights and other universal public goods. The second is to continue support to ongoing work, aimed at improving humane development, particularly in order to include the poor countries in this process. The inputs to this process have mainly been provided by the OECD countries, which are also pushing these issues forward. In this field, as in many others, it is important that the poor countries are also included and feel they are part of the process. A third aspect is to improve the capacity of poor countries to participate in normative and institutional processes, in a proactive rather than a reactive role. This may also reduce the present fears of these countries that increased provision of global public goods would reduce total resources for traditional development assistance. Here, different interests in the poor countries may emerge. Some support the introduction of new transnational or international institutions that could protect citizens in a particular state from repression from that state. Governments may be more inclined to ask for an increase in traditional development assistance, as a large proportion of this is channeled through government structures.

Should a more significant change take place in the landscape of sovereignty, it is most probable that the framework of development cooperation would change and that a larger share of budgets for development cooperation would be used to improve human rights and other public goods institutions at the international level. Falk gives three examples of such new institutions: the International Criminal Court to be based on the Rome Treaty of 1998, the proposal for a Global Peoples Assembly and proposals for upgrading International Rule of Law, including the introduction of international tribunals in specific areas such as trade, the oceans and human rights.

There is no reason why international institutions of this kind should be financed only by funds allocated for development cooperation. However, there may be cases when it can be argued that such funds should cover the costs of poor countries' membership contributions to these institutions and to efforts at national level in such countries to prepare and improve the quality of their membership.

A post-Westphalia world, including upgrading of the rule of law and with individual security strongly defended also increases the legitimacy of external interventions when human rights and democracy, as defined in UN declarations, are threatened.

Such a development would enhance the present trend of allocating an increasing share of total official development assistance to improvement of democracy, human rights, governance and related issues. International institutions for providing public goods in these domains would increase their share of total ODA at the expense of traditional aid from multilateral organisations, including IFIs, and bilateral aid agencies to governments. It would also change the balance between institutions with only the richest and most powerful countries as members, with G8 as one example, and institutions that are also accessible to poorer countries.

Concluding Comments

History does not end here and there is no ultimate world order. The emerging world order will take features from all four governance frameworks provided in this volume as well as from other trends not covered here. The outcome will depend upon the balance between the political, social and economic forces that support the alternative cases. It will be used by the aid-providing countries and the international organisations in accordance with their respective norms and political objectives and they will change over time, as they have done during the post-world war era.

The main qualitative change over the last decade, of which we have not yet seen the full effect, is the change in the security concept and the emergence of individual security, providing legitimacy for new types of military, police, political and aid external interventions. As we have seen in the governance models included in this study, the scope for judging the role of development cooperation in this context is wide. It remains to be seen how much of a backlash there will be in the human security concept in relation to the perceived need for states to guard themselves against various forms of terrorist warfare.

Finally we would like to mention that readers of the draft versions of the chapters in this volume have often suggested that we would have to indicate which of them that is considered to be most plausible. However, the very point of asking an author to "purify" the effects of a specific world order is that by doing so, he or she moves away from trying to create a realistic mix of trends. We therefore feel that it would not be helpful to try and balance the four scenarios against each other according to how realistic they are supposed to be. Furthermore, unexpected world events continuously affect the potentials for one or the other of the frameworks, as is discussed in the introduction. The balance between them will be differently experienced in various geographical areas, by people from different social classes and depending on the sectors and areas in which one is active.

This is also applicable to development cooperation. The matrix below is one attempt to summarise some of the possible major implications of the four governance frameworks on development cooperation that have been discussed in this chapter.

Form of governance	Aid instrument for	Via the following processes
The liberal globalist case	Increased economic integration. Improved macro-economic policy.	Improve the environment for trade and investments. Open up markets in the North. Macroeconomic policy in line with the position of the international financial institutions.
Durable disorder	Control of the borderlands by the centre.	Technologies of risk, performance and auditing to create the securitisation of aid. As the gap between this technological approach and the reality of new wars is so wide, this is not feasible.
Multi- and plurilateralism	Improving global governance in an era of changed norms. Reducing global inequality.	Reforms of international institutions, provision of public goods. Increased hybrid governance. Support to pro poor growth policy and the HIPC initiative.
Humane global governance (post-Westphalia)	Upgrading the role of law, strengthening human rights and democratic governance internationally.	Reform existing international organisations and create new norm-based institutions. Increase the capacity of governments in poor countries and transnational civil society to participate in this process.

References

Anderson, M., 1996, *Do No Harm: Supporting Local Capacities for Peace Through Aid*, Cambridge, MA: Local Capacity for Peace Project. The Collaborative for Development Action, Inc.

Collier, P. and A., Hoeffler, 2000, *Greed and Grievance in Civil War*, Policy Research Working Paper, 2355, Washington D.C: Development Research Group. World Bank.

De Melo, J. and A. Panagaryia (eds.), 1993, *New dimensions in Regional Integration*, Centre for Economic Policy Research, Cambridge, Cambridge University Press.

de Waal, A., 1997, *Famine Crimes: politics and the disaster relief industry in Africa*, Oxford: James Currey.

International Commission of Global Governance, 1995, *Our Global Neighbourhood*, New York: UN.

Kaplan, R. D., 1994, "The Coming Anarchy: How Scarcity, Crime, Overpopulation and Disease are Rapidly Destroying the Social Fabric of our Planet", *Atlantic Monthly*, pp. 44–76.

Luckham, R., Ahmed, I., Muggah, R. and S. White, 2001, *Conflict and Poverty in Sub-Saharan Africa: an assessment of the issues and evidence*, IDS Working Paper 128, Sussex: Institute of Development Studies.

McGrew, A., 1998, "Conceptualizing a Moving Target" in *Understanding Globalisation. The Nation State, Democracy and Economic Policies in the New Epoch*, Stockholm: Ministry for Foreign Affairs.

OECD/DAC, 1997, *DAC Guidelines on Conflict, Peace and Development at the Threshold of the 21st Century*, Paris.

OECD/DCD/DAC, 2001, *Helping Prevent Violent Conflict: Orientations for External Partners* (2001).

Ohlsson, L., 2000, *Livelihood Conflicts – Linking Poverty and Environment as Causes of Conflict*, Stockholm: Environment Policy Unit, Sida.

Ohmae, K.,1995, *The End of the Nation State: the Rise of Regional Economies*, London: HarperCollins.

Rosenau, J., 1998, "States and Sovereignty in a Globalizing World" in *Understanding Globalisation. The Nation State, Democracy and Economic Policies in the New Epoch*, Stockholm: Ministry for Foreign Affairs.

Teunissen, J.J., (ed.), 1998, *Regional Integration and Multilateral Cooperation in the Global Economy*, Forum of Debt and Development (FONDAD), The Hague: FONDAD.

Notes on Editors and Contributors

Indra de Soysa is Senior Research Fellow, Center for Development Research, University of Bonn, and leads a research group on Democracy, Rule of Law, and Governance. He has recently published articles in *Journal of Conflict Resolution, American Sociological Review* and *Journal of Peace Research* and is completing a book on *Globalization, Democratization, and Development* to be published by Routledge.

Mark Duffield is Professor of Development, Democratisation and Conflict at the Institute for Politics and International Studies, University of Leeds. His research interests include the political economy of the new wars, and understanding humanitarian intervention as a relation of global governance. He has worked in Africa, the Balkans and Afghanistan. During the 1980s, he was Oxfam's Country Director for Sudan.

Rickard Falk is currently Visiting Professor in Global Studies at the Santa Barbara campus of the University of California. He retired from Princeton University in 2001 after forty years on its faculty. Falk has served in recent years on the Independent International Commission on Kosovo and on the UN Human Rights Inquiry Commission for the Palestinian Territories. His most recent books are *Human Rights Horizons* (Routledge, 2000) and *Religion and Humance Governance* (Palgrave, 2001).

Nils Petter Gleditsch, Research Professor at the International Peace Research Institute, Oslo (PRIO), editor of *Journal of Peace Research;* Professor of International Relations at the Norwegian University of Science and Technology since 1993. Among his recent work are: *Environmental Conflict* (edited with Paul F. Diehl, Westview, 2001), *Globalization and Armed Conflict* (edited with Gerald Schneider and Katheryn Barbieri, Rowman & Littlefield, in press), articles in *American Political Science Review* and *Political Geography*.

Björn Hettne is Professor at the Department of Peace and Development Research, Göteborg University. He is the author of a number of books and articles on development theory, international political economy, European integration and ethnic relations.

Bertil Odén holds a position as counsellor/economist at the Swedish Embassy in Dar es Salaam, Tanzania. He worked as Secretary to the EGDI 1999–2001 and conducted a research program on Southern Africa at the Nordic Africa Institute, 1989–1998. He has edited and contributed to some thirty books on the political economy of Southern Africa, aid, development economics and international relations. He has also worked with Sida, Ministry of Finance in Tanzania and the Planning Commission in Mozambique.

Raimo Väyrynen, Professor of Political Science, University of Notre Dame, Indiana; Senior Fellow, Joan B. Kroc Institute for International Peace Studies. He served in 1978–93 as Professor of International Relations at the University of Helsinki and in 1990–93 as Dean of its Social Science Faculty. His research interests include global conflict and security issues, international political economy, and international relations theory. He has published twenty-four authored or edited books and over 200 scholarly articles, most recently a co-edited volume *The Prevention of Humanitarian Emergencies* (Palgrave, 2002).